GREAT BALLS OF FIRE

How Big Money Is Hijacking World Football

GREAT BALLS OF FIRE

John Sugden and Alan Tomlinson

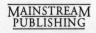
MAINSTREAM
PUBLISHING

EDINBURGH AND LONDON

First published in Great Britain in 1999 by
MAINSTREAM PUBLISHING COMPANY (EDINBURGH) LTD
7 Albany Street
Edinburgh EH1 3UG

ISBN 1 84018 126 5

A catalogue record for this book is available from the British Library

Typeset in Galliard
Printed and bound in Great Britain by Butler & Tanner Ltd

CONTENTS

PREFACE

The idea for this book started with conversations with journalists and friends working in other areas of the media after the publication of our academic book, *FIFA and the Contest for World Football – Who Rules the Peoples' Game* (Polity Press, 1998). They convinced us that some of the themes which ran through that book needed to be developed and made accessible to a wider audience.

A deep concern for the future of football led us to France for the duration of the 1998 World Cup finals to observe and investigate at first hand the power struggles which are consuming the world's most popular sport. The power players of world football administration and commercial exploitation always gather for the biggest beanos and France '98 was the biggest beano of all. We wanted to be there as they buried their noses in the trough.

Why should the way world football is run matter? In the last 25 years FIFA has overseen (or turned a blind eye to) football's transformation from the people's game to the plaything and cash cow of big business and multinational capital. Behind the rhetoric of world development and national representation, from its tax-haven fortress in Switzerland, without transparency, democracy or accountability, FIFA has brokered this transformation.

Having spent much of the last five years watching at close quarters the behaviour of FIFA's leading luminaries, we have grown to be deeply suspicious of those who purport to speak 'for the good of the game' (FIFA's motto). As recent events within the cloisters of the International Olympic Committee (IOC) have reminded us, the administration of international sport is vulnerable to exploitation by tinpot, pompous and vainglorious carpetbaggers. Football is no exception.

The guardians of world football have a duty to care for a precious cultural product. While its leaders do not trumpet the hypocritical ideals of the Olympic movement, FIFA nevertheless has a moral obligation to abide by democratically established sporting ethics such as equality, representation, responsibility, fairness and accountability. Even if they want to run football like a business, they should at least follow a code of good practice. As it stands, FIFA plays by its own rules.

The profit-driven logic of the contemporary game, if left unchecked, will see world football turned into a meaningless global circus, with fewer and fewer genuine fans either capable of or interested in getting inside the big top to witness what would be by then no more than an increasingly dehumanised spectacle. They may as well stay at home and fiddle with the Play Station.

This book is not an epitaph for the people's game. We have written it because we believe that information is power. Pointing out the truth about who is doing what to *your game*, we believe that we can make a valuable contribution to the growing resistance and reaction against the total commodification of football. The Monopolies and Mergers Commission's ruling that Rupert Murdoch's BSkyB could not buy Manchester United is a good example of what can be achieved when enough well-informed people take to the barricades.

We believe that world football should be run by able and honest men and women who put the game first and the bank balance, personal power and prestige and the high life some way down the list. It's time the people got their balls back and did something to get rid of the freeloaders by backing up those who call for reform. We hope this book will help.

As far as possible, we have drawn on our own, exclusive research materials. We are grateful to many people for informing our project. Many are 'insiders' who, understandably, are reluctant to see their names in print. We have done as much as possible to respect their anonymity. We are particularly grateful to those who agreed to be named and quoted.

Despite the issues and concerns articulated in the following pages, we are grateful for assistance received from personnel in all of the six regional confederations which administer world football, and from those within FIFA itself. While the FIFA family jealously guards its secrets, during the course of our research it became clear that some members recognise the need for wider and more honest dissemination of information.

Converting what was written in an academic style to something more accessible and populist was much more difficult than we anticipated. Our readers will judge the extent to which we have been successful. Either way, we are deeply indebted to Andrew Jennings and Clare Sambrook for their efforts in helping us find our populist voices. If the lyrics don't work and our tone is flat, it is our fault.

Special thanks go to Alys and Rowan Tomlinson who contributed to text and photographs and to Ron Maughan who contributed images for the book's cover. And to Bill Campbell of Mainstream Publishing for his faith in the project and his patience while we completed it. Finally, thanks to Chris, Alex and Jack Sugden and Alys and Rowan Tomlinson for sustained family encouragement and support.

John Sugden and Alan Tomlinson
Eastbourne and Brighton
July 1999

1. JUDGEMENT DAY

The clerks in the offices on the other side of this usually quiet street in the suburbs on the south side of Paris have never seen anything like it: cameramen, TV satellite trucks, skeins of cables criss-crossing the pavement, reporters idling. And not a football or a player in sight. We are flotsam in a swirl of hundreds of expectant notebooks. The philosophers in our ranks say we are here this Monday morning to report the battle for soccer's soul. The sceptics remind us that today's winner will walk away with the numbers to FIFA's Swiss bank account.

It's a simple two-horse race. We have conflict, we have drama and we have what one staring-eyed delegate to this morning's epic, 51st FIFA congress in the Salle d'Equinox insists is a choice between democracy and dictatorship. And we have to take sides.

Inside the drab convention centre and already working the floor is Switzerland's Joseph 'Sepp' Blatter. Chubby-cheeked still at 62, with his sparkling eyes and fixed grin, Sepp is soccer's top bureaucrat, general secretary of FIFA since 1981. It's no secret that he badly wants to step up today to the pinnacle, to become president – no, emperor – of the football globe.

Who loves Sepp? He certainly enjoys the embrace of secretive Swiss marketing company International Sport and Leisure, once revered as the biggest wheeler-dealers in sports politics. They've received 17 per cent of the tickets for the 1998 World Cup finals – 436,000 of those crisp cardboard-and foil-darlings – and around 20 per cent of the zillions of pounds the global marketeers have paid to make this World Cup their own.

The duteous Sepp for nearly two decades has trotted five respectful paces behind Brazil's despotic João Havelange, who swept to soccer's presidency 24 years ago, so some say, on a tide of promises. Now the

Big Man wants his boy to follow him. The Big Man usually gets his way.

It's zoo time: they're inside the ring of steel – a six-metre-high fence and matching gate of vertical iron bars, rolled back just enough to admit each new delegate as they stroll up in the morning sunshine. All we can see of the last minutes of what may turn out to be the most suspect campaign in the history of world sport politics is a squadron of blue blazers and neat grey slacks with government haircuts, checking credentials.

Behind them, half of President Havelange's personal payroll wander the carpark, cell-phones shrilling, muttering arithmetic as they try to work out if they now have the numbers to beat the other big man. And he is very big – a slightly paunchy but still blond Viking in his late sixties, the Swede Johansson who even now comes strolling expansively down the pavement.

'Good luck, Lennart,' some of us call and immediately feel foolish because we've known all along that decent as he undoubtedly is, vital as his plans are for making FIFA democratic and transparent, from the day that Blatter, blessed by the Big Man, declared his candidature, Johansson had little or no chance of winning.

A memory: The Big Man must be in pain. For six hours he's had to gaze awkwardly upwards, his neck retracted, his ears rammed back into his shoulders. This discomfort is thanks to that kindly Mr Johansson, who drew up the seating plan. He and the 14 members of UEFA's executive committee who control European soccer, the most lucrative football franchise on the planet, are smugly comfortable, high on the platform rigged up in the ballroom at Jury's Hotel in the Ballsbridge suburb of Dublin.

Here at their own congress, six weeks before the showdown in Paris, the UEFA executive can do what they damn well like. They beam down at their honoured guests' plump buttocks overflowing from the rows of little gilt chairs below them.

Today is supposed to be a two-yearly business meeting for European soccer. But it has been stage-managed as a Johansson campaign rally. The carefully scripted components appear to be: getting European delegates on side and behind Johansson for the Paris vote next month; seeking to bond with honoured guests from around the world; and being less than respectful to the Most Honoured Guest.

The Big Man is today's Most Honoured Guest and they've

positioned him in the absolutely central position of the front row. It must seem a conspicuous humiliation, dumping him on the floor, not elevating him to the platform. He's so close to the platform you'd think he could hide his feet underneath it.

He can't miss one word from above. That must be deliberate too. Sometimes he's called 'Dr' Havelange; other times speakers refer to him as the FIFA president – as if he wasn't there, large as life, in their midst, bloodhound blank-eyed and blank-faced.

The speeches romp across the diverse world of UEFA's competitions, the tons of money they generate – and the political purchasing power it gives them in impoverished Africa and Eastern Europe. There's one recurring, unifying theme: every five minutes, on average, someone from the platform puts the boot into Havelange.

Could it get worse? Yes, and it's happening now. Without warning the two giant video screens on the wall above his tormentors flicker into life with the beaming features of soccer's only living God. Pelé's huge grin lights up the room. He's making a political speech, delivered with cheek. 'I have met many kings and queens, presidents and stars in my travels around the world,' he chirrups. 'But I have never met anyone who cares more for the honesty and transparency of the sport of football as my friend Johansson. I hope deeply in my heart that he becomes the next president of FIFA.'

Pelé sets the tone. We love him as he swats aside the Havelange legacy without ever mentioning the Big Man or Blatter. Again and again he stresses democracy, transparency. Every reverberation of these words seems like a jab at the Brazilian 'Dr'. The screens darken, wild applause, Pelé is gone.

Havelange sits tight for a few seconds, raises his hands as if to pray, then touches the palms together silently, just the one time. Don't get mad, get even.

Still undead? His enemies in Paris, given the chance, would have carved a stake from a goalpost at the Scotland v Brazil opening game on 10 June and stabbed it through the Big Man's heart. For his fan club, reduced these days to the queue of monarchs, presidents and prime ministers desperate to bring the World Cup to their capital cities, he remains a man to be flattered and adorned with state baubles.

To soften the blow of his departure, Havelange has allowed himself to be awarded the title of Honorary President. For life and from his retirement home, he'll endeavour to keep tabs on his protégé Blatter and world soccer. In the business of FIFA, you fear, he will forever be eyeing and involving himself in the fat of endless TV contracts.

João Havelange, autocratic, charming and ruthless and now 82, has dominated the politics of world soccer for nearly a quarter of a century. Born in Rio midway through the First World War, he swam for Brazil at the 1936 Berlin Olympics. After the war, aged 40, he played water-polo at the Helsinki Games.

The tall, energetic entrepreneur with the aquiline nose and piercing eyes moved into insurance and transport and, as the money rolled in, shed his sports kit to become a sports suit. This suit had style. What had gone before was rough tweed; this suit was slick and silky. While the players were still wearing heavy boots, you can imagine Havelange's feet cosseted in crocodile.

He was in the right place at the right time, taking control of Brazilian soccer just before its stars zapped the world, lifting the cup three times in twelve years. But he wasn't keen to share world domination with the likes of Pelé, the team and the rest of the planet; João wanted it all for himself. Here's how he did it.

World soccer was led by Sir Stanley Rous, the English refereeing expert who would have felt more at home in a cold bath than a jacuzzi. He presided over the people's game for 13 years. That was his unlucky number when he faced re-election at FIFA's Frankfurt convention in 1974.

Waiting in ambush, clutching a red card, was the Brazilian adventurer. The Big Man realised that FIFA's apparently democratic one-member, one-vote system for electing presidents – with the vote of the oldest and biggest soccer nations being worth no more and no less than the votes of FIFA's newest and smallest member countries – could be easily influenced, particularly when the voting was through a secret ballot.

Then Havelange did a most unsporting thing – he went on the road campaigning for the job. Countries as yet without television and who had never been visited by Sir Stanley suddenly found that their local cloggers were promised more opportunities to play the top teams, in new tournaments for younger players, possibly in an expanding World Cup finals. Maybe there'd eventually be a friendly against the world's finest, Brazil! At home! God, think of the gate receipts! Who would *you* vote for?

The Third World countries were restless. They wanted Eurocentric soccer to give them some respect. They hadn't the resources to fight their own battle, so the challenge was led by the cosmopolitan Havelange from the Second World. As he traded in the rhetoric of anti-imperialism, few noticed at the time that Havelange was backed by tough capitalists in Europe and America.

The Africans – with 37 out of 122 votes – held the balance of power in 1974. They wanted a bigger World Cup, more facilities, more coaching and a leadership that would slam the door in apartheid's face. Poor old Sir Stan just didn't get it. He wasn't consciously a racist, just a blinkered British paternalist, believing (like the demented Mrs Thatcher did later) that the anti-apartheid movement in South Africa must be 'communist'.

Meanwhile big João was pulling levers that Stan didn't know existed. World soccer had never seen such goings on. Delegates unlikely to support Havelange found themselves left at home; politicians or diplomats based in Europe were drafted into Frankfurt for the vote.

A senior London soccer reporter alleged, in those days when few frowned at such language, that success came partly through 'small brown envelopes going into large black hands'. Nobody sued.

Stan was no longer The Man. He went home to write his memoirs. The new FIFA president Havelange discovered he hadn't got the money to keep his election pledges. Soccer was put up for sale. Havelange didn't have long to wait for a buyer.

Once upon a time in Bavaria in the 1960s lived a brooding genius who disagreed with his mum and dad about how to run the family store. So he crossed the border to Landersheim in France and set up his own subsidiary making football boots and running shoes. He was wildly successful, made piles of money, went back, took control of the family business and became the most powerful man in world sport. He was Horst Dassler and the company was Adidas.

He created the infamous Adidas group that spent the 1970s and 1980s gladhanding their way through world sport, arranging elections and putting Dassler's protégés in the presidents' chairs at the Olympics, at track and field, swimming and boxing. They did similar deals with Dassler. He either got them elected or helped keep them in power. Then they shook hands with his International Sport and Leisure company and signed contracts handing over the marketing rights to their world championships.

Dassler became immensely rich and the presidents used their share of the new money to distance themselves from the fans and the athletes, treating themselves to a lifestyle of private jets, motorcades and luxurious hotel suites. It was such a good life, too good to let go, so they abolished contested elections and every few years, at choreographed conventions, hand-picked minions jumped to their feet and begged them to serve a further term. Then the brass necks had the cheek to call this a 'mandate' from and on behalf of the football (or athletics or swimming or boxing or Olympic) family.

Rough woollen suits were never seen again at sport's top tables and the people's game ever since has had a sponsor's label on it. Whoops, that's a taboo word – we're supposed to call them 'partners'.

By the late 1970s Havelange's expenses were running at £100,000 a year. Within five years his Rio office was costing £250,000. In 1982 at the World Cup in Spain, FIFA officials explored new levels of comfort and ran up a bill of £2 million – nearly as much as it cost to fly all 24 teams to the finals and accommodate them in Spain.

Within a year of the Big Man taking soccer's throne, Horst Dassler found him an assistant. Sepp Blatter was employed as a mouthpiece, charming the press on behalf of Swiss Timing-Longines who were contracted to count the seconds at the Olympics. He was taken to the Adidas offices in Alsace for special training.

'For six months he lived in Landersheim, being taught how to run soccer and becoming very friendly with Horst,' recalls another graduate of the Dassler charm school. After a few years spent organising soccer competitions, he was made top pen-pusher at FIFA.

On the way, unbelievably, Sepp married the daughter of his boss, the dear old Dr Helmut Käser, who eventually stood down as general secretary to be replaced by his son-in-law. The marriage didn't last.

Every concentration of power initiated by Havelange has been implemented meticulously by his servant Blatter. Old traditions seemed to count for nothing when it came to stacking soccer's committees with Havelange's family and friends. TV contracts were signed with other friends and the executive committee was told later. The protégé did as he was brought up to do.

Did Blatter mix with the Adidas team of operators during his training? Did he learn any techniques from them? Maybe, because when Havelange's presidency faltered in 1994, Blatter thought himself wily enough to point the dagger at the Big Man's back. He turned up at UEFA's congress in Holland and, behind closed doors, announced: 'Dear friends, I will be your candidate to get rid of this old schemer. Elect me president of FIFA!'

It didn't work. Most UEFA delegates, even though they were keen to get rid of Havelange, saw through Blatter's opportunism. Worried about his master's reaction, Blatter rushed to the notebooks outside and assured them he was not a candidate. 'I will not stand – it's the media saying these things, not me,' he claimed.

So why did Havelange still want Blatter as his heir? Is it because after serving Havelange for two decades Blatter cannot, like Johansson the reform candidate, demand that independent organisations are called in to examine FIFA's records? Havelange couldn't afford to sack Blatter in 1994 because his protégé knew too much. This is why the Big Man threw his weight so aggressively behind Blatter's 1998 campaign.

As one veteran FIFA watcher told us, 'They are chained together.' If one goes down, he'll pull the other with him. Behind closed doors Havelange told Blatter that he must stand and that he must win.

And look who else is backing the dapper Swiss. Back in Paris the steel-barred gate is sliding wide open. Is it for the champagne tanker? No, it's to allow the regal entry of the president of the Saudi soccer federation. He's transported in a long black Mercedes but it's hard to catch a glimpse of him because jogging in columns on each side of the car are even more government haircuts, all of whom have those little earpieces with wires disappearing inside their collars which, together with their blank faces and narrowed eyes, suggest they've got more than mobile phones hidden inside their jackets.

A flash of traditional Arab robes in the back. It's Faisal bin Fahd of Saudi Arabia. A son of the King, himself one of the legendary seven sons whose father soaked the desert in blood to make Saudi's oil wealth forever theirs. A prince as rich as Faisal is of course a member of the International Olympic Committee but he habitually misses their meetings and Games. The rules say he should be expelled, but this could never happen to a Saudi prince. What mission has drawn him and his platoon of sharp-eyed, short haircuts to a narrow side street in the Paris suburbs this Monday morning?

He's going to cast a vote. He probably has to ask for help marking his X for Blatter (all of us know by now what's going on) because it may be the only time he's ever voted in his life. The Saudi soccer team floundered in France but even if they'd beaten Brazil 10–0 in the final they still wouldn't get to vote back home. It's illegal.

Lennart Johannson announced several years before that he would stand against Havelange in 1998. The big Brazilian was unimpressed; he planned to stay until he was at least 86, at least until the World Cup of 2002.

Johansson went on the road, building alliances, especially in Africa, promising to reform FIFA and hand power back to the members. Blatter kept his head down. What would his boss do?

As it turned out, the boss didn't have a choice. He screwed up by backing Japan against Korea for the 2002 competition and was dragged, sulking, into compromise. Then he legitimised the foul and isolated dictator Abacha by visiting Nigeria, just as the scaffold was erected for the country's poet and dissident Ken Saro Wiwa and the Ogoni Nine. The world cried 'shame' and imposed sanctions. This was an arrogance too far and Havelange was forced to promise to quit in '98.

Blatter waited . . . and waited. He waited until there were only ten weeks before the election and then announced he had little choice but to submit to pleas that he, not Johansson, should lead the sport.

This left little time for his manifesto, such as it was, to be scrutinised. He couldn't criticise the recent past under Havelange because he was complicit – so he had to divert attention from the dictatorship he had so enthusiastically served.

His major offering was to enlarge the executive committee, which sounded like a move towards democracy – until those reading the small print discovered it would meet only twice a year. So it wasn't a democratic reform at all. Stiffening his assault on the few fragments of democracy left at FIFA, Blatter proposed a kitchen cabinet of seven leading officials who would meet monthly and take most decisions.

Aware of restlessness in the ranks about the high living enjoyed by senior officials like himself, Blatter was edgy when the former French star player Michel Platini announced: 'What does FIFA mean to today's players? Nothing. The people they see are figureheads, staying in five-star hotels and eating in expensive restaurants. We want to change that.' The news conference was held in the plush surroundings of the French Olympic Committee, with champagne and ritzy hors-d'oeuvres on offer afterwards.

Blatter toured Africa. As had happened in 1974, this was where the election would be won and lost. He soon picked up pledges in minor soccer nations like Guinea, Sierra Leone, Mauritania and Liberia.

French president Jacques Chirac also reportedly backed Blatter, putting in persuasive calls to the French-speaking African nations.

Blatter boldly promised that the continent would stage the World Cup of 2006, even though he didn't have the authority to make that decision. And, to help get the English behind him, he and the Big Man dropped in on Prime Minister Tony Blair and announced that the 'home of soccer' should be the host of 2006.

In Beijing, he seemed to run out of give-aways so, as Reuters dryly reported, 'Blatter promised China instant help if he won the election, though he did not elaborate.'

As the campaign intensified we scanned the wire services, looking for references to Dassler and to Blatter's past. We couldn't find a word about either. The profiles harped on about him being a former colonel in the Swiss army and dwelt in that jovial way that male sports reporters do on Blatter's recorded preference in 1971 for women to wear garter belts and stockings rather than tights.

Back in Dublin our big Swede, then thought to be well ahead in the contest, is asked who was paying for Blatter's campaign. We all know the rumours of oil dollars from the Gulf so he only has to state, very slowly, 'I presume Mr Blatter has his own private finances.'

Johansson pounds the same themes from the UEFA podium. Every time we hear 'transparency', we know it's time to open FIFA's books. When 'democracy' is mentioned, we know that Havelange's wilful manipulation of FIFA committees must be stopped.

Havelange likes this even less than he liked Pelé. As Johansson ends, the 'Dr' touches the flat of one hand on the table, once. Praise doesn't get any fainter.

At last he's up from his cramped seat to be given one of those pointless awards that sports leaders invented for decorating each other and which we've never heard of. For the record, if anybody's bothered to keep one, this trinket is called UEFA's diamond pin of merit. He then walks the length of the platform shaking hands with every committee member – a valedictory review of the troops.

There's just a little more agony. The charismatic Issa Hayatou from Cameroon says bluntly that Africa knows who its real friends are and that together Europe and Africa will win the battle of Paris. Oceania's Charles Dempsey pops up to promise ten certain votes. Havelange's torture is almost all over, but not before the Swede announces that each delegate will find upstairs a gift in his hotel room: complimentary tickets, passage and accommodation for the 1998 Champions' League final in Amsterdam. At last Johansson has learned the rules of the game, but it's far, far too late.

The Big Man strides up the long aisle to the back of the hall, stopping briefly to shake hands and mutter an aside to an old associate. Despite his 82 years he keeps up a fierce pace and one of us is breathless climbing over chairs, following this setting sun along corridors and out into the hotel foyer. He never slows. Now he's outside in the carpark, sliding into Dublin's biggest Mercedes and away through the gates.

We've just watched a major exercise in self-delusion by the Johansson camp, but nobody, apart from the Most Honoured Guest, yet knows it.

Johansson is devastated in Paris when, soon after lunch, the result is declared. He had believed it would be a close run thing, but defeat by 111 votes to 80 leaves him fumbling. He does the gracious-loser speech and then heads off with his UEFA team to figure out why so many promised votes evaporated overnight.

At the victor's press conference, the smirk slides off Blatter's face when a reporter says, 'There's talk that your campaign was corrupt,' and 'There was talk of $50,000 in envelopes.'

Blatter's face clouds. 'The match is over,' he replies, adding, with barely concealed anger: 'The players have already gone to the dressing-room, I will not respond.'

But, yes, Blatter had some intriguing assistance. Pressed about his campaign, the new president admitted that in order to promise his way swiftly around the planet he had been airlifted in private jets belonging to a Swiss sponsor and a sheikh from the Gulf.

And then it all got very confused with Blatter's and Johansson's retinues separately briefing groups of reporters. Johansson's mouthpiece announced that his boss had 'at no time made any accusations of bribery against Joseph Blatter. He dissociates himself completely from these allegations.' Then his camp produced a press release saying he didn't want to speculate about the rumours but 'should these alleged irregularities become fact, we will take the matter up'.

The *Washington Post* reported that Blatter 'did not deny the distribution of $50,000 in envelopes, but said they were cash prepayments of previously agreed-to disbursements to national federations'.

This is scarcely believable. Cash in envelopes? Surely, this isn't how FIFA does business. What's the receipt – a wink?

Then FIFA put out a press statement: 'Mr Blatter vehemently refutes the allegations and will investigate the source of such malicious reports. He reserves the right to take legal action against those seeking to defame him.'

That night we prowled the lobbies of the FIFA hotels, trying to find delegates who could explain how a couple of dozen votes promised to Johansson had been prized away and ended up in Blatter's favour.

By the early hours, the dishing out of the $50,000 in envelopes by FIFA officials was still a pervasive theme – but another, more shocking, story had emerged. The previous evening, it was rumoured, a private jet had arrived in Paris. This was definitely not Prince Faisal. Nor was it the Kuwaitis, who had made it clear that they didn't want to be part of whatever was going on.

But it was a sheikh with more bank accounts than camels. His burnouses, so said the grapevine, patrolled the FIFA hotels looking for African delegates, who were then made the most sophisticated of offers. This was an offer you couldn't refuse – because nobody could ever prove you had accepted. On the table, delegates were told, was $2 million to be shared between the Africans if Blatter won. Nobody had to promise to vote for him and they could back Johansson if they wished. But the offer was there and this, the dirtiest of dirty tricks, might have cost Johansson the presidency.

Horst Dassler had died in 1987. Eleven years later his spirit won the battle of Paris and his legacy, in football, is set to rule far into the twenty-first century.

2. THE BLAZER-AND-SLACKS BRIGADE

'Football's coming home' was the adopted anthem of the 1996 European Nations Cup in England, the same mantra used by England's campaign team in their bid to host the 2006 World Cup finals. Nice try, but world football came home in 1998 when the French hosted the finals.

England claims to be the birthplace of football, but it was not one of the founder members of the world governing body, FIFA, when it was set up in 1904, and nor did it make it to the first World Cup, in Uruguay in 1930.

The World Cup's creator was a Frenchman, Jules Rimet. From 1921 to 1954 he was president of FIFA. It was this self-made professional and religious do-gooder who dominated the growth of international football – not the English who, apart from for a few years in the early 1900s, stayed out of FIFA, refusing to have anything to do with a bunch of foreigners trying to mess with 'their' game.

Like so many senior sports administrators, Rimet was trained in law. As an older man, the bearded, bowler-hatted and thoroughly bourgeois Rimet was an established figure among Parisian society. But he came from humble origins, born in 1873 into a modest family in rural France, and from an early age helped his father in the family grocer's shop.

From the age of 11 he was raised in Paris where his father had moved in search of work. He lived in the heart of the city, learning to survive and play football on the street. He was a conscientious and able schoolboy.

The young Rimet worked his way towards a full legal qualification, and was active in encouraging football among the poorer children of the city. He was a philanthropist who saw sport was a means of building good character. He was Christian and patriotic. His love of God and France came together in his passion for football. He believed in the universality of the church and saw in football the chance to create a worldwide 'football family' welded to Christian principles.

Like his countryman, Baron Pierre de Coubertin, the founder of the modern Olympics, Rimet believed that sport could be a force for national and international good. Sport and football could bring people and nations together in a healthy competitiveness, he thought. Sport could be a powerful means of both physical and moral progress, providing healthy pleasure and fun, and promoting friendship between races.

Rimet resisted the development of continental confederations and the empowerment of football confederations in Africa and in Asia. He argued that decentralisation would destroy FIFA, and that 'only direct membership will retain FIFA as one family'.

Heading FIFA during its formative years, he gave the organisation a clear mission: to produce a global football family. But he found it difficult to overcome Europe's imperiousness. Europeans still looked down their noses at their poor South American relations, for example. At the first World Cup in Uruguay in 1930 only four of the 15 competing teams – France, Belgium, Yugoslavia and Romania – were from Europe.

Uruguay had shattered the world football establishment by winning the Olympic football championship in 1924 and 1928. These were the most dramatic achievements of the emerging football superpowers of South America. Football was also well established in Brazil and Argentina, where the game had been growing for half a century. It thrived initially in the ranks of nomadic British diplomats, planters and engineers who took balls and boots and a Football Association rule book wherever they went. The colonials' love of the game soon spread among the local, poorer classes.

The sport took hold most strongly around the River Plate and games between Argentina and Uruguay were played regularly from the turn of the century. The South American confederation, CONMEBOL, records its founding date as 1916, long before any other continental confederation. In its early days FIFA was so Euro-centric that no need was seen for any separate European organisation.

Uruguay's Olympic victories encouraged the country's diplomats to lobby for the first world football championships to be held. Rimet was flattered and excited at the prospect of spreading the FIFA gospel on the other side of the world.

Even in its inception the World Cup, for a chosen few, was one of world sport's greatest junkets. The Uruguayan authorities clinched the event by pledging to cover travel and hotel costs of all the competing teams. They also constructed the Centenario Stadium. The date chosen to launch the finals, July 1930, was a political decision rather than a sporting one: it was the centenary of the adoption of the Uruguayan constitution.

The hosts outplayed all rivals to add to their Olympic laurels. Argentina defeated a US team by six goals to one and, because the US included five Scots and an Englishman, the Argentinians claimed to have thrashed a side from football's birthplace. When 20,000 people huddled under loudspeakers in the middle of Buenos Aires to follow the match against the US, they were cheering more than just a football result. They were asserting their national identity against the Anglo-American oppressor. This was symbolic vengeance. Such dramatic victories fuelled the nationalist passions of supporters.

Argentinians herded onto the ferries across the River Plate, from Buenos Aires to Montevideo. They joined the crowds of Uruguayans flooding the main artery of the city, climbing through the city's central park to the massive, modernist Centenario Stadium. There were no sponsors' hospitality villages or armies of media and reporters to get in the way.

This first World Cup was a politically motivated statement by a national government. It was staged by a small country anxious to show its bigger neighbours how well it could perform on a global scale. There were national benefits in communication and transport. And in both staging and winning the event, Uruguay strutted the world stage as champions, world-beaters, modernisers. In Uruguay Rimet's FIFA laid the foundation for the next World Cups in Italy in 1934, and in his native France in 1938.

In between, in 1936, Hitler staged what became known as the Nazi Olympics in Berlin. He took his lead from Italy where Mussolini first mobilised sport in the service of fascist ideals. The fascists developed élite performers, exploiting big events for mass publicity. In Italy they did this with the World Cup and brought together private capital with public money to build new stadiums.

Mussolini's hard men adhered to the Italian principle and practice of *transformismo*, the use of bribery, coercion and threats as a way of combating opposition. As Italy bludgeoned its way to the 1934 World Cup title, ugly scenes in big games, weird refereeing decisions and fanatical crowd scenes showed that *transformismo* was rife on the field of play as well as in Italy's corridors of power.

Italy held on to its title in France in 1938. Only three non-European sides competed. Argentina, weakened by the loss of Italo-Argentinians to the big-spending Italian clubs and insulted at not being allowed to host the finals, decided to stay away. Uruguay also didn't turn up. Central and South America were scarcely represented.

With little serious opposition (the great 1930s Austrian side was crippled by Nazi Germany's annexation of six of its top players) the Italians won again, handsomely repaying their fascist leader and government for the resources poured into international sport.

The Second World War and its consequences changed the face of international football. Global communications improved dramatically, and the British were forced to realise that strong and vibrant cultures existed beyond their island shores.

During the war football had been a popular diversion for troops from many countries. British soldiers returned home with fresh memories of the skilful and enthusiastic way in which the peoples of the world played football. One such man was Stanley Rous and it was he who led the Home Associations back into FIFA in 1946. Rous's rationale was simple enough: 'If you can't beat 'em, join 'em; and if you have to join 'em, you may as well lead 'em.' So it was that first in Arthur Drewry and eventually through Rous himself, an Englishman stood at FIFA's helm during football's golden years.

Stanley Rous, although not assuming the FIFA presidency until 1961, was an influential force in the game after the Second World War, holding the post of secretary of the English Football Association from 1934 to 1961, for example. Rous took over at FIFA in his mid-sixties, the age at which most people retired, and he grasped this new challenge with typical energy and commitment.

Walter Winterbottom, the first man to be appointed as manager of the England team, says that 'in our own country he took us out of being an insular Association Football League and got us back into world football and this was tremendous'. Winterbottom also praised Rous's exceptional charm and diplomatic skills.

A son of the middle classes, his father had planned for him to go to Emmanuel College, Cambridge. But, after service in Africa during the First World War, Stanley studied at St Luke's College, Exeter, and then taught at Watford Grammar School.

Rous was not born into the establishment but through football he became an establishment figure. For him, teaching and football were acts of public service. He played football at college, then in the army during the Great War. Though he may have been good enough to play the game professionally, his commitment to amateur ideals denied him the chance to be paid for playing. Instead, Rous became a referee of international repute. This is where he made his first impact on world football. His rewriting of the rules of the game was immensely influential. In administration, he went on to modernise the English game, establishing a more efficient bureaucratic base, introducing teaching schemes for all levels of the game – coaching, playing, refereeing.

But this mission was about more than just football. Britain was in crisis after the Second World War, losing its empire and looking for a role to play in the modern world. Educating football players as coaches and practitioners was one way of restoring British prominence.

The FA had left FIFA in 1928 and Rous believed that it was time for Britain to be reintegrated into the world football family. In a paper which he presented to the Football Association, first drafted in May 1943, he claimed that the activities of the FA's War Emergency Committee had boosted football's international profile by fostering relations with government departments and by establishing links with influential people through co-operation with the armed forces.

Recognising that Britain's formal political empire was about to shrink dramatically, he saw in football a chance to retain some influence over world culture. 'The unparalleled opportunity which the war years have given the Association of being of service to countries other than our own,' pontificated Rous, 'has laid an excellent foundation for post-war international development.'

A self-styled moderniser, he remained trapped in an anachronistic set of values. 'We used to look upon it as a sport, as a recreation,' he once said in a BBC interview. 'We had little regard of points and league position and cup competitions. We used to play friendly matches, mostly. There was always such a sporting attitude and the winners always clapped the others off the field and so on.' Ruefully he added, 'That's all changed of course.'

From the old world of the English middle classes, but negotiating the volatile world of post-colonialism, Rous's life and philosophy were a bundle of contradictions. He could be both innovative and traditional, adventurous yet crabbily cautious, modern yet steeped in traditional values.

The 1950s and early 1960s were modern football's brightest years. In Britain, continental Europe and South America, stadiums bulged with massive and largely orderly crowds of fervent supporters making their weekly pilgrimages to cheer on local heroes. With high attendances and relatively modest salaries for players, domestic professional football was self-sustaining and provided a stable basis of the development of national representative sides.

On this foundation FIFA's World Cup flourished. During the decisive game of the 1950 World Cup finals in Brazil, the highest ever crowd in the history of football (199,854) turned out to watch Uruguay beat the hosts 2–1 in the imposing Maracaná Stadium. Earlier in the tournament, England had been left in no doubt of the threat posed by foreign football when they were unceremoniously knocked out by the USA, who won 1–0 (though not many people in the USA knew about the match or even cared).

That threat was driven home in 1953 when the majestic Hungarians, inspired by Ferenc Puskas, beat England 6–3 at Wembley. It was England's first defeat at the national stadium and the already-dented façade of invincibility was shattered once and for all.

Hungary were unlucky 3–2 losers to West Germany in the 1954 finals in Switzerland. By the next World Cup in Sweden in 1958, the majesty of the Hungarians had been eclipsed by the rise of Brazil, and Puskas's mantle as the world's greatest player had been stolen by Pelé. Brazil won both that tournament and the 1962 World Cup in Chile, establishing themselves as the greatest team in the world.

In those days there were few bidders for the job of hosting the event. Decisions regarding where the World Cups should be held were made in smoke-filled rooms by the FIFA president and a few cronies. Bidding later became more competitive, but was nothing like the frenzy of today. England based its successful 1966 bid entirely on existing facilities. FIFA president Sir Stanley Rous had been secretary to the Football Association when the decision was made, but was very close to the English president of FIFA, Arthur Drewry. At the 1960 FIFA Congress in Lisbon, England won a close vote over West Germany to host the 1966 finals.

When England won the trophy, the political symbolism of national sports victories was not lost on the prime minister, Harold Wilson, who made sure he was photographed with the victorious English players. And the idea that political gains could be had from hosting the finals was becoming stronger and more widespread.

Rous was concerned at the economic shenanigans and interpersonal pressures which surrounded the bids of Argentina and Mexico to host the 1970 finals. To curb this, he developed a planning cycle for the event. He called this 'the long look ahead', and designed it to give adequate notice to those committing themselves to such a major event. He wanted to give hosts the advantage of a 12-year lead-in, and at FIFA's 1963 Congress in Tokyo, a future list for post-England 1966 was confirmed: Mexico 1970; West Germany 1974; Argentina 1978; Spain 1982. Colombia got the same 12 years of notice, at the end of Rous's presidency, for the 1986 finals (they ended up having to pull out). Rous foresaw the co-hosting role, and proposed that FIFA's long-term plan should envisage zoning the finals, suggesting that the event could be split between three or four countries.

Television executives were wising up to the worldwide popularity of football and the World Cup. This worried Rous, for more pitches and stadiums would be needed. Press and TV facilities would be demanded and, in the age of expanding sport tourism, accommodation would be required and security expected. The emerging cultural and media industries were becoming more and more crucial to the event. This was not the comfortable colonial world of the baggy-panted international referee Rous, dispensing his schoolmasterly wisdom to the needy of the world. Sir Stanley was never comfortable with the intrusiveness of the broadcast media. It invaded the cosy spaces of his football bases in the house gifted to him by FIFA, in Ladbroke Road, London, and in the sleepy villa in lush suburban Zurich.

Harry Cavan, senior vice-president of FIFA during Rous's reign, recalled that before Havelange arrived on the scene, Rous was 'probably the most travelled man in football in the world in those days. He had the right connections, he had the right influence and, above all, he had the ability and the skill to do the job. And of course he was clever. He was generally one or two moves ahead of most of the others.' But 'most of the others' were like-minded fellow Europeans. Rous was ill-equipped to deal with the charismatic Brazilian, João Havelange, and his ambitious and ruthless pursuit of the presidency in 1974.

When he stood for re-election as FIFA president, claiming that he wanted 'just a couple of years to push through some important schemes', Rous either had a confidence which was misplaced, or he had miscalculated the institutional politics of FIFA. Ten years on he put his defeat down to the limitless ambitions of his rival: 'I know what activity was being practised by my successor, the appeals that he'd made to countries.'

Rous's reflections are only half right. Yes, Havelange did run a ruthless and aggressive campaign which, as some believe, may have been seriously questionable. But it was the perception of football administrators in the Third World that Rous viewed them and their problems through Colonel Blimp's binoculars which did him most damage. In the years leading up to the 1974 elections he had plenty of chances to challenge and change the perception of him as old-fashioned, imperious and even racist. That he chose not to, cost him his job.

3. GOODBYE, COLONEL BLIMP

Sir Stanley Rous lived a stimulating but lonely life. For most of his career with the English FA and at the helm of FIFA his wife was an invalid, but he left her at home as he travelled the world spreading the gospel of the game. Work was Stanley's passion and football was his work.

Trying to piece together a picture of the Rous years at FIFA, we spoke to the English FA librarian David Barber. 'Might the FA cellars or archives have any of Rous's FIFA papers?' we asked.

'Oh, no,' David said, 'we haven't room for that kind of thing. Anyway, Rosemarie's got all Sir Stanley's papers.'

For most of his life after taking up the FIFA presidency, Rous's personal assistant and companion was Rosemarie Breitenstein. In photographs taken of the globe-trotting FIFA president in the 1960s and 1970s, the slender and attractive Rosemarie frequently appears by his side, his loyal and faithful right-hand woman.

We asked where in the world could we find Rosemarie. 'You'll find her upstairs,' said the librarian. 'She's Graham Kelly's secretary.' We were hardly able to believe our luck. After a quick phone call she came to meet us in the library.

Close to retirement age, Rosemarie is an attractive woman who carries herself with finishing-school elegance. She speaks perfect English, but with the slightest Germanic inflection. Behind bright eyes, her memories of her days with Sir Stanley remain vivid. During regular visits to the FA, we sat enthralled as she gave us insider accounts of the career highs and lows of world football's first great moderniser.

Rosemarie had dutifully filed away thousands of papers from Sir Stanley's FIFA years in the cellar of the Ladbroke Road home that he bequeathed her on his deathbed. This was the same house that was gifted to him by FIFA once he retired. We told her what topics we were interested in and she would stuff the files into a shopping bag before bringing them down and leaving them with us next to the photocopier in the FA library.

Reading Sir Stanley's immaculate longhand annotations on drafts and original documents, we suspected he was becoming increasingly out of touch and out of place in a changing post-colonial world in which newly independent nations saw football as a means of gaining status and worldwide recognition. He could neither ignore nor control the political and commercial forces swirling around his beloved game.

Havelange planned his challenge to Rous on this basis. He plotted his campaign to seize FIFA's throne with military precision, planning to exploit the one-nation, one-vote system which FIFA employed for presidential elections. He could bank on the full backing of South America's ten members, including the big three of Brazil, Argentina and Uruguay. The emerging Central and North American block was dominated by Mexico, where Havelange had cultivated business and sporting links. He could expect considerable support from this quarter, but he would still need more votes if he were to overcome Rous and the Europeans.

The Brazilian worked out early that if he could win over FIFA's numerous marginal members, the world of football could be delivered into his hands. He saw that the support of the poor and developing football nations could be bought by the highest bidder. There would be promises to keep, but Havelange would worry about these once he became president.

He concentrated his campaigning on Africa and Asia. He told them that it was time for a change, for a new and visionary leadership from beyond the privileged and haughty shores of the developed European world. It was time to break the stranglehold of the former colonial masters. He was helped by the resentment which was felt towards the blimpish Rous in the far-flung corners of the FIFA empire.

Rous's plea that 'block' interests be avoided had little effect. In addition, he soon encountered difficulties monitoring the South Americans' activities and claims. In November 1969 his general secretary sent him, from Zurich to his London address, a full briefing letter for a forthcoming congress. This correspondence catalogued a long list of backstage manoeuvrings which were read as threatening to FIFA's central (but European-based) authority.

The FIFA general secretary, Helmut Käser, expressed surprise that the South American federation wished to change completely the administration at the end of a presidential term of office: 'There will be no continuity in administrative business . . . Possibly this is the South American way of thinking.' He added: 'As usual South America is pretending that FIFA is giving preference to European referees and that South American referees are neglected.'

A 'very delicate matter' could arise, Käser pointed out, concerning referees for World Cup preliminary matches. The delicacy arose from a remark made by a member of the South American referees' committee member that 'it is customary in South America to make "pilgrimages" to the referees' countries'.

On one trip to the Central and North American confederation in 1971, Rous called for the member associations to clean up their act – to make sure that financial resources were effectively and correctly used, to improve slack administration, make committees properly representative and to take more care in nominating referees.

This was quite a list – dodgy delegates, crooked refs, financial irregularities. This strong schoolmasterly ticking-off hardly endeared Rous to the FIFA family in this part of the Americas. His style evoked stereotypes that were to be played upon with brilliance by Havelange.

As Havelange mobilised his support, Sir Stanley noticed that the Brazilian wasn't always playing with a straight bat. By early 1973 Havelange was turning up at confederation congresses. FIFA queries on this were brushed aside. North and Central American confederation president Joaquin Sorvia Terrazas – one of those who had ignored Rous's ticking-off – denied that Havelange had been invited to take part in or attend the congress, or that he'd been present at any of the meetings. 'Unfortunately,' Terrazas told FIFA, Havelange's 'spontaneous visit to the Mexican Football Confederation coincided on the same dates as our Congress'. Passing off such a visit as coincidence strains credulity.

Football officials in Argentina and Uruguay had proposed that Havelange become the South American candidate for the FIFA presidency. Accepting this, the dynamic businessman then moved fast. With the backing of most of the South American countries, he spent 1971 to 1973 in worldwide canvassing. Preparing for the 1974 FIFA election, he visited 86 countries, concentrating on Africa and Asia. Havelange made personal calls to FIFA members to talk up his manifesto. He made eight promises. He would increase the numbers of participants in the World Cup finals. He'd create a junior, Under-20 World Championship. FIFA would get a swish new head office. FIFA would provide materials to underdeveloped associations and help them construct and improve their stadiums. He pledged more courses for sports professionals and the provision of extra technical and medical expertise to underdeveloped countries. He also promised to introduce an inter-continental club championship. With the exception of the promise to build new headquarters, all the other proposals can be read as developments which would bring most benefit to those at the margins of world football.

Lobbying effectively, and pledging these commitments, Havelange – 'a very clever man, a very skilled politician', in Ulsterman Harry Cavan's words – aimed to become FIFA's first non-European president. His candidature was cleverly pitched, harnessing the resentments and aspirations of South and Central American, southern European, Soviet, African and Asian footballing nations.

No candidate for any sports post had ever run a campaign like this. 'It was such a radical change suddenly to have this dynamic, glamorous South American character, brimming with *bonhomie*, travelling the world with the Brazilian team, travelling with the likes of Pelé,' recalled Patrick Nally, former business associate of the late Horst Dassler of Adidas. It was Brazilian carnival time and Havelange led the main parade.

With Central and South America already in his pocket, wooing the African football nations became crucial to the Havelange election strategy. Rous's FIFA made this easy for him. By the mid-1960s, even though the membership of the African confederation (CAF) had increased to more than 30, African representation in the World Cup finals could be achieved only by a play-off between the winners of the African Cup of Nations and its Asian equivalent. Opposing such obvious discrimination, Dr Kwame Nkrumah, then president of Ghana, successfully persuaded CAF members to boycott the qualifying tournament for the 1966 finals in England.

This action shocked FIFA and, at the pre-tournament congress in London, African representation in future finals was granted. This was still fresh in the memories of many of the African delegates as they prepared for the 1974 Frankfurt congress. If it was not, Havelange lost no time in reminding them.

Through the political machinery which he had put together to manage his African campaign, Havelange shrewdly exploited the antipathy between the former British and French colonies. As the 1960s wore on more and more African countries gained independence; as this happened, unnoticed by Sir Stanley Rous, the balance of power within CAF shifted from English-speaking to French-speaking Africa.

One of Havelange's main collaborators in Africa was Jean-Claude Ganga from Congo, who was the first secretary of the Supreme Council for African Sport which was founded in 1966. According to Oroc Oyo, the first secretary of the Nigerian Football Association after independence, 'Ganga mustered Africa for Havelange'. There was little love lost between Rous and Ganga and the latter appeared to be only too willing to use his influence to persuade fellow Africans to support Havelange.

'I remember the 1974 elections very vividly,' explains Oyo, who had trained under Rous at the English FA. On the eve the 1974 elections Oyo was running one of Africa's largest and most influential football associations and was at the centre of the tug-of-war between Rous and Havelange. He recalls attending the CAF congress in Egypt in 1974. After the congress Havelange invited African delegates to a cocktail party hosted by the ambassador of Brazil in Egypt. 'All of us were invited. The plank of Havelange's campaign was to ostracise South Africa, because this was the clarion call of African football. This was a carrot which Dr Havelange brandished before Africa.'

Of all Rous's mistakes, Oyo believes that his misreading of South Africa was the most serious. FIFA suspended South Africa again in 1961, pending an investigation into the mainly white Football Association of South Africa (FASA). Rous visited the country in January 1963 along with Jimmy McGuire, the secretary of the United States Soccer Federation, and produced a report which suggested that the FASA 'was not – or by its rules should not have been – concerned with the government's policies and attitudes'. His official report concluded: 'FIFA cannot be used as a weapon to force government to change its internal sports policy. To do so would wreck FIFA's true purpose.' Rosemarie Breitenstein claims, bizarrely, that Sir Stanley believed that football conditions in South Africa were widely available to all, whatever their background or colour.

In truth, apartheid poisoned sport as it did every sphere of society in South Africa. In an attempt to appease the international community, in 1971 Premier Vorster introduced a 'multinational' sports policy: officially sanctioned racial categories (whites, Indians, Africans and coloureds), under certain circumstances, could play against each other at an 'international level' and play touring international teams.

In South Africa in the early 1970s there were separate administrative bodies for Indian soccer, coloured soccer, African soccer, non-racial soccer and white soccer. And the whites lobbied aggressively to be recognised as the commanding voice for South Africa in the world arena. This was the bizarre zenith of sporting apartheid, even leading to an absurd proposal that South Africa would rotate the racial mix of the national team as it attempted to qualify for successive World Cup finals. They would enter a black team for England in 1966, a white team for Mexico in 1970, presumably a coloured team for Germany in 1974 and so on.

Rous's dogged determination to stand by his antiquated views on the separation of sport from politics flew in the face of pan-African sensibilities and played into Havelange's hands. Mawad Wade, then secretary of Senegal's football association, admits to being one of those in the African confederation who helped Ganga with Havelange's campaign. 'Why? Because of apartheid in South Africa. I was talking to Sir Stanley Rous in the Sheraton Hotel in Cairo. I told him, "If you are elected, can you keep South Africa out of FIFA until apartheid goes down?" He says to me, "I can't promise you because I follow my country, the United Kingdom." I say to him, "In this case, then, we will never vote for you."'

Wade got the answers he wanted from Havelange. 'I met Havelange in the same hotel,' recalled Wade. 'He says to me, "Okay, so long as I am in charge and apartheid still exists, South Africa will never come into FIFA."'

From his earliest days in the presidency, Rous sided with the white football establishment in South Africa. In the early 1960s the FASA faced a challenge from the multiracial South African Soccer Federation (SASF). In its January 1963 visit to South Africa, Rous's two-man commission held interviews with many sports organisations and received full submissions from the two football bodies. In its scathing critique on its multiracial opponents, the whites-only body exploited Rous's naïveté, claiming most of its opponents were 'uneducated, and not fit to assume positions of authority in any sphere of life. I do not desire to enter into any political discussions, as I am aware that

your body does not allow politics to enter into any of its delibera-
tions.'

Rous and McGuire 'unreservedly' recommended that the
suspension of the FASA be lifted. 'The members of the dissident
Federation whom we interviewed, would, in our opinion, be quite
unsuitable to represent Association Football in South Africa. We
found that they desired to hinder and to act contrary to government
policy, which clearly indicates their inability to foster and propagate
the game of soccer in that country.'

The Rous-McGuire recommendation was supported in the
executive committee by 13 votes to five. Despite this substantial
majority, Rous began to think that he was losing control over his
executive. He wrote to Aleck Jaffe of the FASA: 'The votes against
were all from the left wing and for the first time those members
demonstrated their solidarity as a block.' His worst fears were
confirmed the following year at FIFA's Tokyo Congress, when
members took the unprecedented step of overturning the 1963
executive committee decision, and by 48 votes to 15 suspended the
FASA for 'the practice of racial discrimination'. This should have
been a warning to Rous about the growing might of the Third World
vote, but he was either too blind or too arrogant to take heed.

South Africa was to haunt Rous throughout his presidency. At the
Eighth Ordinary General Assembly of the African Football
Confederation in Addis Ababa, in January 1968, the president
addressed the assembly, warning delegates against the sports politics
subversives in South Africa. Referring to a letter received from the
South African Non-Racial Olympic Committee (SANROC), Rous
enraged many African delegates when he said, 'In fact you should
take no notice of their letter. I know these peoples. I have been in
South Africa to meet them. In fact this group is more interested in
communist politics than in football.'

In response, the Kenyan delegate spoke of 'the unwarranted attack
of Sir Stanley Rous against the general secretary and the AFC' on the
South Africa question. 'We in Kenya wish to see that all means
possible are used to bring about a change in South Africa so that our
brothers there may enjoy the freedom of sports we have.' In the eyes
of most of the African delegates, Rous was a racist.

As late as 1973 he was still working to bring South Africa back into
the world footballing fold. He organised a postal ballot supporting a
'special dispensation' for the suspended association to stage a South

African multiracial sports festival. SANROC, from its exiled base in London, wrote back condemning this as 'a dubious postal vote which is not in conformity with rules'. Yet again, Rous misread the international response to such a gesture.

The African confederation roundly condemned his action. Rous argued – in response to a query from Dakar – that 'this gesture was made as an experiment to overcome apartheid in sport'. The dispensation was withdrawn by Rous and FIFA, claiming to have been misled on the make-up of the teams, but the damage was done. His support for such racist schemes was to sink him in the following months.

Granatkin of the USSR telegrammed Moscow's 'categorical' opposition to FIFA's support for the event. It was not the last Rous would hear from the Soviets that year. His relations with the communists were further damaged through the position he adopted over the World Cup qualifying match between Chile and the Soviet Union, scheduled to be played on 21 November 1973 in Santiago's National Stadium.

Chile was governed by a military junta headed by General Pinochet, which had overthrown the democratically elected Marxist government of Salvador Allende in September of that year. Pinochet's régime had brutally eliminated political opposition and it was well known that dissidents had been rounded up and held captive at the National Stadium, where they were tortured and murdered. The Soviets argued that under these circumstances, the game should be played in a neutral country.

In October 1973 Rous sent a FIFA delegation to Santiago led by vice-president D'Almeida and general secretary Dr Käser. The FIFA officials were put up in one of the capital's finest hotels and provided with a chauffeur-driven limousine for the duration of their three-day visit.

It is obvious from their report that D'Almeida and Käser failed to look further than the guided tour provided for them by Chilean officials. 'In reply to our precise question concerning the stadium,' the report states, 'we were told that in a couple of days the stadium will be at the disposal of the sports organisations as it is expected that the interrogation of the remaining detainees will be terminated and most of them will have gone home.'

Between them, Käser and D'Almeida made what was effectively a concentration camp sound like a holiday resort. 'The stadium is at present being used as a "clearing station" and the people in there are not prisoners but only detainees whose identity has to be established.'

'The stadium is under military guard and entry is only possible with a special pass,' they went on. 'Inside the stadium itself the seats and pitch were empty and the remaining detainees were in the dressing and other rooms. Outside the stadium approximately 50 to 100 people were waiting for news of relatives who were still detained. Inside the outer fencing everything seemed to be normal and gardeners are working on the gardens.'

'The grass on the pitch is in perfect condition as were the seating arrangements,' D'Almeida and his colleagues cheerily concluded. 'In Santiago, life is back to normal.' Let the game go ahead.

Without hesitation the FIFA executive accepted these recommendations. The Soviets were furious. From Moscow, Granatkin despatched a telegram to Rous at his London home:

> WELL KNOWN THAT AS RESULT FASCIST UPHEAVAL OVERTHROWN LEGAL GOVERNMENT NATIONAL UNITY NOW IN CHILE REVEALS ATMOSPHERE BLOODY TERRORISM AND REPRESSIONS . . . NATIONAL STADIUM SUPPOSED BE VENUE HOLD FOOTBALL MATCH TURNED BY MILITARY JUNTA INTO CONCENTRATION CAMP PLACE OF TORTURES AND EXECUTIONS OF CHILEAN PATRIOTS STOP . . . SOVIET SPORTSMEN CANNOT AT PRESENT PLAY AT STADIUM STAINED WITH BLOOD OF CHILEAN PATRIOTS STOP . . . USSR FOOTBALL FEDERATION ON BEHALF SOVIET SPORTSMEN EXPRESS DECISIVE PROTEST AND . . . REFUSE PARTICIPATE QUALIFICATION MATCH AT CHILE TERRITORY AND MAKES FIFA LEADERS RESPONSIBLE FOR IT STOP

FIFA received many other outraged objections to its ruling. A personal letter to Stanley Rous from a youth football organisation in East Germany said that a Santiago match would be like playing at Dachau. The president of the East German football federation, Reidle, asked Sir Stanley how he could expect any nation to send their athletes to arenas 'saturated with the blood of noble and honest men'. Complaints rained in from Africa and Latin America. Sir Stanley ignored them all.

On 6 November the following cable from the USSR football federation was delivered to Rous's home address, 115 Ladbroke Road:

DECISION ABOUT VENUE OF MATCH NOT ACCEP-
TABLE FOR SOVIET FOOTBALLERS WHO CONFIRM
REFUSAL TO PLAY GAME IN CHILE STOP REGRET
THAT DID NOT FOLLOW COMMON SENSE AND NOT
RECONSIDERED ITS DECISION

Rous prepared to face the consequences through the ballot box. 'The Russian attitude may well have repercussions outside Europe, since their political muscle extends wide,' he recalled in his memoirs. 'While a sitting president has certain advantages, there were several "political" issues militating against me, because I was not prepared to connive at ignoring its [FIFA's] own statutes.'

Rous believed he had a sizeable proportion of the African vote in his pocket. In 1971 Oroc Oyo, then the secretary of the Nigerian Football Association, a man who'd spent a sabbatical with Rous at the English FA in the late 1950s, promised him that Nigeria, perhaps the most influential country in West Africa and one of the continent's strongest football nations, would support him. However, as Oyo himself told us in 1996, 'I went to his room and pledged him Nigeria's support. Being British trained and since I had some tutelage under Sir Stanley Rous, I did not favour Dr Havelange's drive, I was for Sir Stanley Rous. But unfortunately, when they went for that election in 1974 I had a brush with the Nigerian Football Association and I was sidelined.' The Nigerian delegation 'swallowed the bait of Dr Havelange and Ganga's Supreme Council and that was how he won the election', concluded Oyo.

Right up to the vote in Frankfurt, just prior to the 1974 finals in West Germany, the Europeans did not realise that they had been outmanoeuvred and remained confident that Havelange's challenge would fail. Rous played what he saw as a fair match in the presidential election, but in the conclusion to his April 1974 last-minute campaign brochure, in a thinly veiled critique of Havelange's campaign, he said he would not stoop to vulgar electioneering, emphasising his belief in the 'president's role as world ambassador for football', and playing up his honourable motives and style: 'I can offer no special inducements to obtain support in my re-election, nor have I canvassed for votes except through this communication,' Rous pontificated. 'I prefer to let the record speak for itself.' Unfortunately for him, the needle was stuck on this particular post-colonial record and the sounds were coming through too softly and too late.

Many Asian friends of Rous also sensed the tide turning. For all his respect for Sir Stanley's accomplishments, the young Peter Velappan, then secretary of the Malaysian Football Association, was one of those to take Rous by surprise. Velappan recalls that the president was widely respected, but 'I think Sir Stanley did not take the election too seriously. He didn't believe in campaigning. But Dr Havelange and his people did a lot of groundwork, and specially promising Asia and Africa many benefits.'

The 79-year-old Sir Stanley Rous put his 12-year tenure of office and Europe's monopoly of the world body in the hands of 122 delegates, of whom 37 were African. It was a close-run contest, but Havelange edged over the required mark in a second ballot, with the Africans and Asians behind him.

According to Peter Pullen, a senior official in the Brazilian foreign office and a long time associate of Havelange (Rosemarie Breitenstein recalled him as 'Havelange's agent in England'), there was a hidden irony in this result. Some time before he launched his own campaign for the FIFA presidency, Havelange, in his capacity as president of the Brazilian Sport/Football Federation (CBF), had warned Rous of the increasing power of the Third World. Havelange counselled that Rous should consider changing FIFA's constitution in such a way that the votes of the more established nations of Europe and Latin America would weigh more than those of the newer members from Africa and Asia. Rous, thinking that he had the votes of the British Commonwealth nations in the palm of his hand, turned down Havelange's proposal – a decision that was to haunt him after the Frankfurt congress.

This result shattered Rous, whose response is recalled by his secretary as 'certainly one of deep upset, and in some senses as a betrayal'. Over a century earlier, the prime minister, Disraeli, commented that Britain's colonies had become 'a millstone round our necks'. In 1974 Rous and European sports' other power-brokers harboured similar thoughts.

Letters of condolence poured into Rous from the upper echelons of world sports administration, such as Lord Killanin of the IOC, some referring to the 'dark forces' which had engulfed the world's top sport in the figure of the Brazilian bogeyman. People whispered that Havelange and his cronies had spent £500,000 on his campaign (equivalent to around £4 million today).

Havelange had warned Rous of what was to come. He claims that he did not want at first to contest the presidency, but others 'were very insistent'. So Havelange visited England to dine with Sir Stanley: 'I told him that of the two of us there would be only one winner, and as I was originally a swimmer I told him there would be only one medal. Either I would win the medal, or he would win the medal. He put his arms around me, as a grandfather would a grandson, and I think he didn't believe it.'

Rous, and he was far from alone in this, did not realise that in this historic moment the Grandfather was on the way out, the Godfather on the way in.

4. THE BIG MAN

The most powerful men in the world never walk alone. So it was when Dr João Havelange, FIFA president, swept through the lobby of Cairo's luxurious Marriott hotel on the banks of the Nile. Flanked by bodyguards, trailed by an entourage of factotums, the 81-year-old strode athletically towards the hotel exit like a much younger man.

The Big Man was in town to open the Under-17 World Championship finals, and to chair one of his last executive committee meetings before completing his 24 years at FIFA's helm. In his long-standing role as International Olympic Committee member he would, in a few days, be jetting back to Switzerland to cast his vote and give Athens the 2004 summer Games.

FIFA's executive brings together the heads of its worldwide family. As he took the chair in the main committee room of Cairo's modern exhibition centre, Havelange's piercing steel-blue eyes scrutinised the executive, the men who lead a global football industry reckoned to be worth more than $250 billion.

There was Sepp Blatter, FIFA general secretary, Havelange's one-time apprentice, long-term confidant and soon-to-be anointed successor. Dr Mong Joon Chung of South Korea was there, representing Asia's interests. Dr Chung was not just a football man. He was also a member of Korea's national parliament and head of Hyundai heavy industries, a man who sees within his football mission a greater prize: the unification of Korea, perhaps under his own political stewardship.

Cameroonian Issa Hayatou spoke for Africa, with the potential to control more than 50 African congress votes. Abdulah-al-dabal, Saudi Arabian football supremo, brought with him the power and influence of the oil-rich Gulf states and the will of Saudi's royal family.

Veteran FIFA committee man David Will, a little-known Scottish lawyer, was there for the UK associations. The North and Central Americans were represented by flamboyant entrepreneur Chuck Blazer, general secretary of that confederation and controversial successor to the deceased Guillermo Cañedo, a veteran executive member, senior FIFA vice-president and Mexico media baron. Finding it pretty peaceful here in Cairo away from the threats of the Russian mafia was Viacheslav Koloskov, one-time head of the mighty Soviet football federation.

Julio Grondona, arbiter of South American interests and defender of Argentinian football during that country's recent political turbulence, was at the table. New Zealander and Scottish expatriate Charlie Dempsey CBE was also there. Dempsey calls himself just 'an old Glasgow street fighter', but he was tough and wily enough to get Havelange to recognise Oceania as a full confederation.

Perhaps Havelange's gaze rested longest on the man who would be king, his bitter rival, the burly Swedish truck boss Lennart Johansson, president of the European federation. Johansson led Europe's resentment at Havelange's manipulation of the world body for his own selfish ends. The Swede had threatened to open up the FIFA books, democratise world football and conduct FIFA business with a modicum of transparency.

While Pelé may be remembered as the most influential footballer of the twentieth century, off the field it is this other Brazilian who did most to shape the destiny of the world's most popular sport. After many failed attempts to get an interview with Havelange, we were eventually summoned to his temporary headquarters in a suite in another, even more exclusive, hotel, the Cairo Sheraton. We stepped nervously past two guards brandishing machine-guns and negotiated our way past Havelange's glamorous personal assistant before being ushered in for an audience with the Big Man himself. Havelange is not really that big – no taller than five foot ten – but he has a big presence. He has the air and the physical charisma of the dictator and has not been slow to use this in his presidential role in FIFA.

'Havelange had such an aura about him,' recalls David Will, 'people were actually physically scared of him, were frightened of him, in a one-to-one situation. He's devastating. His control of himself is amazing.' A painful look crosses Will's face as he recounts a recent brush with the Big Man. 'We've had situations recently where he's been shouting at me, because I was supporting the voting procedure in the Congress.' Havelange never loses his composure, though. 'At the end, when we stand up to leave, he says, "Sorry, David," shakes my hand and kisses me on both cheeks. He's in total control of himself.'

During our meeting, Havelange recalls with relish and self-congratulation how he made his way in the world. The son of a Belgian industrialist and arms trader, Jean-Marie Faustin Godefroid Havelange was born on 8 May 1916 in Rio de Janeiro. He joined his father's arms company as a youngster and learned the rudiments of business administration. His father died when he was 18, and he went to work and studied part-time: 'I wasn't earning very much, but I was learning something for life.' He worked for an iron and steel company which had a Belgian link, before working in law for a couple of years. He told us how, early in life, he decided that he could not work for anyone else. After six years, he went to the company director and told him that he was resigning and never wanted to work for another boss in his life: 'I have never had another boss in my life, except maybe my wife,' he said. He branched out on his own, building a business empire in the transport and financial industries of a modernising Brazil.

In 1997 he could boast that 20 million people a year were transported by his company, which he'd been with for 57 years (53 as chairman). He had also been a director of the biggest insurance company in Brazil: 'When I became president of FIFA,' he claimed, 'I had to take a step down in that company.'

Havelange displayed a deadly seriousness – even his attempts at humour were delivered with the grim earnestness of someone who finds laughter a sign of weakness. As he built Brazil's and then FIFA's football empires, he had little time for laughter. He would leave a trail of defeated rivals, victims and dependants as he extended his influence beyond his home nation, the continent and across the entire globe.

Young Havelange was an athlete of some distinction. He had played junior football with Fluminense, the amateur sporting club for Brazil's élite. To join this club, it was necessary to belong to a family of means – which meant being white. When a famous mixed-race player, Carlos Alberto, sought to pass himself off as white by powdering his face in the locker-rooms, they called it the 'face-powder club'. Now, of course, Fluminense is a professional club, one of the most famous and successful in South America.

Professionalism would later bring more opportunities for non-whites and also herald the end for mediocre upper-class footballers like Havelange. Not good enough to play alongside the talented professionals, he redirected his energies to swimming. From the mid-1930s to the early 1950s he competed at the top of his two chosen performance sports, representing Brazil in the Olympics in Berlin in 1936 in swimming and in Helsinki in 1952 in the water-polo team. He said that 'water-polo served to discharge my aggressiveness and all my occasional ill-humour', and it is a common boast of his that he swims every morning of his life.

Havelange's memories of the Hitler Olympics are extraordinary. 'The first thing I remember is that the organisation of the transport was perfect, and the equipment and the facilities for 25,000 people were very well arranged.' He also recalls the convivial hospitality provided by the Nazis and the seven visits some athlete guests made to hear the 700 musicians playing in the Berlin Philharmonic. 'From the start it was a pleasure to be in Berlin,' Havelange said. Like many others, he received the travel and other privileges that Hitler's and Goebbels's friends in the Olympic movement laid on. Train tickets could be booked at a 75 per cent discount, and the 20-year-old saw 25 different cities. He didn't suffer in Hitler's Germany.

Brazil declared war against Germany and Italy on 22 August 1942. It joined the defence of the South Atlantic against Axis submarines and also sent an expeditionary force to Italy in 1944, which conducted itself courageously in several bloody engagements.

Back home, Havelange spent the years of his peak sports performances building up business and social contacts in São Paulo. The young entrepreneur – son of an arms dealer, a chip off the old block – sensed some real business openings in the transport industry. The state had taken over public transport and this would be re-privatised after the war. Brazil had nuzzled up to the US during the conflict, giving its powerful ally the use of naval and air bases. In exchange, the two countries signed a number of agreements for economic development and for the production of Brazilian raw materials.

With the state in temporary control of the economy and a black market thriving, it was a good time to be a young businessman on the make. The city government requisitioned the transport system, creating a municipal company. This was not to Havelange's liking, nor in line with his individualist market philosophy. In his own words, the post-war years were for him ones of opportunity for fighting government interference in the market. 'Since I did not want to be a public servant, I and some friends founded the Viação Cometa in 1947.'

Highway construction was top of Brazil's post-war agenda of modernisation. When most of a country's people can't afford cars, how will they travel on the highways? In buses, of course. It didn't take Havelange long to see this crucial, expanding market. On the eve of the twenty-first century, it is still the vehicles of Viação Cometa that fill the urban hinterlands of São Paulo and Rio de Janeiro. Go and view the stunning movie *Central Station* to see how the moderniser's buses still dominate and scar the Brazilian landscape.

By the mid-1950s Havelange had established a power base in national business networks. His time with the steelmaking company Belgo-Mineira helped him learn how to oil the wheels of bureaucracy. Senior partners realised that if they wanted to speed their imported buses through customs, young João was the man to help them. Although no more than a minority shareholder, Havelange was chosen as director-president of Viação Cometa.

The sports world was fertile ground for big-business contacts, too. During his São Paulo years, Havelange had swum and played water-polo at the Espéria rowing club, cultivating and consolidating friendships with some of the country's leading industrialists. From his mid-20s onwards, he was displaying the qualities of the dealmaker and fixer that would serve him well throughout the following half-century. No one else had combined sports and business networking and interests so closely, so early in the era of modern and global sport.

In Havelange's view, simply being Brazilian made him the man for FIFA's top job. 'It was an advantage for me when I became president of FIFA that since a small child I have lived together with all the different races and understood their mentalities. It is nothing new for me to be in FIFA's multiracial environment,' he told us.

He makes it sound as though he was brought up in Rio's *favelas*, the notorious slums. 'I had the good fortune to be born a Brazilian, which is a multiracial society – Indians, blacks, Arabs, Jews, Europeans, Japanese, Koreans, Latinos, everything. All the various races of the world joined together to make a multiracial world.' It sounds good, but he refuses to disclose how much social contact he has with Brazil's lower classes and the poorer immigrant groups.

He warms to his theme: 'In São Paulo and Rio there are streets with Arabs on one side and Jews on the other side and they live in the same street in perfect harmony.'

Havelange points out that Brazil is the eighth industrial power in the world, that São Paulo is a city just like those in Germany. Yet the northern part of the country is less developed, 'a little like Africa'. Havelange claims that Brazil is both a mid-point and a microcosm of the world: a leader of the non-aligned nations with aspects of the First, Second and Third World. This allows Havelange cleverly to position himself as representative of the developed world, as much as of the Third World – but with an empathy for the entire planet.

Trading on his achievements in the swimming-pool and his associated networks and contacts, in the late 1950s Havelange brought his business and administrative skills into Brazilian sport. His base in the Brazilian Sports Federation (CBD), gave him authority over all the country's major sports, including football. 'I brought to the federation the entrepreneurial skills and the business skills from my own company,' he told us. 'There were just [sports] coaches, but I brought in specialist doctors and administrators for the federation to give it a wider basis. This is what made the difference and why we won the World Cup in 1958, 1962 and 1970.'

He recognised the potential football had to promote Brazil's international image, and his own global profile in both sport and business. He used his experience of restructuring football in Brazil, with an expanded national and regional league and cup set-up underpinned by commercial intervention, as a model for the expansion of the world game when he seized FIFA's reins of power from Sir Stanley Rous in 1974.

His election to the presidency was a watershed moment in the history of world sport. Already a key member of the International Olympic Committee (IOC), Havelange eased the passage of Spain's Juan Antonio Samaranch into the Olympic family and helped him to secure the presidency of the IOC. Similarly, Italy's Primo Nebiolo rose to the top of the increasingly influential International Amateur Athletic Federation (IAAF), confirming a new Latin dominance in world sport. Once at the FIFA helm, Havelange set about taking control of world football away from its established Northern European, Anglo-Saxon stronghold. To do this he would have to fulfil the promises he had made to the developing world during his election campaign.

When Havelange took over at FIFA, operating from its modest headquarters in Zurich, it was little more than a one-man operation run on a shoestring. The organisation had fewer than a hundred members and operated one tournament only, the World Cup finals, for which only 16 nations could qualify to take part.

After a quarter of a century, when Havelange stepped down in Paris in 1998 on the eve of the first ever 32-nation senior competition, FIFA, according to its president's estimate, had more than $4 billion heading into its coffers. As a global industry, he reckoned football to be worth in the region of $250 billion annually, way in excess of General Motors' $170 billion. This huge expansion, including the addition of a series of world championships for youth players and women, was achieved in partnership with transnational media partners and business interests including such global giants as Coca-Cola, Adidas and McDonald's.

Havelange, with the help of his close ally and confidant, the late Horst Dassler, was the first to recognise the full commercial potential of sport in the global market. He opened the gates and the money flooded in, along with the media and marketing men with their own ideas about the scale, structure and presentation of the world's most popular sport.

Havelange was a consummate political operator who ruled FIFA in autocratic style. Henry Kissinger, having acted as spokesman for the USA's failed bid to host the 1986 World Cup, experienced the president's managerial style. 'It made me feel nostalgic for the Middle East,' he said dryly. British sports minister Tony Banks declared that compared with Westminster, the politics of FIFA in the Havelange era were 'positively Byzantine'. Former FIFA media director Guido Tognoni said that on a clear and sunny day, 'Havelange could make you believe that the sky was red when it was really blue'.

People have talked about Havelange's almost supernatural powers of strength and concentration. 'He was a master of managing meetings,' Tognoni told us. 'He was also a master of making people feel that they are important without actually giving power away. He was just a master of power.'

There is a physically competitive side to this use of power. 'He was always the toughest guy, and even when he was tired he didn't want to stop the meetings,' said Tognoni. 'He was always fully informed about everything – whereas the members, they were not professionals, they had to eat what was served.' After a reflective pause, Tognoni concluded that the Big Man 'had the power to do everything that he wanted'.

When Havelange rang FIFA House in Zurich from his office in Rio, it was as if his physical authority came down the telephone line: FIFA staff have been known to stand to attention at such times. So too have presidents and monarchs, as Havelange in his prime dispensed patronage and spouted pledges of support to countries scrambling for the privilege of hosting the World Cup finals. Morocco and the USA were rival candidates to stage the event in 1994, for example. Both countries fought to outdo each other's hospitality. Havelange enjoyed an audience with President Reagan in the White House and received the Grand Cordon Alaouite from King Hassan of Morocco.

In the late 1980s, at a time when Switzerland was considering bidding for the 1998 tournament, the Swiss Football Association nominated Havelange for the Nobel Peace Prize, praising him for his achievement in turning FIFA into a 'world power binding all nations'. The announcement of this proposal generated a standing ovation from many delegates at the 1988 FIFA Congress in Zurich. The French and the Moroccans remained in their seats. Jacques Chirac claimed during his successful presidential campaign that he had been promised by Havelange that France would be given the 1998 World Cup *before this had even been considered by FIFA's executive*. Havelange, with Chirac in Paris, stated, 'I would be happy to see the committee look favourably on France's candidature,' knowing that Morocco would run again, as well as Switzerland.

The FIFA president did not mark out France as a favourite in his early pronouncements on the race to host the 1998 finals. In late 1988 – within five months of receiving his Nobel nomination – he praised Switzerland for its good transport network, telecommunications systems, hotel provision and stable currency. He told the Swiss what they wanted to hear – that it was 'able to organise an outstanding World Cup as in 1954, but brought up to date'. The stadiums would require to be extended and renovated, but 'given the financial strength of the country', he could foresee no problem there. Each of the bidders translated Havelange's remarks as a clear endorsement of their chances rather than those of their rivals.

Havelange welcomed the president of the French football federation to Zürich. The French felt that they had to move quickly to counter the Swiss Nobel proposal. Worse, the French FA feared problems in the relationship between their new prime minister and Havelange. The FIFA president had backed Barcelona over Paris in the race for the 1992 Olympics and he was seen as part of a Latin monopoly of world sports leadership. In East Berlin in 1985 when he was mayor of Paris, Chirac – seeking the support of the Eastern European lobby – accused Havelange of bias and threatened to use his influence in Africa to ensure that the Brazilian was not re-elected president of FIFA. Tensions had simmered between the two men since. Awarding the winter Games to the French venue was a clever IOC strategy which meant that Paris could hardly be awarded the summer Games too. The sequence of voting was reversed so that the decision about the winter Games was taken first – so scuppering the Paris bid and putting Barcelona in prime position.

The people of the Swedish city of Falun were the real losers in this story. They had several times sought to host the winter Games and had polled a promising 31 votes in the ballot for the 1988 games against the 48 votes of the eventual winner, Calgary. IOC members urged the Swedes to mount another bid. 'You will have my full support,' Havelange told them. In fact, Samaranch persuaded Havelange to change his mind and lobby for Albertville, which he did. Albertville romped home with 51 votes against Falun's 11.

At the time, Havelange's transfer of support from Falun to Albertville worked against the greater French interests, and the Brazilian could be seen to be blocking Chirac's ambitions. A successful outcome to the French bid for the '98 World Cup would be quite some consolation for this. Reminded by FIFA spokesman Guido Tognoni that it was FIFA and not a national prime minister that awarded the finals, Chirac nevertheless told the nation that France had 'a good chance of being awarded the World Cup finals. And I will do everything I can to ensure that we get them.'

There were still four years to go until FIFA had to make this decision. In France the media provided free advertising to the level of an estimated 25 to 30 million francs. After September 1991 the French football federation was ready, in the last stages of the bid, to spend six to seven million francs in courting the FIFA committee members who were to award the finals.

By November 1991 Havelange was 'very, very unhappy' about the Swiss candidature, saying that 'FIFA could not accept the temporary tubular steel grandstands proposed for stadiums'. At the same time as he was dismissing the Swiss bid that he had so consistently encouraged in the previous five years, the French campaign was reaching its climax. In a piece of shameless vote-catching, Havelange was inducted into France's Legion of Honour – the country's highest decoration – by the country's president, François Mitterrand. In a ceremony at the presidential palace, Mitterrand praised the Brazilian as 'one of the great figures of today's sporting world'. Enraged observers thought otherwise, describing the award as 'disgraceful'.

Like many other sports leaders, Havelange said a lot about promoting world peace through sport. He claimed to have done much through football to bring China fully into the world's economic and political embrace. He declared high hopes for the positive impact on international relations in East Asia of the co-hosting arrangement between Japan and South Korea for World Cup of 2002. One of his final ambitions was to organise an international 'friendly' match between Israel and the fledgling Palestinian state to be played in New York, the seat of the United Nations, to show, in his words, 'that football can succeed where politicians cannot'. This was initiated by Vice-President Al Gore, who approached Havelange during the 1994 World Cup finals in the USA. Havelange recalls that Gore was 'very upset' when the suggestion was not received with great enthusiasm, the FIFA boss initially saying, 'No, we are a sport, we are not politics in that sense.' Magnanimously, in his own telling, Havelange reconsidered and through the liaison of Prince Faisal he communicated with the Saudi King, Fahed, who 'offered to give the Palestine Football Federation a hundred million dollars to get them going. Now things have moved on and Palestine is a more clearly defined political entity.'

Within a year, he was seeking to arrange this game for the end of 1997, though it never took place. Palestine, however, was accepted as a full FIFA member at the June 1998 Congress. It was a defining moment when the Palestine delegate carried its flag around the Equinox Centre, welcomed along with a few other nations as the newest members of the FIFA family. There were no doubts as to where its vote would go in the election for the presidency later in the day.

Havelange claims that FIFA is truly democratic, with each member country having one vote. But the secret ballot, one-member, one-vote system gives him a great deal of control. Vanuatu, the tiny island republic in the Pacific with a population of 150,000, has the same voting rights in a FIFA congress election as does Germany with 80 million inhabitants; the Faroe Islands have the same voting weight as the mighty Brazil. For years this has worried more powerful football nations, as the outcome of elections can be assured from the accumulated commitment of tiny constituencies. Achieving the majorities necessary to change the rules, procedures or statutes of FIFA is exceedingly difficult.

In the 1970s, it was clear that if world football was to become truly global, it needed a man like Havelange. By fulfilling his 1974 election promises and making football a truly world game, he achieved much. The Brazilian himself is not slow to claim credit for the way he personally remodelled FIFA to do this. He matter-of-factly writes that in his time 'the FIFA administration may be considered perfect'.

FIFA claims to be non-commercial as well as democratic. Under Swiss law it has non-commercial, almost charitable, status – despite the $4 billion in its coffers – and escapes the usual company reporting requirements. This provided the perfect set-up for the Big Man's operations.

A FIFA document claimed in 1984 that Havelange was a 'football magnate who combined the qualities of far-sightedness and openness, an entrepreneur in body and soul', who 'in no time transformed an administration-oriented institution into a dynamic enterprise brimming with new ideas and the will to see them through, so that now the administration is managed in the form of a modern firm'. Guido Tognoni, though, said that 'people say that he was leading FIFA like an industry – but he was leading FIFA like a private enterprise, like a proprietor'.

'As if he owned it?' we queried.

'Yes, exactly,' replied Tognoni.

As late as the end of the 1990s, deals regarding the sale of the television rights for the World Cup finals of 2006 were completed by Havelange, Blatter and their FIFA lackeys without reference to the executive committee. 'It's depressing,' David Will recalls. 'I think we just have to keep chipping away at this. The first task is to have the committees properly chosen, and not to have them packed with pay-offs. We don't know how the [2006 television] deal was made.' He sighs. 'Per Omdal [Norwegian fellow committee member] and I have seen the contracts, but we asked that they be laid before the executive committee for final approval, and instead we were told at the executive committee that the contracts were signed that day.'

So Havelange's 'perfection' has come at a price. Pelé, amongst others, criticises him for over-expanding football in Brazil, to the point of crisis in the finances of the domestic game. Similarly, in exposing football to the overwhelming influence of market forces, Havelange has helped to hand the world game to people who view the sport as no more than an opportunity to make big money.

Havelange has faced a torrent of allegations. Most recently, investigative writer David Yallop, in his book *How They Stole the Game*, confirmed that during the year that Havelange gained the FIFA presidency, he submitted accounts to the Brazilian Treasury, claiming that the CBD was in surplus, when in fact it had a deficit of $1.7 million, the equivalent of more than $5 million today. Yallop reports that during the 16 years of Havelange's reign at the CBD, from 1958 to 1974, over $20 million dollars in today's values 'vanished without trace'. Some in the Brazilian junta wanted to put the balme on Havelange. The Big Man rode the storm, however, and in the end a state-owned bank paid the missing sums for 1974 into the federation's bank account, debited to the Social Assistance Fund. Yallop's investigations also show Havelange dealing in Rio de Janeiro's lottery and in the arms trade and related industries.

Throughout all of this, Havelange has kept his football empire together. It has had as its binding theme the idea of the family, inherited from Jules Rimet, but inflected in the modern era with a dose of the president's own philosophy, the imperative of *omertà* by which the real truth is what is most of all kept within the family.

Even as he planned for his retirement in 1998, Havelange worked ceaselessly behind the scenes to ensure that the régime which he had installed at FIFA would continue through the election of Sepp Blatter. We were there to see it happen.

At FIFA's watershed conference in Paris's Equinox Centre in June 1998, the riches of world football were kept in the family when Blatter routed his rival. On confirmation of that result, the Big Man embraced his protégé and successor. The family treasures were secure.

In the huge exhibition hall in Paris where the future good of the game was passed on into the hands of the Havelange-backed candidate, we wondered for whose good the whole self-indulgent pantomime was staged – for football people, for regional cabals, for ruthless and power-hungry individuals?

Havelange believes that he has done nothing wrong. In response to the fierce criticism which followed his visit to Nigeria just as dissident Ken Saro Wiwa was heading for the gallows, the Brazilian gave away perhaps more than he intended to with regard to his own personal philosophy: 'I don't want to make any comparisons with the Pope, but he is criticised from time to time, and his reply is silence. I too am sometimes criticised, so explanations about such matters are superfluous.'

Silenzio, Signor Dr Havelange. It's official – *omertà*. We couldn't find it in the statutes, but here it is – FIFA's own brand of presidential infallibility. Above the law of nations, above conscience, he has simply been used to doing what he wanted to do. Even after his withdrawal from formal office, FIFA still bears Havelange's indelible stamp. On or off the throne, he continues to cast a shadow over the football world.

5. THE PREDATOR AND THE PROTÉGÉ

High above the Champs-Elysées, as if proclaiming its conquest of France '98, the blue-and-white banners of Adidas fluttered atop the company's exclusive retreat in the heart of Paris. Mingling with the élite, we made small talk, nibbled delicate hors-d'oeuvres and quaffed Bolly with them in their penthouse suite. We were there to hear the official announcement of Adidas's major sponsorship role in the Women's World Cup finals, USA 1999.

On and off the field there had been many battles fought during France '98 – between teams, between fans, between touts, among the media and among FIFA wannabes and has-beens. But possibly the greatest conflict was the war of the sponsors.

The FIFA hierarchy turned out in force for Adidas's party. Sepp Blatter was there to address the sycophants and hand over the official Adidas match ball to the captain of the American women's team. But for its pretty blue-and-pink – for girls – design on the exterior, the ball was identical to the one that few male players had been able to kick properly during France '98. Like the men's edition it had been laboriously hand-stitched by child labourers in the sweatshops of northern Pakistan. In our hyper-technological age, the sporting-goods industry's claim that a machine capable of stitching leather casings for footballs cannot be made sounds farcical. Low labour costs in China and the Indian sub-continent seem a more plausible rationale for continuing the practice of hand-stitching. (We took one home for the lad, who eyed its pinkish exterior suspiciously before taking it down to the park for a kickabout with his mates. 'Too light,' he pronounced when he returned home. 'It kept getting stuck up in the trees, so we played with Tom's Mitre instead.' Adidas balls may get FIFA approval, but they get a big thumbs-down from Ratton Rangers Under-11s.)

On a plinth in the entrance hall of the Adidas Club, next to the World Cup match ball, the latest example of the Predator football boot was on display. For some, its sleek looks brought to mind outrageous free-kicks from outside the penalty-box curling into the top corner of the net, beyond the reach of a flying, flapping keeper. For us, in this setting, the Predator reminded us of a man who, along with Havelange, played a major role in turning world football into big business – Horst Dassler.

Once he ousted Sir Stanley Rous, João Havelange had a big problem. He didn't have the money to keep his election promises. Unless he found filthy-rich financial backers, his African and Asian allies would prove to be fickle friends. Enter Horst Dassler, the German sporting goods manufacturer and fixer.

'Can you give me any justification as to why a football boot manufacturer should wish to decide who should become the president of FIFA and control world football?' former British sports minister Denis Howell asked the president of the Adidas empire in 1983. The answer is obvious: to make a lot of money. In order to add to a fortune which, thanks to the Olympics, was already considerable, Dassler offered his sports networks and his vision of global marketing to the new boss of FIFA. Havelange's cash-flow problem was on the way to being solved.

Television was central to Dassler's plans. For Rous, the medium had been nothing more than an educational tool – you might use it for teaching the laws of the game, or as a coaching aid, but little more. With Dassler to guide him, Havelange saw television's potential as a money generator. Together they plotted to harness the broadcasters' increasing interest in football to the marketing interests of multinational companies.

Crucial to the success of their plan was the way in which Dassler and Havelange, through the mediation of Patrick Nally, secured Coca-Cola as a global partner for FIFA and its main asset, the World Cup. Nally had been involved, with the commentator Peter West, in the early growth of sports sponsorship in Britain. Through an advertising agency and then their own company, West Nally, they had established sponsorship deals with brewery companies, Green Shield Stamps, Benson & Hedges, Kraft, Ford, Esso and Cornhill Insurance.

Nally proved useful to Dassler. He was well established in the UK sports sponsorhsip market, with a unique portfolio of powerful clients. Dassler's British agent, John Boulter, the runner, involved

Nally in promoting Adidas's Arena swimwear line. This was fronted by Mark Spitz, exploiting the American's astonishing haul of gold medals at the 1972 Munich Olympics. Adidas was expanding its textile and clothes range, and in late 1974 Boulter arranged for Nally to meet Dassler.

The German had a unique vision: he could see that international sports federations were going to become very important, as old amateur beliefs gave way to professionalism and commercialism in Olympic sports. He knew an opportunity when he saw one. With Rous on the way out and Havelange on the way in, he realised that FIFA and the World Cup were there for the taking. 'Sir Stanley suddenly woke up to the fact that he was about to be bumped off by this Brazilian,' said Nally. 'Dassler had seen the election of Havelange as being a watershed – here you had the gentlemanly "old school" of Sir Stanley Rous suddenly ousted.' A new style of opportunistic leadership was in charge at FIFA House and Dassler was soon knocking on the door. Havelange, already aware of the German's skills in international sports networking, was quick to invite him in.

Dassler was trained in a tough school of sports business. The young Horst was dispatched by his father, Adi, to the 1956 Melbourne Olympics to market, by any means possible, the company's sports equipment, particularly the shoes with the distinctive triple stripe. Adidas achieved a near monopoly of brand marketing at that event, and Dassler admitted that he paid amateur athletes to wear the Adidas brand.

In cut-throat competition with Puma (founded by his uncle, in bitter family competition), Horst Dassler also managed to persuade dockers in Europe and Australia to slow down or prevent the dispatch or import of any Puma goods. To the multilingual salesman, this was normal business practice. 'He became very adept at moving around and understanding people,' Nally remembers. 'He knew how to get things from people. In other words, he always knew who he could approach and offer money to and who he could approach and *not* offer money.' According to his one-time associate, Dassler knew whether the offer of an IOC membership was more attractive than a straightforward bung. Nally claims that Dassler even offered to broker an IOC membership for UK Sports Minister Denis Howell. Shortly before he died, Lord Howell told us that this allegation was 'certainly not true', but recognised that Dassler's brazen approaches and sharp practices had few limits.

A small, squat man with a harried look, Dassler was driven by the suspicion that someone was always trying to do him over. He was also secretive to the point of paranoia. As Patrick Nally recalls, 'He would have spies. All of his sports people who were out there to look after the athletes would always spy on the opposition. They'd all be trained to bug telephones. They'd all be trained to go into other people's briefcases.'

Like an old soldier recalling his favourite campaigns, Nally talks about his time with Dassler with barely concealed pride. 'It *was* the shoe wars. You were out there to do what you could to the enemy,' he said. 'You would get people drunk, you would be trained to investigate and find out what other people were up to.'

Dassler recognised how to control the riches of the growing sports market. He made deals with administrators in the international federations, and was aware of the big prizes that would flow from gaining and holding power and influence in the biggest organisations of all, the IOC and FIFA. He saw 'what Havelange needed to help him make his dreams a reality', said Nally. 'The man Havelange went to was Horst Dassler and the man Horst Dassler went to was me.'

Nally travelled the world for 18 months, negotiating with key figures in Coca-Cola. He was the first sports marketing man to view the entire planet as his market, rather than just separate countries or regions. His main contact, Al Killeen, was number two in Coca-Cola. Killeen had been hooked on football ever since he had been persuaded by one of England's greatest-ever players, Sir Stanley Matthews, to pump some of the company's money into coaching camps in Africa. But the Coca-Cola company had a federal structure and did not usually make centralised decisions concerning worldwide policy and investments. Cunningly, Nally took Killeen to a match at Brazil's Maracaná Stadium. 'It absolutely blew his mind,' recalls Nally. 'He couldn't believe there were 110,000 screaming Brazilians there for the warm-up, even before the real match.'

Killeen realised that if soccer could mobilise commitment and passion on such a scale, it had huge marketing potential for his product. Dassler got Havelange to impress the Coca-Cola people, at the company's world headquarters in Atlanta, by flying in on his private plane to meet them. Killeen fought to convince the board and, backed by the company's number one, J.P. Austin, pushed through his ambitious plan to tie Coca-Cola to the world's most popular game. Or was it the other way round?

All of the regions would contribute. They weren't asked, they were told. They had to contribute a small percentage of their income to a central pot in Atlanta which the Coke headquarters would then pipe to FIFA and its various competitions. 'Previously, each country and local bottler had made their own sports sponsorship policy,' explained Nally. 'Killeen was brave enough to dictate to the whole Coke world that they would back one sport – football.'

Havelange's eight-point manifesto in his campaigning brochure, as mentioned in Chapter 3, was both too broad and too vague, a long way from a development programme. Nally claims he had to make things up as he went along, under the tutelage of the wily Dassler. Horst introduced him to another German, teacher and sports administrator Klaus Willing. Together they produced a strategy that would accelerate global football development. It would also increase FIFA's and Havelange's power and, crucially, expand Coca-Cola's markets. They sent administrators, coaches, medical experts and trainers into Third World countries as part of the development philosophy. They wrote the regulations for the new World Youth Championship. Their development programme exported the knowledge of the strong soccer nations to another hundred countries. Prime targets Africa and Asia, 'all those places where the votes were important', as Nally wryly noted. And places where the Big Man was in debt.

Dassler also recognised that the FIFA administration as it stood was not equipped to make this programme work. Havelange had inherited a Dickensian set-up from Sir Stanley Rous which operated from a small house in Zurich with 'Dr Käser, his secretary and the dogs', as Nally disparagingly caricatures it. The personnel had to go and a new headquarters was needed.

Tommy Keller, who worked for Swiss Timing-Longines and ran the international rowing federation as well as the General Association of International Sports Federations (GAISF), introduced Dassler to Joseph Blatter, an administrator working for Swiss Timing. Dassler head-hunted him to manage the football development programme. Blatter was trained at Landersheim for a number of months. Shadowing the master, he learned how Adidas worked, before moving on to become Dassler's preferred choice in FIFA. When the new FIFA House was under construction, former press boss Guido Tognoni recalls, 'Blatter worked from premises made available by Dassler.'

The manner of Blatter's appointment to FIFA demonstrated the characteristic Havelange style. The Brazilian announced the appointment ahead of the date set aside for FIFA's executive committee to make its decision. Blatter had impressed Havelange and other FIFA officials by administering the Coca-Cola-sponsored World Youth Championships in Australia and stepping in and saving the local organisers from chaos. On the spot, Havelange telexed his decision to FIFA that Blatter was the man for the job.

Havelange recognised how important the sponsors were to football's future development. The Big Man wanted to be in a position to take control of any such potential relationship. He could see that Blatter had the qualities that were needed: he was a skilful communicator, fluent in five languages; he could flatter and charm the right people; and, if necessary, he could undermine rivals.

The result of the Coca-Cola deal was an extensive FIFA programme giving Havelange the means to honour his election mandate – to develop Africa and Asia, create a World Youth Cup and bring more Third World countries into the main tournament.

Blatter was there at the beginning of this new phase of football finance and global development. Dassler's protégé learned fast, and so well that he would have to commit himself to keeping FIFA family secrets for the rest of his working life.

For Patrick Nally, persuading such a big name such as Coca-Cola to join the soccer programme was crucial because it gave the game massive credibility and attracted the attention of other top brands. 'If you're into Coke, you're into the biggest blue-chip company on a global basis,' he explained. Bringing Coca-Cola into the sponsorship of world soccer 'became the blueprint for everyone who wanted to try and bring money into international federations through this source'.

The multi-million-pound investment package put together for FIFA concentrated initially upon the new Under-20s Youth World Cup, first held in Tunisia in 1977, and followed up by tournaments in Asia, the Soviet Union, South America and the Arabian Gulf. The inaugural Under-17s World Championship was held in China in 1985. Like the Under-20s competition, it too was hosted in regions which were peripheral to football's main Western European theatre but central to Coke's global marketing strategy. In Blatter's hands, Havelange's programme worked like a dream. Football expanded its playing base, Coca-Cola extended its market penetration, and FIFA got richer and richer.

However sceptical the established football nations might have been about such events (some seeing them as tinpot, in comparison to their own apprenticeship systems and fully developed professional leagues), the FIFA initiatives offered valuable international experience and competition which were to stand Asian and African footballing nations in good stead on the larger stages of the World Cup and the Olympic Games.

By using Coke's money to create such platforms for Third World countries, Havelange fulfilled his electoral pledges. He also guaranteed a sound basis for his five subsequent uncontested presidential nominations. First World finance secured the future of the Brazilian and the expansion of football in the Third World.

Coke cash also supported a worldwide soccer skills programme, ensuring even more widespread publicity for the sponsor. The company were so happy with their new love affair with football that they pumped more than $10 million into the 1978 World Cup in Argentina.

The upfront negotiations with Coca-Cola were conducted by Nally, but the internal fixing was accomplished by Dassler and Havelange. 'He wanted all the politics handled through him and his team,' says Nally. This included grooming Blatter at the Adidas base and convincing Havelange to place the Swiss at the centre of FIFA's future plans.

Nally and Dassler established sponsor clients' exclusivity in all aspects of merchandising and franchising. This was all controlled through FIFA House. By the first World Cup of Havelange's presidency, in Argentina in 1978, Nally had contracted six major sponsors to FIFA, including Coca-Cola, Gillette and Seiko, though he was still juggling the advertising billboards of companies contracted with different national teams. This was soon to be streamlined, in FIFA's template for what became the Olympic Programme scheme in the case of the Olympics. From then on, the only option open to sponsors was the complete marketing package. Dassler and Nally knew that the cost for companies was so high that many could not get near the scheme, but this suited them. It made it easier to work with those élite global brand names who could afford the stake. This new scale of football finance involved the acquisition and distribution – with minimal accountability – of huge sums of money.

Once he got the sponsors where he wanted them, Havelange had to feed them. One way was to increase the number of FIFA competitions. The Youth and Under-17s tournaments were augmented by the Indoor World Championships and the Women's World Cup. Another way was to expand the senior World Cup itself. Nally's task was to create a marketing programme to fuel this expansionist programme. Dassler, in turn, committed vast sums to the FIFA president.

As the 1982 World Cup in Spain approached, big money was needed to convince 'the Spanish to take the tournament up from 16 teams to 24 teams as part of Havelange's commitment to get more Asian and African teams in', said Nally. 'In Spain, in the Palacio de Congresso, in the gentlemen's toilets, Horst said the going rate with the Spanish organising committee wasn't going to be the $4 million which I'd already negotiated and agreed. We had to pay an additional $2.4 million.' In men's rooms all over the world, the new élite of the FIFA family was reshaping football for ever.

Nally argues that the Coca-Cola connection gives sports organisations an aura of respectability, generated by the company's global image of corporate cleanliness. But behind the scenes, without Coca-Cola's knowledge, there is skulduggery. 'There's no government checking on them. There's no auditors checking them. Nobody's trying to see where the payment goes or what the individuals get,' explains Nally, 'so somehow the IOC and the IAAF and FIFA are totally beyond reproach.' And, so they think, beyond the law.

Being the president of a rich and unaccountable international federation suddenly meant first-class air tickets, hospitality and awards around the globe. 'It certainly beats sweeping out the back of the garden at the weekend,' grinned Nally, 'if you're flying first class everywhere to major international events.'

How did Horst Dassler hold together an operation on this scale? He provided lavish hospitality, the 'compulsory Adidas dinner' at every international sports federation meeting. He invited sports administrators to Adidas's residential and catering complex at Landersheim. And, mostly for Africans and Asians, he opened up his sports shop and restaurant with other hospitality, social and personal services in Paris's Montmartre district.

Dassler and Havelange looked after loyal family members and retained people in specialist capacities. Harry Cavan, the Northern Irish football administrator and FIFA vice-president, had worked closely with Rous, but soon shifted loyalties to Havelange. The eloquent Cavan had the look and persistence of a door-to-door salesman. Dassler made him a 'shoe consultant'. Twenty years on, in the urinals of the top hotels of Europe, there would always be a FIFA comrade on hand to help the emaciated, shuffling and Parkinson-afflicted Cavan open and do up his flies.

The booming world of sport sponsorship and marketing worried Denis Howell when he was Britain's sports minister. Chairing a Central Council for Physical Recreation inquiry, he questioned the role of sports agencies. Mark McCormack's International Management Group, for example, staged events, represented performers, sports bodies and sponsors, negotiated television rights and even commentated on events. To a streetwise Old Labour man raised in the municipal politics of Birmingham, this looked like too big a concentration of power: 'Such a situation is pregnant with conflicts of interest and cannot carry public confidence.' McCormack, though, refused to meet with Howell's committee of inquiry to discuss these matters.

Howell and his committee also expressed some astonishment when they learned that 'Adidas had undertaken an extensive programme of education in Africa on behalf of FIFA, the most powerful governing body in world sport'. The committee recommended that such initiatives should be monitored by agencies with public accountability. Howell, a top referee in the professional game in his younger days, wanted to ensure that FIFA and its partners were playing by the rules. His recommendations have never been taken up.

Dassler's empire was beyond the reach of the likes of England's quaint Central Council for Physical Recreation. Howell did not fully understand the scale of Dassler's grip on the organisation of world sport and the collusive nature of his relationship with the network of tame sports organisations. Dassler promoted the creation of the Association of Summer Olympic International Federations (ASOIF) to counter the influence of the independent General Association of International Sports Federations (GAISF). He manipulated the Italian fixer, Primo Nebiolo, into its presidency, and later into the presidency of the International Amateur Athletics Federation. By 1986 the GAISF gained as its president the Korean Kim Un Yong (Mickey Kim), nine days after he became a member of the International Olympic Committee. Kim, a former agent of the Korean CIA and the hard man of international tae kwon do, would later gain notoriety in the bribery scandals that shook the IOC in the late 1990s.

Dassler infiltrated world sports organisations with a cadre of ruthless and greedy individuals like Kim. It has been reported that Nebiolo mustered $20 million for his IAAF from the organisers of the 1988 Seoul Olympics for changing the times of track-and-field events to suit the broadcasters NBC, having initially proposed schedules wholly inappropriate for a mass American television audience.

Lord Howell died in 1998. The previous year he told us, 'I think that the finance of professional sport has now become obscene and is totally destroying what I call the soul of the game . . . people have been trying to buy the soul of the sport, and therefore corrupting it, with disastrous results.' By then his judgement sounded like an anthem for a lost age.

Dassler constructed an international espionage system. He collected files on all of the movers and shakers in world sport. The apparently independent publication *Sport Intern* was in fact his personal propaganda machine. From 1980 until his death seven years later, this publication was an important part of his political armoury.

Dassler was persuasive and, with cash in hand, could overturn cherished beliefs overnight. The Welsh Rugby Union, for example, was furious with him for sponsoring the boots of individual amateur players. Dassler went to Cardiff and, one meeting with the WRU later, he had arranged comprehensive team sponsorship. The administrators, in Lord Howell's words, 'totally embraced Dassler and changed their attitude. He paid the Welsh Union for the right to supply boots and pay the players, and they totally changed the whole of the ethos of their sport.'

Dassler told Howell that he had in his office a tremendous computer and records department, with information tabulated from every periodical and newsletter issued by every sports body round the world. He said it was very natural that if anyone wanted to pursue a career in world sport, they would come to him to get the names and addresses of all the contacts. Rous was above this trade, but Havelange was only too happy to use Dassler's files and networks to get football's top job.

Some sports administrators saw what was happening. Philippe Chartrier of the International Tennis Federation wrote, 'The control of sport could shift from the international federations due to the pressure of money,' and argued that the federations should be properly organised and given the means to do their job. But Dassler's records and little black book of deals and debts were by now the main influence on the big business of world sport. His clinching coup was the formation of the sports marketing company International Sport and Leisure in 1982. It was part-owned by Adidas's Japanese partner, the advertising giant Dentsu. Dassler's Monaco-based advertising company SMPI had combined his capital and contracts with Nally's ideas and marketing nous: ISL became its successor, apparently autonomous but little more than a front for Dassler's operations.

One of Dassler's assistants at Adidas, Klaus Hempel, was the figurehead. By mid-1983, just months after its formation, ISL was handling merchandising and stadium advertising rights for FIFA and the European football federation. Soon after, the International Olympic Committee appointed the company to manage its new fund-raising programme. A few more months and it had gobbled up the merchandising, licensing, sponsorship and supplier rights for the local organising committee for the Seoul Olympics of 1988.

ISL boasted, in a special supplement to *Time* magazine's European edition at the end of 1983, of its successes in attracting sponsorship for its football marketing programme. Canon, Camel, JVC, Seiko, Fuji, Air France and Cinzano joined Coca-Cola on the list of World Cup backers. Sponsors also provided services to the media – a harried press person could borrow photographic equipment from Canon and photocopy on a Canon machine, for example, take a refreshing drink of Coca-Cola for next to nothing, check the scores on television monitors provided by JVC and keep an eye on copy deadlines via the official timekeeper, Seiko. With Dassler's networks in place, ISL rapidly dominated world football marketing in this formative phase of the industry.

Dassler was the mastermind behind the marketing of world sport. Though he and Adidas were not technically a part of ISL, it was indisputably his baby. Blatter was close to the German, and the Adidas chairman, Robert Louis Dreyfus, stated in the mid-1990s that in those early days part of Blatter's FIFA salary was paid by Adidas. Right up to his sudden death in 1987 Dassler was in control of the vast fortunes and those who would generate and dispense them in world sport and football.

Blatter was the head of public relations at the Swiss Association of Sport for two years before joining Swiss-Timing Longines. There, he says, ' I worked in marketing . . . and it was there that I entered into contact with the big names of the sports world and the great name

Adidas.' Joining FIFA – 'it was an old house, there wasn't yet an office here, I went to Landersheim, to the French section of Adidas, and I worked there from August until December 1975' – he became technical director from 1975 to 1981, when he was promoted to general secretary. 'For six years, I was ambassador or itinerant missionary for football. I did the development programme Futuro together with Coca-Cola and Adidas. If we hadn't had Adidas and Coca-Cola, who both supported us during this period, we would have never entered the world of football with such a fantastic programme of development . . . I will never forget Adidas . . . without them we wouldn't have had this development programme. Without Adidas I think that FIFA would not be where she is today.'

Horst Dassler is recalled with enthusiasm by Blatter: 'He was an extraordinary man, a man of courage, of initiative, a visionary. He went at the age of 20, in '56, with a small suitcase, the first to try to make well-known athletes identify with the brand name Adidas . . . he was the father of sport sponsoring. One can never repeat this enough. It is he who said that one must associate the product, develop the product, with the sport, and equally to increase sales of sports equipment.'

Dassler was an obsessive workaholic who slept little and showed few signs of tiredness. He was an exceptional motivator, with high expectations of all who worked for him, and did not hesitate to call on personal loyalty. 'Each person was truly persuaded that he was part of the family and not just part of the company – and this was wonderful.' Blatter saw him not only as 'a great salesman but also a great diplomat', who could have resolved problems in world sport, had he lived: 'He always knew how to fix things when there were differences.'

Dassler and Blatter grasped the vast potential of football in the world's burgeoning global markets, and were effective salesmen pitching their product at the world's top companies. Guinness was one that didn't bite, but that didn't deter them. Blatter knew there were big bucks to be found. Together they approached food companies, banks and insurance companies to fund FIFA's development programmes and pay Havelange's debts. But Blatter concedes that it was almost by chance that FIFA fell in with the Coke empire: 'By accident we found that we'd drunk Coca-Cola with a bit of rum in Paris, I remember. I drank Coke, and he [Dassler] said, "One thing you should have is that – everyone drinks Coca-Cola." That day in the same restaurant in a hotel in Paris there was a guy who worked for Coca-Cola in England, and that was how it began.'

When Blatter talks of Adidas, he uses the word 'we'. Recalling the company's dip in fortunes after Horst Dassler's death in 1987, he claims it was because 'we did not pay attention to the market, we didn't see the waves, and we sold this business for a morsel of bread'. In Dreyfus, Adidas's new owner, he sees a strong man in the Dassler mould, a man fit to re-establish and strengthen still further the close ties between FIFA and the company. He sounds angry when fielding questions concerning this close relationship. 'Those who make such reproaches are people who don't know the ethical and moral value of business and of sport.' Blatter's morality means that Adidas gets special treatment, and that if the company is outbid in its sponsorship deal by another sports equipment manufacturer, it is unlikely that the law of the free market prevails. Blatter makes sure that FIFA remembers its debts and honours old loyalties. 'I presented this report to the finance commission, to the executive committee, to tell them that the moral value of the Adidas company was worth more than the difference in the financial plan the [American] competitors were offering. If a journalist says that it was biased, it's not true. It is simply that it is necessary to think again that someone has made a particular effort over the years. Since I began they were really committed.' He draws upon tradition to account for the FIFA–Adidas cosy relationship: 'The wider family of football is everyone who is in football, including the economic partners like Adidas, Coca-Cola, the other manufacturers of sport articles, and the media. The media are just as much our economic partner, and also make up the family of football.'

After Dassler's death, FIFA confirmed that it had assigned to ISL all of the marketing and sponsorship rights for every World Cup up to and including France '98. An option was included in this deal for the 2002 tournament. ISL even got the merchandising rights for FIFA logos, which had been in the hands of a rival outfit, Sport Billy Productions, whilst John Boulter took over as head of promotions at Adidas and for a while it was business as usual in the global industry of world football. But Horst Dassler's four sisters didn't see things like that. They had been useful to brother Horst, sleeping partners in a quiet boardroom. But by the end of 1990 they had sold off their 80 per cent share of the empire and the husband of one of them became president of the holding company which was the majority

(51 per cent) owner of ISL. Dassler's sisters approved the appointment of Jean Marie Weber as chief executive at ISL.

Within two weeks, two key figures at ISL had had enough. Klaus Hempel and Jürgen Lenz were gone by the autumn of 1991 to set up their own rival operation. Hempel and Lenz set up what became TEAM (Television Event and Media Marketing), just across the road from the ISL headquarters in Lucerne. It was all very cosy in Switzerland – FIFA was up the road in Zurich, the International Olympic Committee was not far away in Lausanne, and the European football federation was just a couple of hours down south, on the shore of Lake Geneva. They were sure that there would be plenty of cash to go round and that the bonanza in sports marketing could fill a few more bulging Swiss bank accounts.

Jürgen Lenz is a star graduate from the Dassler school of sports business. He has a massive presence in the lobbies of the hotels where the football glitterati gather. His grey silk suit is top of the designer range. He's only – and very comfortably – a little overweight. His eyes are blue and his hair is blond. We don't need to set up a specific appointment. 'Find me in the lobby. I am always in the lobby,' he said, courteously but firmly, caressing his mobile phone discreetly, Swiss politeness blending with German efficiency.

This is a man in charge of his patch. He'd swept us in with him at the VIP entrance to the Champions' League Village at the Real Madrid *v* Juventus game in Amsterdam, little Jim Rosenthal from ITV left behind and looking peeved on the wrong side of the coolly clad bouncers.

Lenz asked us what we thought of the Boyzone performance during the pre-match proceedings. He'd personally selected the Dublin quintet, looking for something entertaining but snappy, fun but without the kind of overkill and razzmatazz you get at the Superbowl, Olympics or World Cup. We told him he'd got it just about right for us, though we weren't too sure what the mass of the Spanish and Italian supporters had made of it.

Lenz's professional pedigree was in marketing, where he ran accounts for an international advertising agency. In 1977 he moved to Adidas to work for Dassler and five years later was one of the first to join ISL, as chief operating officer to Klaus Hempel's chief executive. Dassler gave Lenz the job of developing ISL's marketing concept and business plan. Dassler, not formally in ISL at all, liaised with the International Olympic Committee, 'doing the sports political side', whilst Lenz devised the Olympic Programme sponsorship concept.

Lenz and Hempel proposed a management buyout of ISL after Dassler's death. 'We realised the situation was a little bit like what Princess Diana said – three in a marriage gets a little bit tight,' he told us. 'With the representative from the family, we decided that it gets a little crowded here.' But the sisters never responded to their offer.

The two men didn't hang about. They negotiated a release, including a clause preventing them from working with Olympic clients. But they had a free run at the burgeoning football market: 'We knew where the good business prospects were, and there were certainly more in football.'

Hempel and Lenz didn't rush things. They took a three-month break and then met up again to consider the possibilities. 'To get a sharp mind you've got to get in shape body-wise,' lectured Lenz. So he and Hempel headed south into the hills, spending four weeks at a health farm, exercising for four hours a day and dedicating another four hours to working up 'a blueprint of what a future sports marketing concept in an ideal world would look like'. They then filed away the blueprint, formed TEAM and before they knew where they were, they had brushed ISL and IMG aside and won the tender for the television and marketing rights to the relaunched European Cup, the Champions' League.

They had been taught well by the German master. They had the three key Dassler insights: make and use the right connections; always have sufficient finance for a fallback position if things don't go according to plan; and use a very short decision-making process. They were able to do what the European Broadcasting Union considered impossible and got 24 national broadcasters to accept a match schedule on a regular weekday evening slot, broadcast live in prime-time. They were backed by start-up finance of $100 million, provided by a German entrepreneur. Once the television deal was in place, the sponsors were queuing up at their door.

The TEAM work on the Champions' League has rebranded European football. The company's aim has been to make the product easy to recognise for the consumer. Music, logos and regular scheduling achieved this. 'These are simple things,' laughed Lenz. 'You don't have to be a brain surgeon to get these things. The accomplishment is not in thinking them up, but in putting them in place, in actually doing it.'

Doing it is not at all simple. The orchestration of hundreds of outside-broadcast vans, thousands of press and media and thousands of VIP guests is event management of the highest order – and that's before the spectators are even considered. Lenz calls the Champions' League 'a product for the people', available on 'free TV'. He believes that it would be a huge mistake to allow it to fall into the hands of media companies which are geared totally towards satellite and digital television. And he calls upon sports bodies to retain their influence and not simply allow the marketeers to take over. (Dr Michel D'Hooghe, chairman of FIFA's sports medical committee, has admitted that sport's priorities can be railroaded by broadcasters' interests. Talking about the midday kick-off time for a game in Orlando during USA '94, he said, 'I deplore that the rights of television are now stronger than the arguments of the doctors.')

ISL, in association with the German firm Kirch, gained the FIFA World Cup marketing and television rights for 2002 and 2006. The price for 2002 was £600 million, for 2006 £800 million. FIFA retained a power of veto over how these rights might be sold on. Blatter said that this could be used to guarantee that the World Cup remains 'accessible to viewers who do not possess expensive satellite or cable systems'. But £1.4 billion is a lot to recoup. Bids may well come in that reduce the power of veto to a fond memory.

Things did not go perfectly in France '98. Too many companies got in on the act, conceded ISL's Glen Kirton. In 2002, FIFA and ISL will together control the whole marketing programme. They will find ways of funding the local organising committee, which will no longer be able to fix up its own rights deals. These were the issues preoccupying the football men at France '98 – finance as much as football.

Back at the Adidas Club, like generals following the progress of a major battle, Adidas's senior executives could gaze down from their penthouse vantage-point upon the ant-like, rival armies of football consumers flowing backwards and forwards between the Place de la Concorde and the Arc de Triomphe. Looking south-west, they could glimpse the action around their central stronghold, the Adidas Park across the Seine from the Eiffel Tower. If they used their binoculars, they could make out the campaign headquarters of their main rivals, Nike, whose own theme park dominated the spacious square beneath the appropriately futuristic Grande Arche de la Défense.

The new FIFA president defends the sponsors against those who accuse the companies' guests of taking a disproportionate share of the seats to the detriment of the public and undermining the traditional atmosphere of the match. 'There are not enough directors to fill the stadiums,' Blatter insists, adding that many of the sponsors gave the tickets to children. 'The people with ties bought the tickets,' he expands, 'and distributed them to the young people. So those who say that it was only the people of caviar, well, I was there for nearly all the matches and I didn't see a gramme of caviar in the stadiums.'

The sponsorship war between Adidas and Nike at France '98 was a close-run thing. Nike had its deal with the Brazilian team. Adidas was official World Cup sponsor as well as supplier, the first time one company had ever got this. Adidas came out top in a market research poll of six European countries, with a 35 per cent recognition rating. Nike came a brilliant second (for a company which hadn't sponsored the championship at all) with 32 per cent. Blatter recognises the dangers of sponsors' direct influence on the game, and was worried that Nike, not an official World Cup/FIFA partner but sponsor of the Brazilian team and of Ronaldo himself, had abused its access and position by interfering in team selection minutes before the '98 World Cup final: 'Nike had access to the entire World Cup, access to a player, and this player wasn't planned to be playing in the final. It is like the organiser of a concert if the principal tenor says, I am a bit off, he says but come anyway, because during the opera you will manage to sing better. It is this that we thought was done with Ronaldo. Adidas would never have done that, they would never have tried to intervene between a coach and the president of a federaton.' Blatter, albeit diplomatically and opaquely, here rounds on Nike as the biggest of those eager to challenge FIFA's exclusive deals with preferred sponsors.

The pioneer Coca-Cola was a distant third with 20 per cent.

Dassler would have liked all this. His pupil Blatter certainly did and, as new FIFA president, was working as closely as ever with ISL. Blatter, the hand-chosen protégé of Horst Dassler, could reflect upon a job well done: Adidas top of the sponsors and ISL in place as FIFA's 'second cash box'. Football finances were secure in the hands of the Dassler legacy.

6. THE BOUNTY HUNTER

Alan Rothenberg sat in the front row at the French Olympic Committee's majestic headquarters in Paris. He was there to support Sepp Blatter's bid to become FIFA's eighth president. It might have been a long way from his Los Angeles law office, but where there was money to be rustled in sport, you could bet that Rothenberg, the bounty hunter, would be riding into town.

Rothenberg was used to backing winners. He'd got the credit for raising soccer's profile in the USA during the 1984 Los Angeles Olympics, and he'd pulled off a major success as the organiser of USA '94. And here he was chatting to Simonet of the French football federation, rubbing shoulders with Chirac's man from the Elysée Palace. As boss of the US soccer federation, he'd nominated Blatter for the FIFA presidency. João and Sepp had backed him in the great American adventure of '94. He was here in Paris to pay his debts.

The sight of the pensive but confident Rothenberg took us back to a sweltering night in June 1994, as we headed into Manhattan during the first week of the World Cup finals. The train in from Massachusetts was quiet, with not a football fan nor a World Cup poster in sight. We were meeting up with some Irish expatriates at a midtown bar between Lexington and Park. The heat at Grand Central station and in the taxi queue was oppressive and we craved the cool of an air-conditioned bar. How could people play football in this crazy heat? Was the World Cup really happening?

To enter PJ's on any night is to step into a twilight world between the USA and Ireland, but on the night before the Republic of Ireland's game against Italy in the Giants' Stadium, it was more like stepping out of, not arriving in, New York, and being pitched into the heart of Dublin. A lot of locals, though, are hooked on the Houston Rockets *v* New York Knicks shoot-out, live from Madison

Square Garden. Suddenly all sport was cut from the bar's TV screens as the channels switched to a bigger story still – a mixture of race, sex and murder. A white stationwagon appeared on the screens, pursued along a Los Angeles highway by a phalanx of black-and-white patrol cars and a swarm of police and media helicopters. One of the US's greatest living sporting legends, OJ Simpson, is in the stationwagon and is holding a gun to his own head. Will OJ shoot himself rather than face a double murder charge for the alleged slaying of his estranged wife and her lover? 'Pull the fucking trigger and get it the fuck over with,' shouts an enraged Knicks fan.

A moderate cheer goes up when NBC switches back to the basketball just in time to see the Knicks wrap up the fourth quarter and go into a 3–2 lead in the best-of-seven series. The local New Yorkers are ecstatic. The Dublin half is happy to join in the celebrations, if only as a warm up for their own ceilidh tomorrow night.

USA '94 may be under way, but NBC shifts its focus to Olympic wrestling in the Gay Games, currently taking place in Manhattan. All week in the pages of the *New York Times*, the Gay Games and the World Cup will vie for fourth place behind OJ Simpson, ice-hockey's Stanley Cup and the NBA play-offs. At the same time, there's something utterly logical about the staging of football's quadrennial fest in a country where it's widely regarded as a bit of a joke.

Sepp Blatter delivered an upbeat verdict on the tournament: 'The 1994 World Cup produced a turnover of $4 billion with 32 billion television viewers. I mean no disrespect to other sports by saying that even the Olympic Games cannot compare. The World Cup was a fabulous success.' Success, though, is gauged in economic terms, couched in the statistics so vital to FIFA's commercial and media partners.

Penetrating the generally uninterested US sports market has been one of FIFA's biggest challenges. The USA is part of CONCACAF, along with Mexico, the traditional power base of football in that region. One of Havelange's long-term allies, the Mexican media magnate, Guillermo Cañedo, had been an important figure in FIFA since 1962 and became one of its vice-presidents in 1971, three years before Havelange's accession to presidential power. Cañedo was to become senior vice-president, Havelange's number two, and chairman of FIFA's media committee. His last major task was to chair the organising committee of the USA World Cup finals. Cañedo got into the heart of FIFA at the expense of Curaçao's Mordy Maduro, who complained of 'quite a few irregularities' in the election process.

FIFA could do little about such complaints. Rous and his officials had suspected that results of matches in World Cup qualifying tournaments were manipulated, but the federation's administrators simply ignored the letters referring to a particular country's protest. FIFA's general secretary, Dr Käser, wrote to Rous: 'Quite a number of "incomprehensible decisions" were taken in connection with this tournament but all of them were finally endorsed by their congress with the exception of the above mentioned Surinam *v* Haiti case which happened after the congress was over.'

By the early 1970s key positions in confederations and FIFA itself were being pursued by powerful individuals representing interlocking sets of interest within and across confederations. These new power-brokers took little notice of FIFA's protests, snubbing scheduled meetings where Rous raised the usual problems – financial irregularities and inefficiency, dubious refereeing appointments, dodgy delegates and organisational unaccountability.

When Havelange replaced Rous as FIFA president he was helped by his Central American allies, to whom he would grant the 1986 Mexico World Cup finals after Colombia was forced to pull out. The USA was written out of that deal but got its turn eight years later, and with it the chance to exhibit the sport to the biggest consumer market in the world.

The USA team had performed well and reached the semi-finals at the first World Cup in 1930, though with the help of six former British professionals. Its greatest moment was at the 1950 World Cup finals, beating England 1–0. We talked to Sir Walter Winterbottom, England coach/manager, about that historic game in Belo Horizonte, Brazil. 'You cannot make excuses,' he said and proceeded to make several. 'We got beaten, but really it is ridiculous. Now that was a referee who was badly influenced by the crowd. The crowd were all for America simply because they were the underdogs.' So bad refereeing and a partisan crowd were to blame.

'It wasn't a big ground, it didn't hold that many spectators at all,' he continued. 'Why we had to play there God only knows, but the pitch was in dreadful shape. The grass was high and thick, it was Bermuda grass growing in small clusters and it spreads and it sits the ball up.' The ref, the crowd and now the pitch.

Winterbottom relived the agony. 'We hadn't had any practice on it of course. What is happening is the ball is teed up and you are hitting shots over the bar. They were going over the bar. We hit the wood-work eleven times. Eleven times, that's absurd.' Too much paint on the posts cost England the game!

Then, of course there were the perfidious foreign Johnnies whom England were playing against. 'We were shooting in, virtually, and they were doing all kinds of things. They were handling Stanley Mortensen outside the penalty area, you know, tackling, rugby tackling him when he was running through.'

'But here's the real reason,' said Winterbottom, lowering his voice. 'We scored a genuine goal, Mortensen claims and all our players do. What happened was that the ball was going into the net but Mortensen decided he'd head it and he deflected the ball and the goalkeeper fell back into the goal. He was a basketball player, he caught the ball in one hand and threw it out from the back of the goal, and the referee didn't give the goal.' That's it! England didn't really lose the game at all, they were cheated out of it. 'Oh dear,' sighed Sir Walter. Oh dear, indeed.

Whatever, the result entered the record books and the country that gave the people's game to the world was humbled by a makeshift team of immigrants from a country where the game was treated as a cross between a joke and a freak show.

A soccer boom of the late 1970s and the early 1980s was short-lived, and financial backers as well as fans lost interest as the New York Cosmos's all-star, international but ageing side – featuring Pelé, Carlos Alberto, Beckenbauer and Chinaglia – was not replaced by players of comparable world stature or even by high-level 'home-town heroes', as soccer league pressman of the time Jim Trecker explained. Expenses had became so high, he told us, that 'the League just sort of imploded on itself in financial instability'.

Carlos Alberto, captain of Brazil's World Cup-winning team of 1970, declares that very few people know why professional soccer in the United States finished. The problem, he believes, arose when a barely documented Mexican bid succeeded in winning the 1986 finals and, according to Carlos Alberto, that spelt the end for big-time soccer in the US. 'America was the candidate. Soccer in the US seemed to be booming and was backed by Warner Communication,' he told us. 'The Warner people [couldn't accept] the FIFA decision that Mexico replace Colombia. Mexico was the host as recently as 1970.' Carlos Alberto's voice rose. 'The World Cup the Americans wanted to host wasn't 1994, it was 1986. If FIFA had placed the 1986 World Cup in the USA, that was the best market. When FIFA decided on Mexico, Warner Communications said, "We are finished. We don't put any more money in."'

Mexico's triumph over the US says much about FIFA mores and the Havelange style. Henry Kissinger, the former US Secretary of State for Foreign Affairs, made an hour-long presentation with a multitude of detail based on commercial analyses to the FIFA committee. He needn't have bothered. The Mexican delegation was already in the lobby of the Stockholm hotel, following up its eight-minute presentation with preparations for a celebration and victory reception.

The success of the Mexicans suited the interests of Havelange's friends in the Mexican media. Guillermo Cañedo was spotted 'arm in arm' with Rafael del Castillo Ruiz, head of the Mexican delegation, before the Stockholm meeting. Havelange's special commission had recommended Mexico.

Kissinger considered suing FIFA for breach of its own articles. The FIFA decision, and the manner in which it was reached, were both disappointing and humiliating to the US soccer establishment, as well as Warner, the main financial backers of the North American Soccer League. With escalating costs and falling revenues at home, and this snub from FIFA and the deal-making networks of world football, it was hardly surprising that Warner withdrew its support.

The false dawn of the NASL meant that soccer would continue to have a low profile in the USA until it was selected by FIFA to stage the finals. Its national side did well enough, in the build-up to 1994, to qualify for the World Cup finals in Italy in 1990. (FIFA had banned Mexico from taking part, accusing them of cheating by fielding over-age players in the World Youth Cup. This decision, of course, was viewed with suspicion – Mexico were a strong team and their absence eased the USA's passage to Italia '90. The Mexican ban had come just after the USA had been awarded the 1994 finals. Costa Rica had topped the qualifying group, so if Mexico had competed, it was more than likely that the US would not have made it to Italy. In the event, the USA lost all three of their games in Italy and finished bottom of their group. But at least they could now claim a World Cup pedigree and this would be a boost for business in 1994.)

The choice of the United States as host for the World Cup finals was greeted with derision and scepticism by journalists, commentators and professionals. At the tournament draw in Las Vegas in December 1993, media pundits commented on the tackiness and vulgarity of the event. The draw opened with welcomes from high-profile television, film and sports celebrities. Jessica Lange and Jeff Bridges were there, and Faye Dunaway was one of the co-hosts. 'Hello world, welcome to the USA' was the repeated line as these celebrities performed limited tricks with a football. Bill Clinton came on to state that the country was 'proud and excited' to host the tournament and that 'World Cup fever' had gripped the whole nation right through to the White House.

The three thousand guests at the Las Vegas event welcomed João Havelange for what the host acknowledged to be one of the most complicated draws ever conducted, linked as it was to a seeding system and the demographics of ethnic and immigrant communities across the chosen venues. The trophy was passed from Havelange to Alan Rothenberg, linchpin of the organisation World Cup '94. Rothenberg stated that it was with 'pride and humility' that he accepted the trophy for the period of the finals, which he was convinced would 'establish a legacy for USA soccer to flourish at every level of play'.

Soon after awarding the finals to the USA in 1988, FIFA had been active in campaigning against the US soccer federation's incumbent elected president, Werner Fricker. It was directly implicated in the election of Rothenberg as his successor.

When we caught up with him in Paris during World Cup '98, Rothenberg boasted, 'I saved the World Cup. FIFA was gravely concerned that the preparations were not going the way it wanted them to and was seriously thinking about taking the World Cup away from the US. That's when they contacted me and asked me whether I'd be interested in getting involved. I said yes, and was told I should become president of the United States soccer federation. I had to admit I wasn't even a member of that organisation.'

This minor technicality did not worry FIFA and, as Rothenberg tells it, 'Within a few short months we figured out the situation, and so in August 1990 I got elected president of the federation, and shortly thereafter took over organisation of the World Cup.'

At the Las Vegas draw, Roberto Baggio of Italy was presented with not just the Player of the Year award, but also with the Adidas Energizer trophy. Mickey Mouse introduced the viewer to the attractions of Orlando, Florida. Nightlife, cars and people were highlighted as the special qualities of Detroit. Nike, Delta and Opel graphics then led into a sustained Nike advertisement – 'You can't live without . . . Just do It' – which mixed soccer, sex and youth style.

At the opening ceremony in Chicago on 17 July, Diana Ross tried to take a penalty, striking the ball with a jerky mechanical swing of the leg. The ball rolled painfully and apologetically wide, and in a memorable anti-climax to the razzmatazz of the build-up the goal itself collapsed.

As it turned out, this was no bad omen. Early concerns at the staging of the event in the USA soon disappeared once the tournament started. It had been feared that, in order to create more high-scoring games, the goals would be enlarged; that, to accommodate USA television advertising, single matches would be divided into four time-periods; and that matches would be played upon artificial turf rather than proper grass. But none of this happened. Indeed, scepticism among some was tempered by an eager anticipation of the effect of some brave innovations by FIFA. A subtle amendment to the offside law was intended to favour attacking play. Stricter interpretation of foul and violent play would promote creativity. A new line on how to deal with injured players and the award of three points to teams for first-round wins were further measures planned to boost the image of soccer in the USA. It was plugged as a free-flowing, creative game with little of the overt aggression characteristic of other top-level professional team sports.

The World Cup had a bigger media impact in the USA than many pessimists had anticipated. It was hailed as the surprise sports story of the year, with television ratings 20 per cent to 30 per cent higher than many expected. Live games on the ESPN cable channel attracted viewing figures equal to the rating for prime-time Wednesday Major League Baseball games, and the final attracted nearly nine million viewers on ABC and another 1.5 million on a cable Spanish-language network. Press coverage also exceeded expectation.

Young people were the primary marketing target. Membership of the United States Youth Soccer Association increased by 9 per cent to 2.1 million. The American Youth Soccer Association's membership went up 14 per cent to half a million. The US soccer federation had 16 million registered players, more than any other FIFA member, and most of them were children.

The professional game may have continued to face difficulties in attracting investors, finding adequate stadiums and setting up local franchises immediately after the USA '94 adventure, but where soccer did thrive was where it had thrived before – in the schools, among particular ethnic communities and among women. This is where the sponsorship had already been targeted. The banana company Chiquita Brands International sponsored the Chiquita Cup, Fair Play, Clinics and Soccer Challenges, grass-roots programmes for youth soccer. Chiquita was also an Olympic soccer and US soccer sponsor, and its World Cup marketing drive confirmed soccer's specific market – children aged 15 to 16, women of 25 to 34, and adults of 55 and above. Soccer sponsors associated the game with a healthy, family image. Thriving Mexican Leagues already played their matches in southern California, and hispanic crowds flocked into the Los Angeles stadium to watch El Salvador take on Denmark. Healthy and athletic women, including world champions and potential gold medallists at the inaugural Olympic women's soccer tournament in Atlanta in 1996, embraced the game. More and more children played it. USA '94 reaffirmed the business community's focus upon these segments of the US sports market.

Staging the event well was a matter of civic pride for many and massive personal profit for a few. Direct comparisons with the Olympic Games can be seen here. At the 1984 Los Angeles Summer Olympics, tens of thousands of volunteers were recruited to help at the peak of global cold-war politics. The organisers refused to give the volunteers free lunches; the Los Angeles Organising Committee reported a surplus of $225 million.

At the World Cup finals ten years on, the same form of exploitation fed in to the event's staggering profitability. No lunches for the idealistic enthusiasts, but the 94,194 spectators at the final in the Rosebowl, Pasadena, paid $43.5 million for their tickets – an average price of nearly $462 per ticket.

The organisers weren't short of a subsidised lunch or two. Scott Parks Le Tellier was featured in the British press in 1993, not just as the managing director and chief operating officer of USA '94, but also as a missionary (with a Mormon background), visionary and evangelist – for football. He became hooked on soccer whilst watching the World Cup in Germany in 1974. Le Tellier and other key players in USA '94 were eager to make the most out of football's US market.

As an ambitious young attorney Le Tellier moved to LA to meet entrepreneurs on the appropriate sports and professional circuits. He played tennis with Mike O'Hara, head of the sports department in the organising committee of the Games, and soon got on to the committee and into the financial side himself. Speaking to journalist Ken Reich in the post-Olympics euphoria in early 1985, he told how he filled in for the boss, Alan Rothenberg, back at the LA Games. 'Alan was the original commissioner,' said Le Tellier, 'but because he was so tied up doing other things and was never there, they figured that the job wasn't going to get done.'

After the successful Games bonuses were paid to employees, in three categories of $2,500, $1,500 and $700. Le Tellier moaned that these were so insulting as to leave a bad taste in the mouth.

A decade on, and working with Alan Rothenberg in a team that seemed to have survived the bitterness and tensions of the Olympic exertions, Le Tellier ensured that things tasted better. For his 50-hour working week in 1991 (for roles of secretary, managing director and chief operating officer), Le Tellier received annual 'compensation' of $174,000, with a further $148,697 for 'other allowances'. In 1992 he got $186,000 and $414,291 allowances, linked to a move to California (where he already was) from an address he'd been using in Virginia.

Three months on from the final game of USA '94, Alan Rothenberg received $7 million in compensation for serving as the World Cup organising committee's chairman and chief executive officer, from the event's preliminary projection of a $60 million surplus. The $7 million comprised a $3 million bonus and a $4 million 'deferred-compensation package for back-pay due', calculated at $800,000 a year, running from August of 1990 through to 1995. Prominent in defence of this decision was board member Peter V. Ueberroth, for whom Rothenberg had worked during the '84 LA Games. One board member was not so supportive, saying, 'I'm against paying a guy for a volunteer job.' Le Tellier, chief operating officer of the World Cup organising committee, was voted a $500,000 bonus.

Rothenberg declined the offer of a $350,000 salary, but took the odd $30,000 in 'other allowances'. The state treasury was told that 'the board of directors has authorised the payment of salaried compensation to Mr Rothenberg. Mr Rothenberg has elected to defer the compensation pending a determination that a sufficient surplus exists from World Cup USA 1994 Inc. operations to satisfy all other obligations.'

Rothenberg has a clean conscience relating to the $7 million lump sum that came his way. 'This sounds terrible,' he said, 'but if you look at the whole eight years that I've been involved, I've been underpaid if you will. I took the job on a non-paying basis, though I was offered a very generous salary. I told them that I wouldn't take a salary. When it was over with they could look at the results, and whatever you think is fair . . . and some very independent high-powered people decided that $7 million was a fair payment.'

A sense of proportion is not one of Rothenberg's qualities. 'The reality is,' he went on, 'my law practice has suffered enormously, so I made a lot less money practising law than I would have otherwise. I'm not asking for people to feel sorry for me, but I saved the World Cup.'

Rothenberg had taken over responsibility for the World Cup organising committee soon after his election as USSF president, and assumed a central position in the tangled networks of the USA's soccer developments, with interests too in the proposed Major League Soccer (MLS) and as president of the US soccer federation. What bothers some people is that MLS, which is headed by Rothenberg, received £500,000 from World Cup USA, whose chairman is Rothenberg, to pay for its business plan which it submitted to the USSF, of which Rothenberg is president. No one was very surprised when MLS beat two other bids to set up the national league and then was given $3.5 million by World Cup USA for start-up costs.

No one seemed very surprised either when the Major League Soccer initiative stalled after US '94. For Rothenberg, it was not so much a football commitment as a coldly logical business decision as to how best to exploit the market. He believes that the North American Soccer League 'tried to do too much too fast, frankly'. So, with his $7 million cheque in his pocket, he felt little obligation to rush to put in place the new professional format for the game. MLS is up and running, but with little sign that it will ever get close to the market share of other big-time American sports.

For Rothenberg, soccer in the USA is still a 'sponsor's dream, a marketer's dream'. But launch such a dream, in its MLS version, at the right time for the maximum niche-market impact, when the family audience, solid white-collar, and the female third of all US players are ready. Rothenberg knows the market and told us that players, parents of players and coaches in the USA number more, proportionally, than the equivalent population of the UK. 'But socially, culturally, we have to be sure that our programmes fit within the American way,' he observed, with reference to grass-roots soccer and the cultivation of home-based talent.

For Rothenberg, the World Cup is as much about personal market worth as love of the game. Such financial transactions at the heart of the USA World Cup administration are fundamental to understanding the basis on which the tournament was held. Like the 1984 Los Angeles Olympics before it, the event was staged to celebrate the ways in which the US could meet a challenge and put on an efficient and spectacular global show. But it was also a goldrush for a thrusting and entrepreneurial professional élite. Veteran FIFA insiders have described Rothenberg as a brash LA lawyer, 'not a football man at all'.

USA '94 generated $4 billion, with a direct profit of over $20 million to the US organisers. But the real legacy of that World Cup was the model of mean, lean and immensely profitable event management. You don't have to like sport to do that. It helps if you do, but the driving force behind USA '94 was a combination of local pride, global posturing and personal and economic ambition.

USA '94 was, in João Havelange's words, a source of 'great pride', boosting FIFA's 'reputation as a dynamic and progressive body alert to modern currents of thought and deed'. Havelange beat his chest, boasting of his all-round satisfaction at the event. 'FIFA can reflect upon universal acknowledgement of its exceptional success. It vindicated totally FIFA's decision to award the finals to a country whose tireless efforts to promote our sport have long earned our respect. The short-term objective – to stage a spectacular World Cup with thrilling football, full stadiums, fair play and a peaceful atmosphere' – succeeded 'beyond question.'

Chairman of FIFA's organising committee, Guillermo Cañedo, joined the chorus of self-praise, writing in the official report on US '94 that the event 'was organised to a degree of perfection befitting the prestige of the tournament itself'. This silenced those who had questioned the ability of America to cope with such cultural and logistical problems. Cañedo also praised the high standards of technology and organisation. Nowhere did the Mexican media baron refer to viewing figures or advertising revenues back home in Mexico. There was no mention either in the report of Rothenberg's bonus, described by Hank Hersch of *Sports Illustrated* as an 'unconscionable' level of personal remuneration for an individual purporting to work in a voluntary capacity for a supposedly non-profit organisation.

Three years after the World Cup, Rothenberg's management of

World Cup USA 1994 Inc. was in the Californian courts. He was being sued by a former World Cup employee for breach of a contract. Rothenberg's own firm, Latham & Watkins, had handled the World Cup's legal matters, and in December 1996 a column in *Sports Illustrated* described him as 'a self-promoter and . . . smug', and called this hiring of his own law firm a 'blatant misuse of power'. Rothenberg was called upon to explain his multi-million-dollar compensation package, the use of Latham & Watkins as World Cup's legal counsel, the hiring of his 20-year-old son Bradford who was paid $107,321 for work on the World Cup, and a licensing contract between the organisation and his wife.

Rothenberg had been taken to court by a former employee, Michael Hogue, the director of the US team's World Cup training site in California in the run up to USA '94, who accused him of 'a blatant misuse of power for personal profit'. Hogue had been brought onto a national committee by Rothenberg in 1990 for developing plans for a national outdoor league. Axed from the World Cup set-up in 1992, he sued for wrongful termination and breach of his employment contract, and intentional and negligent interference with prospective economic advantage. Hogue, who unsurprisingly had to eat his words, claimed that Rothenberg had prevented him working in the soccer industry after his contract was terminated. Hogue was chasing more than $1.5 million, and Rothenberg's side offered, then withdrew, $200,000 in settlement. 'The man has the morals of a bandit,' Hogue told the *Los Angeles Times* in 1994, and stuck to his guns. In September 1997 the jury in a Los Angeles superior court deliberated for just one hour after a five-week trial before 'denying recovery' to claimant Hogue, in a vote of 11–1.

Rothenberg was used to winning. He'd campaigned for only 17 days for the USSF presidency in 1990, but romped home with 343.9 votes against incumbent Werner Fricker's 169.66 votes. Stories still circulate of how workers used tweezers to drag back clippings of a newspaper article about Rothenberg that had been pushed under the hotel bedroom doors of hundreds of delegates. His firm, Latham & Watkins, did a great deal of complicated legal work for World Cup USA '94 to the tune of $2.7 million between November 1990 and December 1994. The company was used to such high-profile clients, acting back in 1984 as general counsel for that year's Olympics organised by Peter Ueberroth, who turned up to testify in support of Rothenberg during the trial.

Rothenberg was a skilful manager of conflicting interests. Ronald Silverman, a former law partner, commented: 'You can't unnerve him, you can't scare him.' He'd controlled the MLS when it had won against two other bidders to the USSF to establish the national league – when he was also the boss of the USSF. 'Joining the US soccer federation was like joining the PTA,' he reminisced. The voluntarist spirit was soon quenched: 'Some of these people had to realise,' he explained, 'there is a big difference between lining the field for a youth league game and running a potentially billion-dollar business.' Not enough of a difference for Rothenberg to change the USSF's status as a charity. USA '94 had more than 400 employees. Many, out of hearing, nicknamed the boss 'Rothenweiler'. The man does little to discourage such stories: 'I don't beat up people because I enjoy beating up people . . . but if I have to leave some strewn bodies in order to win, within the rules, that's the way you have to do it.'

After USA '94 the court controversies did little to hold Rothenberg back. Just before France '98 he bought his way into one of the three sides owned and operated by MLS. At the time that he became individual owner (though in his own words, 'investor operator') of the San Jose Clash, he was still president of the USSF. He formed a $20 million investment group to buy the Clash, bringing in the Japanese advertising giant Dentsu. His long pedigree in sports law and administration – in basketball from the 1960s to the 1980s, and owning the Aztecs in the North American Soccer League – served him well in this latest move to own a team in a league he himself had created and headed. Dana Gelin had branded him, in *Sports Illustrated*, a 'shameless self-promoter'. The LA jury recognised his behaviour as perfectly acceptable. 'I put right on the table . . . exactly what my interests are,' Rothenberg has said. 'I follow the ethical rules that each organisation has.' It helps, of course, if you are in charge of the organisation too.

Football administrators in the USA were still triumphant years after the event about the scale of the success. Sitting at his desk in the USSF's Chicago headquarters, the president Hank Steinbrecher spat bile as he commented on the sceptical climate with which he and others had to contend. 'It was considered a joke, and I heard all the criticisms for so long – the United States could never pull off a successful World Cup, they would never get fans into the stadiums, they never sold sponsorships, they would cut the game into quarters, they have no passion, they have no idea of what it is like to play. Oh, and by the way, their team sucks.' He gave a wry smile, paused and said, 'Well, guess what? All the European press had to eat crow.'

On the field of play, USA '94 was indeed a glorious spectacle. On the day of the final, the walk to the ground – the Pasadena Rosebowl – had a dreamlike quality: sunshine and heat, brightly coloured, jovial – not aggressive – crowds wandering by the sprinklers of the suburban neighbourhoods surrounding the stadium. Entrepreneurial adolescents – California's best – plied a lively trade in cold drinks on the sidewalks, a football-pitch length down from the security of their millionaire homesteads. Less-privileged street vendors offered T-shirts, hats, flags and footballs as well as chilled sodas and beers. Touts looked happy enough, marking up tickets to $800 (£550). It was a far cry from our own memories of youth: the damp and stoic marches through mean streets to Goodison Park and Turf Moor, and the school caps which helped us con our way through the boys' turnstiles for one and sixpence.

The spectacle inside the Rosebowl didn't disappoint. The opening ceremony was lively and entertaining. We wondered what it would be like to be Pelé, who, just because he happened to be a good foot-baller, can hold hands and skip around the Rosebowl with Whitney Houston. Children swarmed across the pitch in the cause of UNICEF. And the Lords of the Rings themselves – Havelange, Samaranch and Nebiolo – were in the best seats in the house to witness this celebration of sport's love affair with consumer culture.

Maybe the match was dull, but who cared? Roberto Baggio bal-looned his penalty over goalkeeper Tafarel's bar, giving the game to Brazil. Cue SFX. Francis Ford Coppola could not have created a more evocative scene than the exodus from the Rosebowl. Fireworks, rockets and Roman candles exploded into the afternoon sky. Heli-copters buzzed up above, clouded by smoke. As Darryl Hall's World Cup anthem 'Gloryland' boomed out, we looked skywards to see a trio of First World War vintage biplanes fly across. Someone stood on a wing of the lead aircraft and waved to the crowd. 'There goes Baggio, making a break for it,' yelled one wag. 'No, it's not – it's OJ,' laughed another.

OJ Simpson had once run fleet-footed around this very stadium, winning the Most Valuable Player award in the American Football intercollegiate championship game in 1968. He'd then won the coveted Heisman Trophy, and gone on to become one of the game's greatest stars. How the mighty can fall. It was a sobering counter to the throbbing and vital street culture of the Brazilian and Italian fans in Santa Monica and other LA bases, where carnivalesque rivalry was the order of the evening.

Forgettable game or not, the final was without doubt an *event*. It proved wrong the cynical and world-weary doomsday predictions of soccercentric non-Americans and soccerphobic Americans. And for some professionals it was the crowning glory of their careers. Tognoni discounts the disappointing goalless scoreline of the final. 'It was a wonderful event and a full stadium,' he told us. 'I said to myself, "First of all I can never do more for an event than I did for USA '94." And maybe it may not be as beautiful again because we will never have, until we go to the US, the big stadium again.'

Hank Steinbrecher, hailing Havelange as 'the father of the rebirth of soccer in the United States', insisted that 'this giant is starting to stir' and made the outrageous boast that 'by the year 2010 the United States will host and win the World Cup'. The USSF/ Organising Committee made $60 million, and hundreds of millions for FIFA. 'Surely,' he concluded, 'they'll be back for more sooner rather than later.'

World Cup '94 reminded sports entrepreneurs of the cultural variety and vitality, global profile and commercial potential of football. Doug Logan, a former promoter of Pink Floyd, The Rolling Stones and Madonna concerts, developed a logo for Major League Soccer which celebrates not just the kick (at the expense of the handling skills so essential to mainstream USA sports), but a 'Pan-Americanism not Americanism', with the dominanting blue and green of the logo symbolising the sky and the pitch of a global game that, finally, some powerful Americans want a piece of.

As 'Gloryland' played over the PA in the Pasadena Rosebowl, it wasn't only football fans who were basking in the sunshine. So too were the Mr Fixits of FIFA and self-confessed 'brash American' soccer entrepreneurs and popular-cultural promoters. They were already counting the benefits of returning to the cradle of consumerism for another World Cup bonanza. Some of the entrepreneurial big boys of the summer of '94 would be prominent in the Machiavellian politics of FIFA throughout the last decade of the century. Rothenberg was one of them. He had come a long way since commissioning Olympic football in '84. It had been one hell of a profitable ride – and the wagon was still rolling.

7. THE BIG BOSS

Only the Havelange aura – and that of Saudi's Prince Faisal when he bothered to turn up to a FIFA event – rivalled the presence of the immaculately groomed Dr Mong Joon Chung. Jet-black hair, tall, lean and trim for his early middle age, you knew when Chung was around. His minders surrounded him as he swept through the palm trees of the Sheraton lobby in Abu Dhabi.

You didn't talk to Chung unannounced over a coffee. First, you were grilled over lunch by his factotum, who'd been with him throughout his adult life – even to Johns Hopkins University in Baltimore, where Chung's dissertation in physics won him his doctorate. Patient negotiation was needed to get access to Chung, and even then we were bounced out of his Sheraton suite as soon as the discussion moved from FIFA history to shadier aspects of South Korea's World Cup bid, and to evaluations of Havelange's impact.

One European-based FIFA-watcher close to the strong man of Korean football knew the real stakes. For Chung, the Korean FA was an apprenticeship for bigger things. The Big Boss usually had a few matters on his mind – like heading Hyundai heavy industries, sitting in the national parliament or profiling Korea in Asian and world football politics.

Chung was used to getting what he wanted. One veteran observer of the Asian political scene, Agence-France pressman Erskine McCullough, told us that if Korea had lost in the race for the 2002 World Cup finals, 'the Japanese Embassy would have gone up in flames'. And World Cup Korea–Japan 2002 was a hard-fought title. To Korea the most important thing was to have their name before Japan's, 'for historical, mainly political reasons', McCullough mused.

A little over six months before the FIFA executive committee was to make its decision on who would host the 2002 World Cup, the

Koreans and Japanese were lobbying for support in South Africa. For years the Japanese had felt that the decision was in the bag. A self-assured confidence brimmed over at their big reception at the Sandton Sun, Johannesburg, on the tail end of the African Cup of Nations in January 1996. Sir Bobby Charlton was on display, plugging the bid. Jim Trecker, PR at USA '94 and US football fixer, lauded the Japanese bid and the qualities of the nation's people. A video relayed football stars saying that if the Japanese did something, they would do it well. The Japanese treated their audience to a hi-tech vision of the virtual football spectacle – it looked as though terraces might be a thing of the past as the country which had done most to accelerate a world media revolution turned its attention to football. How could their bid fail? Hadn't Havelange favoured the Japanese all along? Wasn't the South Korean bid – as we all *really* knew – paper thin? Maybe.

The Japanese were to pay a high price for their smugness when the politically led bid of the South Koreans got stronger as the race went on. The in-house politics of the FIFA family hierarchy were inscrutable to the Japanese, but not to Chung. He was quick to spot a rare moment of vulnerability in Havelange, in the Big Man's contest with Europe's Lennart Johansson. Using all of the resources at his disposal, he struck to catapult Korea into the driving seat.

FIFA vice-president David Will had experienced the race between Morocco and France for the prize of staging the 1998 finals. 'That was bad enough, the pressures on that were terrible,' he told us. But this was nothing next to the summer of 1996, when FIFA was due to select the host for the 2002 finals. The fight for the privilege of hosting the first World Cup of the new millennium, and the first to be staged outside Europe and the Americas, was still more intense.

As Japan and Korea moved towards the decision date, the competitors followed the French example of a last-ditch assault on the motivations and appetites of key FIFA personnel. 'This was so dramatic, this one. This was just unbelievable,' said Will, flinging his arms into the air. 'It was ridiculous. I said to Japan and Korea, "I'm not coming to any more receptions, I am not accepting any more gifts." The stuff was arriving at the door, and of course, what do you do? The postman delivers it. It's just ridiculous. The only thing that was missing was the cash in a plain brown envelope. You know, it was unbelievable.' We imagined the postman's daily struggles up the gravel driveway, burdened with TVs, hi-fis, PCs, movie cameras, ornamental vases and decorative kimonos. Enough is too much for the puritan Scot. 'I am not accepting invitations to Japan or Korea,' he said, reclaiming some of the moral high ground. 'This is not out of discourtesy. I am stopping. And I know that most of the Europeans did the same. They just stopped.'

But what had happened before they stopped? And if, by implication, only the Europeans stopped, what did the others continue to accept from the rival bidders? The UEFA president Lennart Johansson was one of those Europeans. He admits that members of FIFA's executive committee were propositioned by nations seeking to host the 2002 World Cup. 'Yes, there were no limits,' he said, 'a bottle of whisky, a camera or a computer, everything was permissible.' Johansson added that he had returned a computer.

Another FIFA executive committee member, Dr Michel D'Hooghe of Belgium, told us how hotel rooms were garlanded with flowers. More sinister, a lobbyist from one of the bidding countries appeared in the seat next to him on a flight from Brussels to Prague. This fellow passenger didn't stay silent. He talked to D'Hooghe throughout the flight. 'Could this be a coincidence?' the Belgian asked, in a fashion that needed no answer. We responded with a noncommittal shrug. As we left his office we couldn't help noticing the centrepiece of his desk – a magnificent circular green pot, inscribed by Dr Chung, offering his best wishes to D'Hooghe's association.

It's hard to do the arithmetic accurately – we've put the questions to the Koreans and the Japanese, but the face-to-face ones are politely and coldly deflected and the e-mails not answered. Estimates claim that $100 million was spent by Korea and Japan in their campaigns. The escalation and the outcome of the bidding war became enmeshed in internal FIFA politics. They expressed the deep-rooted and simmering tensions between FIFA and the European federation, and the positioning and implicit campaigning of potential successors to Havelange.

In his inimitable style, Havelange had led the Japanese to believe that the World Cup finals were within his individual gift. An Asian venue was very much in his thinking as early as 1986, when he gave an interview to the Swiss magazine *Sport*. There, he spoke in favour of rotation of the finals in Europe and America up until 1994, and 'expressed the wish' that the 2002 event should be given to China.

In the autumn of 1987 Havelange travelled to Beijing for further preliminary discussions with China's sports leaders. His encouragement of a Chinese bid was also linked to his IOC manoeuvres. At the time, he believed that China would be awarded the Summer Olympic Games for the year 2000: 'Anyone who can organise Olympic Games is no doubt capable of hosting the finals of the World Cup,' he announced disingenuously. World Cups are, as he well knew, more demanding – lasting up to five weeks, involving 32 teams, requiring nationwide venues.

Meanwhile, as the Chinese dwelt upon Havelange's overtures, Japan and South Korea expressed their interest in developing bids at a meeting of the Asian confederation. FIFA's general secretary Sepp Blatter had visited South Korea's soccer facilities earlier in the year, and the aggressive and uncompromising tone of the South Korean campaign was set from the start. A summer Olympics the following year in Seoul was presented by the Koreans as a perfect illustration of the nation's ability to stage such events and the Korean press mobilised against the other potential bidders. China's low standard of living would bar it from meeting FIFA's financial criteria, they argued, and Japan's main sport, baseball, would obstruct any plans to stage a World Cup event there during the baseball season.

The successful Seoul Olympics and a concentration by the Chinese upon their bid for the 2000 Games boosted Korean confidence in the race for the 2002 World Cup. By the summer of 1990 Havelange could tell the Xinhua press agency that as well as Korea, additional candidates for the finals were Japan, Saudi Arabia, China and Malaysia. Asian football standards were improving, he stated, and would be close to those of Europe and South America by 2000. An Asian venue was therefore ideal for 2002. This was the classic Havelange and Samaranch tactic, talking up the candidate to stoke the fires of rivalry.

During the World Under-17s Championships staged in Japan in 1993, Havelange consistently gave the impression to the Japanese that they were the firm favourites, his personal choice. Reservations remained over the lack of English-speaking expertise in Japan and the rising costs of accommodation and transport, but the country was the clear front-runner.

The complacent Japanese trusted that the Big Man could deliver, but cracks were appearing in the walls of his fiefdom. FIFA's own committee practices were being transformed, with more committee members – clustering around Johansson – willing to openly challenge Havelange. The accession of Chung to the Asian confederation's vice-presidential place on FIFA's executive committee added another dissenting voice. Unlike so many other members, the Big Boss was prepared to take on the Big Man.

Chung's route to the vice-presidency was trouble free and he had few rivals. Former businessman Tadao Murata was a more genuine football man, but had far too low a profile to stop the Chung offensive. He had worked in the big conglomerates of Tokyo and London and he knew the score in Asian football politics, being a pioneer in the development of the game in Japan. But he was a generation older and shorter in stature, with a less striking presence than his Korean rival. People liked Dr Murata and he is a nice person; up against Chung, though, he was destined to finish last. Two others contested the election for the seat on the FIFA committee. Kuwait's Sheikh Ahmad Fahad knew a bit about tough battles – his father had been murdered by invading Iraqi troops in the Gulf War. Also in the fray from the Gulf was Mohammed Bin Hammam of Qatar. Hammam polled a promising vote but Chung pipped the Kuwaiti Sheikh by 11 votes to ten. Murata got just two and was for a time removed from office back in Japan's World Cup bidding organisation. The Japanese were outplayed in this critical contest for the Asian vote and it would cost them dear.

Chung's election on to the FIFA committee raised immeasurably the Korean profile. He had lobbied and campaigned hard, promising much and ensuring the presence of crucial South Asian delegates at the Asian confederation's election. Insiders in the Asian federation relate how he funded voters on epic cross-desert journeys.

So Chung became one of Asia's representatives at the heart of FIFA. He now had the base from which to raise the stakes in the race for 2002. After the 1994 World Cup, Chung announced that he would receive Havelange in Korea to show the facilities and constantly took the opportunity to promote his country's bid. In a statement of exceptional cheek, he even urged FIFA to act 'to prevent an escalation in the "unnecessary war of attrition" between Japan and Korea'.

Chung showed that he meant business. Groomed for power and victory, the Korean heir to the Hyundai giant was not used to losing. In all of FIFA's circles, he carries himself with the *hauteur* of the born élite. He keeps a respectful distance from Havelange, but occupies his own space, exuding confidence and power. Chung has been born to win, bred for victory. His father, Chung Ju-yung, head of Hyundai, was the real leader of the successful Olympic bid, and five years after the Seoul Games he tried to become president of the country. Chung junior was coming into the FIFA boardroom with an agenda of his own which stretched well beyond FIFA's fixture list.

FIFA and its decisions were being swayed by new influences and alliances. In 1994, Asia's confederation secretary Peter Velappan elicited a commitment from Havelange that FIFA would, after its Chicago Congress of the forthcoming summer, give serious consideration to the principle of awarding the finals to two countries. Havelange agreed to form a study commission for this, but proposed no change to the established rules. Velappan saw co-hosting as a solution to the fierceness of the Japan-Korea rivalry, for neither would be prepared to lose. He also believed that co-hosting would boost the Asian presence in the World Cup, with two host nations qualifying automatically for the finals. As it turned out, Asia was initially given more or less the same allocation for 2002 it had received for 1998, four places including the two hosts. At France '98 Asia had three places, plus a fourth secured in a play-off with the Oceania champions.

Tunisia, Egypt, Mali and Somalia also presented a motion to the Chicago Congress proposing that the World Cup finals be rotated around the confederations. Blatter told the North and Central American Congress in New York that such a plan would fail, as very few countries in the world possessed the required infrastructure, technology and economic basis to stage a 32-team tournament.

Regardless of the scepticism of the FIFA secretariat, such proposals coming from the confederations (including Europe's discussion documents on the future of FIFA) were opening up debate in committees in a way that the dictatorial presidential style of Havelange could no longer stem. However confident the Japanese were in the bidding process, their reliance upon the patronage of Havelange, and upon their interpretation of and trust in the strength of his word, was to prove misplaced. The Japan bid kept to its strategy, backing activities such as courses in Africa. But the Africans were siding with the Europeans, Chung and Charlie Dempsey of Oceania. With no presence inside the central FIFA committee, the Japanese bid lost ground.

With FIFA committees open to new influences, the outcome of

the bidding process for Asia's first Word Cup became unpredictable. By the end of 1994 Havelange sought to stand back, cancelling trips to the Asian Games in Hiroshima and the planned trip to Korea.

Chung, as president of the national football association, organised the Korean bidding committee, of which he was vice-chairman. His emergence as an effective voice within FIFA's major committee gave the Korean bid a priceless boost. He was hardly the faceless bureaucrat, as chief-in-waiting of one of the country's heavyweight *chaebol*. His bidding committee was full of important figures. In the chair was Lee Hong Koo, then the deputy prime minister and the head of the New Korea Party, who doubled as head of the government's unification committee. Men from the foreign ministry joined the team. Korean embassy staff were brought in. The Koreans placed an agent – called a bidding committee secretary – in their embassy in the country of residence of each member of the FIFA executive committee. Business muscle filled other posts. One of these went on to become chairman of the bidding committee, Koo Pyong-hwoi, chair of the Lucky Goldstar *chaebol*, who was also president of Korea's Board of Trade.

The competition for the 2002 finals turned into a merry-go-round of presentations, press conferences, receptions and hospitality events. Men with votes received mailings, deliveries and invitations. Confederation national championships and congresses were the platform for these, as football administrators and sports media personnel were invited to hear yet again the forceful rhetoric and hyperbole of the contestants.

Everyone wanted to get in on the act. At a meeting of the African Confederation executive during the African Cup of Nations in Johannesburg in 1996, some committee members clearly thought that Japanese *largesse* would get them to another 'Japan-related event coming up in Yaoundé'. A minute dashed such expectations, recording that 'trips there would not be free, and it is clear that the occasion was not linked to Japan's bid for 2002 World Cup'.

Sir Bobby Charlton, with business interests in Africa and franchises such as the World Cup Japan/Bobby Charlton International football shirt, backed the Japanese bid. It was, he sincerely believed, in the best interests of the World Cup. We met up with him in Johannesburg. It had been hot work. We were pleased to get him a cold beer when we talked things over with him afterwards. Charlton was genuinely impressed with what the Japanese had to offer. Their big push in Africa had also been a nice little earner for him and his company. Most importantly, he was learning valuable lessons which he would bring to England's bid to host World Cup 2006. A key lesson which he hadn't learned when we spoke with him (but which he'll have digested by now) is that you should never trust a FIFA president.

The build-up to the May 1996 decision was an intense process of lobbying and promotion. The stakes were higher than any intrinsic to the football world itself. As well as criticising from the start the rival bids, Chung and his compatriots discussed the Korean bid in terms of wider political projects, not just football. When in April 1996 North Korean troops entered the buffer zone separating the two Koreas, so violating the truce that ended the 1950–53 Korean War, General Song Young-Shik, the secretary-general of the South Korean Bidding Committee, argued that such a situation reinforced Korea's case to be given the World Cup finals. 'Hosting the World Cup can play a role in facilitating the reunification process,' the General said, proposing football as a means to the peaceful resolution of one of the world's most long-standing conflicts. (Such statements also undercut the Japanese by seeming to remove one of Havelange's objections to the bid. The self-styled ambassador for peace seemed to have erected a huge barrier against the Korean case by saying that the reunification of the two Koreas should be a prerequisite for any successful Korean bid.) With the reunification issue on the agenda, the Korean bid steamrollered ahead. 'I could not find any weak point in this bid,' said Horst Schmidt, secretary-general of the German FA, head of FIFA's delegation to Korea in late 1996. This stunned the Japanese, so confident in their bullet-trains, state-of-the-art stadiums, swish hotels and media know-how.

In his visionary style, General Song emphasised the quality and cheapness of Korea's hotels and transport, praised the country's football heritage, and pledged to gift $230 million to FIFA's national associations – over a million dollars per country, all the projected World Cup profits. A former British diplomat in Seoul described the Korean bid and claims as 'absolute nonsense – there's nothing there outside Seoul and Pusan'.

Things became rather like a school playground stand-off – my bid's better than yours, my ground's bigger than your ground. Rather late in the day the Japanese realised the weight a politician could add, and hauled in the prime minister to endorse the bid. African aid was still on the Japanese agenda – a youth-coaching course here, a bit from Sir Bobby there, how about a medical seminar or two?

The Koreans, meanwhile, played the peace card to saturation point. They framed their bid as 'a priceless opportunity to again make a major contribution to global peace and harmony, promoting unity among all people, including those of our divided nation'. They claimed they could unite the world through football. The rhetoric rose to a crescendo in projecting the finals as 'a catalyst for peace', and linking 'the beautiful game and reconciliation'. FIFA rhetoric was mixed in with Korean ideology. Friendship and peace through football was a sacred FIFA principle. A united Korea was a South Korean – and US – imperative. This was more than just football: 'If the first World Cup of the twenty-first century could help erase the last vestige of the Cold War of the twentieth century, the tournament would be more than a milestone for football: it would be a milestone for mankind.'

So there we have it – up there with the space race. Young Chung had bigger goals in mind than World Cup matches. It was even rumoured that Korean industrial heavyweights had pressurised the European Commission to lean on UEFA to promote the Korean bid. And in early 1999, on CNN, Chung went on record with his ultimate goal – the presidency of the reunited Korean peninsula. As a stepping-stone to this, he also announced his willingness to challenge for the FIFA presidency in 2002. 'I have many friends on the FIFA executive committee,' said Chung.

The bidding process became caught up in the battles for power within FIFA, especially the emerging challenge of Johansson to Havelange. Tadao Murata, back on board after his sentence of shame, confirmed this, describing bitterly the way in which the Japanese had been caught in the 'crossfire between the FIFA and the UEFA presidents'.

As the day of decision drew closer, it became clear that Korea, with the European members' support, could beat Japan in a head-to-head challenge. The Japanese wouldn't budge right through to the eve of the decisive FIFA meeting – after all, a deal is a deal with the Big Man. In the two days before that meeting, FIFA wrote to the Japanese, asking them to consider the possibility of co-hosting. Former prime ministers of South Korea and Japan, Lee Hong Koo and Miyazawa Kiichi, met as unofficial delegates of their respective governments to seek a diplomatic solution.

The co-hosting option had been strongly promoted by the Europeans on the committee, but Havelange remained totally and utterly opposed to the prospect. 'Forty-eight hours before the vote he was saying "over my dead body",' David Will told us. The Big Man, faced with what would have been a humiliating defeat for himself and for the Japanese bid, was at the last minute persuaded to support the co-hosting option.

Samaranch of the IOC was one source of advice, convincing Havelange to give way and so avoid a divisive vote. With a sigh of relief that echoed around the grand avenues down from their headquarters and around the shores of Lake Zurich, the FIFA committee accepted what now became Havelange's proposal for co-hosting. No vote had been needed. No faction was publicly humiliated. Public self-evisceration would not be required.

Japan and Korea were unlikely bed fellows. Early in the bidding war Chung had argued that Japan's belligerent past rendered it unsuited to the role of World Cup host. For hundreds of years the two countries had been enemies. Japan had ruled the Korean peninsula between 1910 and 1945, subjecting the Korean people to dreadful abuse, including having Korean women enslaved into prostitution for soldiers of Japan's Imperial Army. Chung had called this occupation 'the most barbarous in the history of humanity'. The Japanese embassy in Seoul had even warned its nationals to prepare for the worst should Japan win the hosting honour. Hardly a good foundation for setting up a partnership to run the World Cup.

The decision meant that Chung's political ambitions were enhanced – and his company's prospects were looking good too. Close to $1.5 billion was lined up to be invested in South Korea, in stadiums, communications, transport and accommodation. It was the country's leading corporations such as the so-called 'World Cup trio' of Hyundai, Sam Whan Camus and Hotel Shilla which would benefit from this World Cup windfall. The Big Boss was into big bucks.

Korea would stage the opening ceremony and the opening match, while Japan could get the final. Cunningly, Chung, using the French and Spanish spellings of his country's name, manoeuvred 'Corée' into the first billing in the name, as well as the opening credit of the tournament itself.

In France '98, meanwhile, the receptions and the promos continued. To function-weary FIFA folk, and footsore hacks and researchers, getting to the Korea–Japan reception at a hotel in

The hottest ticket in town: a voting card for the FIFA presidency

Counted out: Lennart Johannson (right) concedes to Sepp Blatter after the first-round ballot at the Paris Congress, 1998

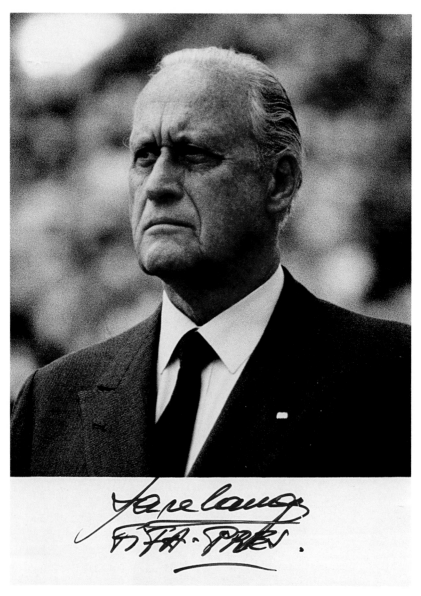

The Big Man: João Havelange

From protégé to president: Sepp Blatter

Mawad Wade, former secretary
of the Senegal FA: 'I was one of
the men in CAF who was in
charge of making a campaign for
Dr Havelange'

Oroc Oyo, former secretary of
the Nigerian FA: 'Ganga
mustered Africa for Havelange'

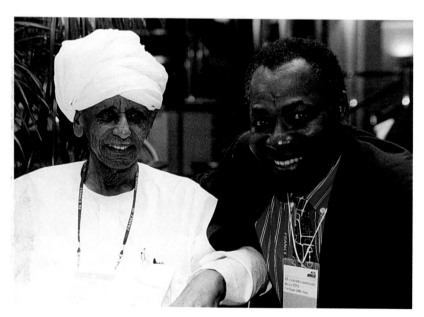

Out of Africa: Dr Halim of CAF and Sudan
with Emanual Maradas, editor of *African Soccer*

'Shell and Abacha go to hell!': at the African Cup of Nations
Johannesburg a fan draws attention to the execution of Ken Saro   va
and the involvement of Shell Oil, one of the tournament's sponso

George Weah of AC Milan and Liberia

Joseph Antoine Bell, goalkeeper of Cameroon and Marseille: 'In France you might expect that $10 of every $100 coming into football would disappear. In Africa, for every $100 coming into football, $90 disappears'

ABOVE: Dressed to sell: fans act as clothes-horses for FIFA's sponsors

RIGHT: Trouble-shooter: Nike had to fly Carlos Alberto, the former captain of Brazil, to the African Cup of Nations in South Africa in 1996 to protect their $10 million investment in football in Cameroon

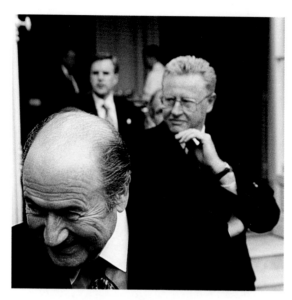

Kelly's problem: former FA secretary Graham Kelly ponders how to gain the ear of the new President Blatter on the lawns of the British Embassy in Paris

Not so wise man: doomed Keith Wiseman
tries to talk his way out of trouble in Paris

The gang of four: Havelange, Blatter, Kelly and Collins (of the Welsh FA) at the Paris meeting of the International Football Board, 1998

David Will, the Scottish FIFA vice-president and representative of the International Football Board

Charlie Dempsey, president of the Oceania Confederation

Chuck Blazer, general secretary
of the Concacaf Confederation

Alan Rothenberg, the man behind USA '94
and the Mr Fixit of soccer in America

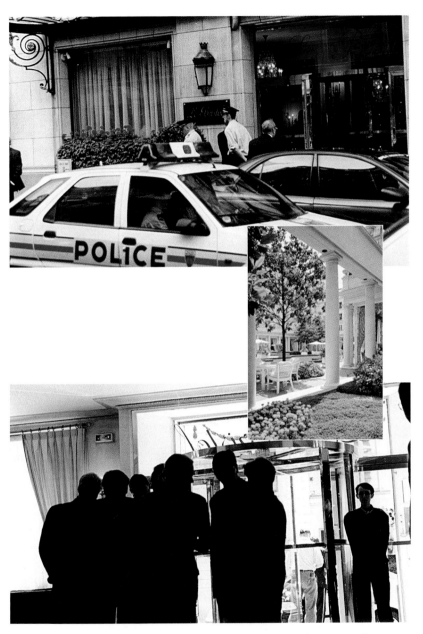

TOP: Safe-keeping: tight security outside Hotel Le Bristol,
the FIFA family's exclusive Paris retreat
INSET: The FIFA Club, the five-star private leisure
wing inside Le Bristol
BOTTOM: The shadow cabinet: FIFA members
plotting in the hotel's lobby

Foreign legions: French riot police outside Marseille's
Olympic stadium await the arrival of England's finest

Fight night: bruised and battered, the lads review the
local papers the morning after the battle of Marseille

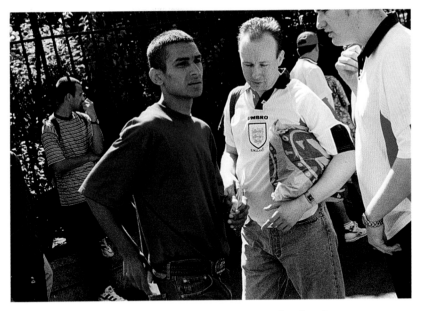

Tickets, please: English fans barter with a local tout

Touts on tour: the fat man stakes out his patch in Marseille

16e Coupe du Monde de la FIFA - FRANCE 98
16e FIFA World Cup - FRANCE 98
16e Copa del Mundo de la FIFA - FRANCE 98

FIFA

For the Good of the Game

COMPOSITION DES EQUIPES	START LIST	ALINEACION

Match N°: 64	Brésil (BRA) : France (FRA)	12/07/98 21:00
Finale		Saint-Denis, Stade de France

Brésil (BRA)

N°	Nom	P	Age	Sél
1	TAFFAREL	G	32	98
2	CAFU	D	28	67
3	ALDAIR	D	32	67
4	JUNIOR BAIANO	D	28	20
6	ROBERTO CARLOS	D	25	51
5	CESAR SAMPAIO	M	30	31
8	DUNGA ✓	M	34	89
10	RIVALDO	M	26	15
18	LEONARDO	M	29	45
20	BEBETO	A	34	72
21	EDMUNDO	A	27	28

France (FRA)

N°	Nom	P	Age	Sél
16	BARTHEZ Fabien	G	27	19
3	LIZARAZU Bixente	D	28	37
8	DESAILLY Marcel	D	29	48
15	THURAM Lilian	D	26	38
18	LEBOEUF Frank	D	30	15
6	DJORKAEFF Youri	M	30	44
7	DESCHAMPS Didier ✓	M	29	75
10	ZIDANE Zinedine	M	26	38
17	PETIT Emmanuel	M	27	25
19	KAREMBEU Christian	M	27	35
9	GUIVARC'H Stéphane	A	27	12

Remplacements ~ Substitutions ~ Suplentes

12	CARLOS GERMANO	G	27	27
22	DIDA	G	24	13
15	ANDRE CRUZ	D	29	29
14	GONCALVES	D	32	31
13	ZE CARLOS	D	29	2
16	ZE ROBERTO	D	24	16
19	DENILSON	M	20	20
17	DORIVA	M	26	9
11	EMERSON	M	22	9
7	GIOVANNI	M	26	14
9	RONALDO	A	21	41

1	LAMA Bernard	G	35	37
22	CHARBONNIER Lionel	G	31	1
2	CANDELA Vincent	D	24	11
14	BOGHOSSIAN Alain	M	27	10
4	VIEIRA Patrick	M	25	8
13	DIOMEDE Bernard	A	24	8
21	DUGARRY Christophe	A	26	26
12	HENRY Thierry	A	20	9
11	PIRES Robert	A	24	17
20	TREZEGUET David	A	20	11

Entraineurs ~ Coaches ~ Entrenadores

ZAGALLO Mario	JACQUET Aimé

Arbitres ~ Referees ~ Arbitros

Arbitre	BELQOLA Said (MOR)	Assistants	WARREN Mark (ENG)
4ème	AL ZEID Abdul Rahman (KSA)		SALIE Achmat (RSA)

G - Gardien Goalkeeper Portero	D - Défenseur Defender Defensa	M - Milieu Midfielder Medio	A - Attaquant Forward Delantero	P - Poste Position Puesto	Sél - Sélection Caps Internacional	✓ - Capitaine Captain Capitán

Canon
Official Sponsor

EDS   HEWLETT PACKARD   SYBASE
Official Suppliers

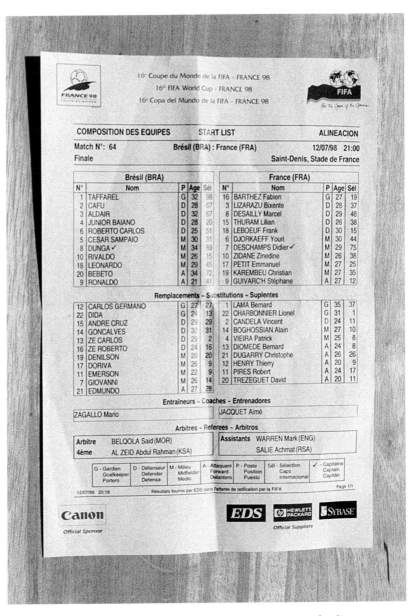

LEFT AND ABOVE: Now you see him, now you don't:
Ronaldo's name miraculously reappears on the Brazilian
team sheet moments before the World Cup final

Hands on the ball: Michel Platini and
Sepp Blatter together for the FIFA presidency

Montparnasse in that dead time between the semi-finals and the final didn't sound like too much fun. It was a crowded schedule, too, with the British Embassy in the diary later in the day putting on a bit of hospitality for the England 2006 bid.

Dr Chung was waiting to greet us all. His niece, elegantly attired in Western dress, was also there. Talking to her later, we discovered that she lived in London, studied at the Royal College of Art and specialised in gold smelting. What could we say? What prescience, though, for the niece of a *chaebol* top man to be getting this skill on the eve of the meltdown of the Asian economy.

Between the refills and the football gossip, the reluctant partners distributed a glossy brochure presenting their progress. It's a book that can never be back to front or upside-down, for held one way it's the right way round for Korea, and held the other way, it's correct for Japan. Equal partnership here means no concession given, no honour lost on either side.

The brochure presents Korea's ten venues. Outside Seoul, it's a voyage of discovery for the football world. Get on to your local travel agent now to beat the rush. Get in there with the bigwigs of world football for a match or two at Sogwipo on the small island of Cheju, off the south-western tip of the Korean peninsula. It's blessed with the nickname 'sculpture of the gods', and boasts 'fields of blooming rapee flowers' every spring. But there's no mention of airports or stadiums. Make sure you check before you set off.

Japan's list of venues doesn't include Tokyo or Kyoto or Hiroshima, but the short commutes from the heart of Tokyo, Saitama and Yokohama will nevertheless be popular spots for the FIFA folk. Oita is another site that might appeal to some of the FIFA chaps. It's on the island of Kyushu, between Japan and Korea, and proudly promotes smiling, naked females occupying the locale's 'famous hot springs' with their 'highly curative effects'. Site supervisors among the FIFA club will be rushing for that assignment.

Football has forced through some initiatives that might have taken a lot longer without the co-hosting. Korea's President Kim Young Sam and Japan's Prime Minister Hashimoto met within months of the co-hosting decision at so-called soccer summits. Heads of state normally attend the opening ceremony of the finals, so negotiations are under way to prepare for the first-ever visit of the Japanese emperor to South Korea. The simmering hostilities of a recent past will not disappear overnight, though. A few games of football will not be enough to make the Koreans forgive the Japanese for their brutality during the occupation of the peninsula. But the symbolic impact will be great, as the Korean head of state opens the 2002 finals in Seoul. Getting that one stage further than his father managed, the world may well see Dr Mong Joon Chung, the Biggest Boss ever, eased into the presidency of the reunited Korea by the time he reaches the epicentre of global football politics.

8. A RUMBLE IN THE JUNGLE

When Nelson Mandela walked out of Cape Town's Pollsmoor Prison in February 1990, his long march to freedom took him to a hero's welcome at Soccer City, a sprawling, modern football stadium on the outskirts of Soweto. Mandela's release heralded seismic changes in South Africa, culminating in the dismemberment of apartheid and the victory, four years later, of the ANC in the country's first democratic elections.

It was apt that Mandela should be fêted in a football ground. Sport was an important weapon in the war against apartheid. Football is the black people's game not just in South Africa but throughout the continent. During times when mass gatherings of non-whites were either banned or heavily policed, South Africa's football grounds were one of the few places where blacks, coloureds and Indians could come together to celebrate common causes.

Six years after his release, in January 1996, Mandela returned to Soccer City, to open the finals of the African Cup of Nations. As a jumbo jet from South African Airways roared low over the open-topped stadium, an adoring crowd gave the new South African president a rapturous welcome. Seated alongside Mandela, surveying the opening ceremonies, were FIFA's President, João Havelange, and the man who wanted his throne, Lennart Johansson. The champion and his challenger both knew that with 51 vote-holding member nations, Africa would be the key to winning or losing the 1998 presidential election.

It had taken UEFA a long time to recover from Sir Stanley Rous's demise, and the Europeans had been little more than spectators as Havelange grew increasingly powerful and dictatorial. They watched as he filled FIFA's most important committees with friends and yes-men. During a period when football in Europe was getting bigger and wealthier, UEFA's top brass were forced to stand aside as more and more of their money was siphoned off to the third world, FIFA and who knows where else.

After suffering this for more than 20 years, in 1994 the Europeans finally decided to fight back. In the New York executive committee meeting following the USA World Cup, Havelange pushed them into the ring. At the very end of the meeting he handed out photocopies of a document which listed FIFA's restructured committees and their new members. Then he closed the meeting. There was no debate, no discussion, no explanation. For the Europeans, who had again lost out in the reshuffle, this was one decree too many.

Europe's biggest problem was in finding a challenger who was smart and ruthless enough to go head to head with the influential and scheming Brazilian. He also had to be trustworthy. Sepp Blatter, FIFA's general secretary, who had offered himself to the Europeans, was not considered. Blatter is clever and ruthless enough, but having worked so closely with Havelange for so many years, he was not likely to be chosen for this particular purpose.

UEFA's candidate was their burly Swedish president, Lennart Johansson. Like Havelange, Johansson made his fortune running a transport business. Unlike the Brazilian, he comes from humble stock, the son of a carpenter and one of six children. He was president of Sweden's AIK Gothenburg before running the national federation and becoming UEFA president. 'I know the smells of the dressing-room,' he says, stressing his grass-roots credentials.

Sweden takes pride in its contribution to world diplomacy and global democracy and Johansson cast himself in this mould. He claimed not to be interested in the power and riches which come with the FIFA presidency. He wanted the job so he could reform FIFA. 'My FIFA would be an international democratic network based on trust, transparency, loyalty and solidarity,' promised Johansson.

Physically, Johansson is a big man, but he lacks the charismatic authority of Havelange. His barrel-chested upper body balances precariously on his spindly legs and, like a bloodhound, his sad face has too much flesh for his skull. When he tells you that he would rather be sitting fishing on a frozen river-bank than running for world football's top job, you believe him. But for the good of the game he stepped into the ring and, like Ali versus Foreman 20 years earlier, the main rounds of this heavyweight contest were fought in Africa.

Oroc Oyo compared this situation to the period leading up to the

1974 elections: 'Africa was now like the bride whose hand everyone is seeking.' The former Nigerian FA chief had been at the 1996 African confederation's congress and had watched Havelange and Johansson at the hustings. 'Each of them at every turn of the road was trying to make his case for the presidency. In every speech I was reading campaign strategies.'

Havelange dropped out of the race before the end of 1996, but before he withdrew his candidature, in a repetition of his 1974 campaign, he tirelessly travelled the continent drumming up support for his re-election. His main strength was that he had delivered on his pre-1974 promises to develop the game in Africa. Under his presidency African representation at the World Cup finals grew from one in 1974 to five in the event in France in 1998. Many African football leaders saw Havelange as a champion of their cause.

Although by 1996 many Africans believed that Havelange had reached an age when he should retire gracefully, had he stood, according to Emanual Maradas, the voice of African football, they might have voted for him out of a sense of duty or 'out of sentimentality – Africans are sentimental people, loyal to those they perceive to have helped them'. Unfortunately, this is a trait that Havelange and many other individuals and groups are only too willing to exploit.

Never a man to leave anything to chance, the Brazilian tried to boost his popularity in the continent by suggesting that an African nation should host the World Cup finals in 2006. Once more he played a South African card, but this was different to the ace he held in 1974. Then his platform had been the continued isolation of that country. Now he was welcoming South Africa back into the football family. 'I have no doubt in my mind,' said Havelange in his speech opening the 1996 African Cup of Nations, 'that with her resources, facilities and expertise, South Africa could stage the 2006 World Cup finals.'

UEFA officials had already declared their intention to support a European bid for the 2006 event. Havelange's intervention on behalf of Africa infuriated them. They viewed his comments in Johannesburg as shameless vote-catching and as part of his attempt to split the growing alliance between UEFA and the Africans.

Havelange's backing for a South African World Cup pleased Nelson Mandela, but the Brazilian's subsequent cosying-up to Nigeria dismayed the South African president and infuriated many others throughout the continent. A love of football is one of the few things which unites Nigerians, and successive governments have shrewdly exploited the people's passion for the game. In 1995 Nigeria had been scheduled to host the Under-20 World Cup finals. This was interpreted as a conciliatory gesture by FIFA to the Africans who were angered by the world body's decision to favour the USA over Morocco as the hosts for the 1994 World Cup finals. It was also planned to ease the re-entry of the Nigerians into world football after the December 1990 ruling which banned them from all competitions for two years after they had been found guilty of fielding over-age players in international youth competitions. To the bewilderment and anger of the Africans, at the eleventh hour FIFA rescinded Nigeria's status as hosts and switched the Under-20 tournament to Qatar. Officials argued that there were too many health risks in this part of West Africa and that the European nations in particular had been unable to obtain health insurance for their travelling teams. Many observers believed that the decision had more to do with world football politics than health. Dr Halim of Sudan called the decision 'one of Havelange's nasty tricks. He had already promised it for Qatar – I don't know why,' hinting that Havelange had done a deal with the oil-rich Arabs at Africa's expense. Whatever the truth of the matter, because publicly the campaign to take the competition away from Nigeria had been led by the Europeans, Havelange saw an opportunity to exploit the situation and improve his standing in Africa at Johansson's expense.

In November 1995 he visited Lagos and met the leader of the military dictatorship, General Abacha, who fêted him like a revered foreign head of state. In return, Havelange apologised for the 1995 withdrawal and pledged to hold the 1997 Under-20s World Cup finals in Nigeria. There were three huge problems associated with this promise. In the first place the 1997 tournament was already scheduled to take place in Malaysia. Havelange's *volte face* infuriated the Malaysians and seriously damaged the ageing president's reputation throughout the Asian confederation. Secondly, decisions of this nature can only be taken by the full executive and Havelange's behaviour was intolerable. It was quickly seen as a potential propaganda coup for Johansson and his supporters, who were already campaigning on the grounds that Havelange was too dictatorial. The affair reached boiling point in Paris on the eve of the 1998 World Cup draw. What should have been a routine debate took on the dimensions of a crisis, as three and a half hours of acrimonious discussion failed to resolve the issue. For the first time Africans and Asians were forced to greet each other coldly. Europe and South America once more found themselves on opposite sides of the table. The vote, when it was eventually taken, was split along straight regional lines: 11 in favour of Malaysia (eight European plus three Asian) against nine in favour of Nigeria (three each from Africa and North/Central and South America). Havelange's *ex-officio* decision was overturned, but most importantly, for the first time he had lost control of his executive. The battle lines were drawn.

The third and biggest problem for Havelange was the appalling timing of his Nigerian visit. Just as he was busy helping to legitimise the corrupt Abacha régime in Lagos, the writer and poet Ken Saro Wiwa and eight other Ogoni dissidents were hanged at the General's behest. Saro Wiwa's crime was to have led a group of activists who were fighting for the rights of the Ogoni people in the face of what was perceived as the exploitation of their traditional tribal territory by Shell Oil. So long as the money poured in, in Abacha's eyes the petroleum company could do what they liked with the Ogoni homeland.

Nelson Mandela led the international outrage at these executions. Until the hangings, the South African president played a major diplomatic role in trying to ease Nigeria back to democracy. Now he made an emphatic call for oil sanctions against Nigeria and urged Shell to suspend its $4 billion liquefied natural gas project in Nigeria as a mark of protest, warning, 'We are going to take action against them in this country because we can't allow people to think in terms of their gains when the very lives of human beings are involved.'

Mandela swiftly persuaded his country's football federation to withdraw Nigeria's invitation to take part in a four-nation tournament due to be held in South Africa in December 1995 as a prelude to the African Cup of Nations. Both the Netherlands and Israel refused to allow the Nigerian team to set up training camps. Only through Havelange threatening to call it off was France persuaded to allow Nigerian representatives to attend the World Cup draw in Paris on 12 December.

Abacha retaliated against Mandela and ordered Nigeria, the 1994 African champions, to withdraw from South Africa's 1996 African Cup of Nations. As a consequence of the champions' withdrawal, the African federation suspended them for the following two African Cup of Nations and fined the federation a paltry £11,000. Unwittingly, by forbidding Nigeria's Super Eagles, the pre-tournament favourites and the team which would go on to become Olympic champions in 1996, to turn up, Abacha had really done Mandela a favour. In Nigeria's absence, with Cameroon in disarray and Ghana not playing to their usual standard in Johannesburg's high altitude, South Africa were able to win the tournament easily. What was made to appear by the international media as Mandela's and the new South Africa's pre-destination, was in fact determined by political forces off the field of play.

Shell Oil was a sponsor of the African Nations Cup. During the final between South Africa and Tunisia, a man in the crowd below the VIP box and Mandela held aloft a placard with a picture of Ken Saro Wiwa on one side and Abacha on the other, under the slogan 'Abacha and Shell go to Hell!'. Meanwhile overhead, and also in full view of Mr Mandela, a light aircraft circled Soccer City in Soweto towing a banner proclaiming, 'Go Well, *Bafana Bafana* [Zulu nickname of the South African team], Go Shell'.

Whatever the impact on Shell Oil of Saro Wiwa's execution, Havelange's proximity to it seriously damaged his kudos throughout Africa. The Nigerian affair was another example of his failing judgement and contributed to his decision the following year not to stand for re-election.

With Havelange reeling, Johansson seemed to have a good chance of winning the African vote. The Swede peddled his 'Visions' pro-posals around the members of the African confederation's executive. Visions suggested reducing the number of confederations from six to four and rotating both the presidency and the World Cup finals around the confederations. Johansson's manifesto stated that he would be happy to see the Africans hosting the World Cup finals in the foreseeable future, with an African at the helm of FIFA.

Johansson made overtures to the president of the African confederation, the Cameroonian Issa Hayatou, a man with a growing reputation as a major player in FIFA politics. If Hayatou were to back the Swede's candidature for 1998 (and so deliver Africa), Johansson would step down in 2002, making way for Hayatou's bid for the presidency.

These initiatives were the subtext to the Meridian Convention, launched in 1994 to foster greater co-operation among footballers and football administrators in Europe and Africa. A treaty was signed in 1997 whereby 'as equal partners UEFA and CAF hereby decide to undertake extensive co-operation in areas of football, based on the principles of friendship and mutual respect, and with the aim of promoting the development of football on both continents'. This meant Africa's best players would continue to play in Europe while millions of the Europeans' Champions' League-generated dollars would flow back to Africa and through to member associations.

A key proposal, which was introduced by Johansson and UEFA, was to give each African team participating in World Cup qualification one million Swiss francs – potentially, a cool 50 million plus. Visions, rotation, restructuring, development were all vague abstractions, but a million in readies is a concept easily understood in Africa. It's also easily misappropriated. As one African soccer expert said, 'Hopefully, the new money for development promised by UEFA will make the national associations stronger and more autonomous, but there is an equal chance that this initiative will only lead to more corruption.'

Critics of both Johansson and Hayatou have argued that the Meridian deal was nothing short of a bribe. But it was nevertheless too transparent and accountable for the money to end up in the pockets of those who would actually vote in the Paris elections. The brown-envelope treatment it was not – which is one reason why it did not work for Johansson.

In return for Visions and the cash, CAF pledged to deliver the block African vote for Europe's man in the 1998 Congress. This was promised by Hayatou at an executive committee meeting in Ouagadougou on 9 February, before the start of the 1998 African Cup of Nations. 'Africa will not present any candidate for the election of the FIFA presidency,' pronounced confederation general secretary, Mustapha Fahmy. 'It is endorsing UEFA's official candidate, its present president, Lennart Johansson. It is an unequivocal position taken after analysing the situation in the government of planet football.'

With Africa's 51 votes in the bag, the FIFA throne was all but Johansson's. But he did not fully appreciate that neither Hayatou nor the members of the African executive could guarantee how the votes would be cast in the secret ballot.

Africa's football politics is not monolithic. In the north, the Arabs hardly see themselves as African at all, following their own agenda and resenting being dictated to by a Cameroonian whom they believe to be over-ambitious. Sub-Saharan Africa is rife with differences and disputes between east, west, central and southern countries, and there is also conflict among the linguistic heirs of different colonial masters. It was always highly unlikely that Hayatou could deliver Johansson's much-sought-after block African vote.

The Swede's camp was working zealously and drafting the election programme. 'The challenges that lie ahead cannot be tackled by one person alone, in his capacity as FIFA president,' stormed Johansson. 'The world football movement is a community. For this reason, FIFA has to further strengthen its democratic governance, as the United Nations of world football.'

Johansson's manifesto made a full-frontal assault on Havelange and his fortress-FIFA legacy. Pleas for democracy, accountability, openness, transparency and trust were all over this document. But some minnows had grown fat on the back of Havleange's FIFA, particularly in Africa. They wanted secrecy not openness, autocracy not democracy, continuity not change. They wanted to keep their five-star lifestyles, and looked for reasons to rebel against the African confederation's directive.

Just then, in November 1996, with his opponent about to throw in the towel, the shadow boxing Johansson knocked himself down in an 'off the record' interview with a Swedish journalist – off the record but the hack happened to tape the interview – reported in the Swedish newspaper, *Aftonbladet*. When asked what sets Africans apart as soccer players, Johansson responded, 'They have rhythm, emotions, dance. They move in that way we don't. I do not know what is built into the black race, but I have noticed that they don't seem to like swimming.' Worse was to come: 'When I got to South Africa the whole room was full of blackies and it's fucking dark when they sit down all together,' chuckled Johansson. 'What's more, it's no fucking fun when they're angry!'

Johansson did not deny these statements. How could he, when they had been caught on tape? He claimed that the problem lay in the translation and that he had not used the term 'blackie' in a racist way. Once his comments hit the African press, Johansson was finished. That the UEFA president had made his racist blunder while in Africa to accept an award from the African confederation for his work on development there made him look foolish. To many Africans Johansson revealed himself as just another white imperious, racist hypocrite.

The damage done by these remarks should not be underestimated. A few weeks later Havelange announced that he would not stand for re-election. Johannson looked like an outright leader, cruising in a one-horse race. But his 'blackies' comments were enough to cause some African associations to switch their allegiance away from him. They gave many others the pretext to break their promises once Blatter and Havelange got to work on them.

Mystery surrounds Havelange's surprise decision. It was a combination of punches rather than a single knock-out blow which took him out of him the fight. The Nigerian affair had him rocking as did the FIFA executive's decision to reject his proposal of Japan as host for the 2002 World Cup. Havelange was in his eighties and the death of FIFA's senior vice-president, his close friend and co-conspirator Guillermo Cañedo, was another setback.

After the publication of his racist comments Johansson struck a melancholy figure on the FIFA circuit. At the Asian Cup in Abu Dhabi in December 1996, he looked uncomfortable in the lobbies of the Sheraton and in the midst of the Arab football schemers who were so smoothly oiling the wheels of the Asian confederation. Little did Johansson know it, but they were also plotting the big Swede's downfall.

For a long time after the 'blackie' affair, Johansson stopped giving private interviews to journalists. We eventually got to talk to him while he was in Cairo for the Under-17s World Championships. The day before we'd had an interview with Havelange. It was more like an audience and we expected something similar with Johansson.

We were wrong. The Swede was staying in a luxurious suite of rooms in the Cairo Marriot, on Gezira island in the middle of the White Nile, a couple of miles away from Havelange's roost in the Sheraton. From Johansson's room on the 15th floor, if he strained his eyes through the polluted haze shrouding Cairo's suburbs, he could just make out the profile of the great pyramids of Giza.

Johansson's faithful retainer, Rudi Rothenbühler, showed us in. The big Swede rose from a long plush settee and greeted us warmly. He was dressed in an open-neck polo shirt and boxer shorts. His broad, care-worn face told how much the challenge for the presidency was hurting him. Johansson confided, in the spacious and lonely opulence of his suite, that he had considered pulling out of the race in the wake of the racist gaffe. He then turned his attention to Havelange, criticising the Big Man not so much for what he had done, but for the manner in which he had done it: 'It's not acceptable that you get a bunch of papers that you are supposed to take a decision on the same morning as you have a meeting.' Johansson also commented on how the general secretary was given so much power by Havelange: 'He is not the "godfather of football". With all respect to Mr Blatter, who does he think he is?'

Johansson was scathing about the way Havelange had used power and patronage to run FIFA like a personal fiefdom. 'Mr Cañedo for sure was in the media business and he was high up in the FIFA hierarchy. He made a certain kind of business through his position. If someone in the future is in that position, it would be most important that he would not be involved in the decision-making process about media contracts. This would not be correct.' Johansson was determined to bring order and transparency to world football and to do this he was determined to rid FIFA of Havelange and his cronies. This, and an obligation to his supporters, is what kept him in the ring.

Half an hour into our interview Johansson sighed, 'Excuse me gentlemen, I have to get ready to attend a function, but please we will continue to talk while I get changed.' The African federation had organised a dinner river cruise along the Nile and Johansson was a guest of honour. So as Johansson walked in and out of his bedroom, first in his underwear, next struggling with the gold cuff-links for his dress shirt, we kept our conversation going.

He looked like a man who would rather be on the terrace back home drinking with his wife and his buddies than cruising up the Nile with football's power-brokers. Former FIFA communications boss Guido Tognoni knows Johansson well. 'He is maybe too honest and too naïve for his job,' says Tognoni. He means this as a compliment. Tognoni knows the Byzantine atmosphere of FIFA. Johansson is too nice to survive there. 'He doesn't want power, he doesn't have any personal ambition. But he is not happy with the style in which FIFA is managed,' continues Tognoni. 'He was convinced by his advisers, by UEFA people and others, that he should challenge the president and take over and change the style.'

Two years before Johansson lost the fight for the presidency, Tognoni gave him little hope. 'He is honest, he is not corrupt,' argued Tognoni, adding that this puts him at a crippling disadvantage. 'He doesn't do it for his personal ambition, not at all. I think he would be more comfortable if somebody would take the weight away.'

But nobody did, and Johansson lifted his big frame out of this trough of doubt and got back on the campaign trail, shaking hands with his comrades from Asia, greeting one and all with the candidate's stage smile. He would not let down those who had put their reformist hopes in him. He might have considered dropping out for a quiet life, but he also recalled his own brand of obdurate toughness: 'Havelange did not realise that the new breed inside FIFA are bright and intelligent people, and they cannot be treated with indifference. He thought he could just sweep the new Swede aside, and after a while he found I was just still there.'

Still there, but slumped in the corner on his stool, gasping for air. Havelange had left the ring, but the canvas would not be empty for long. With much fanfare, Havelange's right-hand man was about to step through the ropes.

9. FROM PROTÉGÉ TO PRESIDENT

When the counting was over for the 1998 presidential election, Sepp Blatter's 111 votes didn't at first seem to register fully on his visibly shaken opponent. Johansson almost deflated, his massive frame drooping with disappointment. He seemed not to see the implications of this first-round rout, and procedures began to be put in place for a second ballot. Technically, with 80 votes, Johansson had prevented Blatter from securing the two-thirds majority necessary for an outright first-round victory, and was entitled to contest a second ballot.

Then it sank in, or it was made clear to him: he would be crucified in a second ballot. Dignified concession was the only option. Havelange, with heavy irony, praised the UEFA president as 'sportsman, gentleman, leader and friend', whose 'qualities and values' would help the football family enter the next century. Rothenberg just stood by and grinned – to him it represented a job well done. Blatter hailed his defeated rival as 'a great personality, fair and realistic' and pledged 'to unite football' and establish 'continuity in the good sense'. 'I am a servant of football,' beamed Blatter. 'I shall play, live and breathe football,' he said. We expected 'and I will drink Coca-Cola' to be his next utterance. Instead, he announced, 'I am deeply, deeply touched, deeply, and offer a message of friendship, openness, understanding, a message of solidarity.' How this phrasing must have weighed on the shattered senses of the Swedish loser.

It is hard to say when the ambitious Blatter began campaigning for FIFA's top job. Perhaps it was as early as the first day he walked into FIFA HQ. One of Johansson's supporters' biggest complaints in the build-up to the 1998 election was that Blatter used his position as general secretary to campaign for the presidency before he finally declared himself a candidate at the eleventh hour. In the years preceding his election, Blatter was always present at world football's most important events. He had access to every kind of insider-information. From the moment in November 1996 that Havelange declared that he would not stand for re-election, Johansson's camp believed that Blatter was secretly campaigning to succeed his old boss.

Blatter had learned well at the feet of the master and he understood football politics in Africa, especially the politics of the belly, whereby there is little or no accountability, and individuals are ruthlessly self-seeking. While Johansson busied himself working on the African hierarchy, Blatter, often accompanied by Havelange, criss-crossed Africa in a private jet provided by a Gulf emir, visiting some of the continent's remotest and poorest countries. From the Cape to Cairo and from Dakar to Mombasa, he made whistle-stop calls on the men in the national associations who would be marking the ballot cards in Paris in June. It was a strategy which had worked for Havelange in 1974 and it was about to work for Blatter in 1998.

As the June 1998 presidential election loomed, Johansson became increasingly edgy. Would his most feared opponent line up against him? If so, when? Would his manifesto for the reform of world football bring the factions of the football family together? Should no one else stand, would a single-slate succession usher in a period of reform, openness and accountability in FIFA?

As the closing date for nominations drew closer, the Johansson camp appeared more and more nervous, with the smart money on a nomination from inside the FIFA camp. Who was there, able to mobilise the global vote, to offer enough incentives to enough national associations, to outflank a Europe–Africa alliance? The football world knew that there was only one answer to this question – FIFA general secretary Joseph Blatter.

Blatter declared his candidature on 30 March, right on the eve of the deadline, Michel Platini, the French football idol of the 1980s and joint chair of the French World Cup organising committee, as his running mate. The place chosen for the announcement of Blatter's candidature was a masterstroke. He had to be away from his own patch, to stand back from his position inside FIFA, to make the public statement that he was not using it as a campaigning base. So the press corps was invited to the Paris headquarters of the French Olympic Committee.

The imposing building juts out defiantly from Avenue Pierre de Coubertin, like an Atlantic liner. In the entrance hall, a bronze statue of Baron de Coubertin greets us. Climbing the marble steps to the communications amphitheatre, taking in the images of a century of sporting achievement, the world's media were left in little doubt as to the seriousness and significance of the Blatter launch. Down below, a champagne reception awaited the hungry hacks after the formal announcement.

Blatter reminded us of his business and administration experience as an organiser of the 1972 and 1976 Olympic Games. He'd headed public relations for a Swiss tourist board in the 1960s, and been general secretary of the Swiss ice-hockey federation. He'd come to Horst Dassler's notice as director of PR at Longines, but his relationship with the German didn't feature in the biographical profile distributed at the launch.

Blatter had a campaign slogan – 'FIFA for all, All for football' – and what he called 'a programme, an ideology, a message'. The main emphasis in the message was upon 'the extended football family comprising the crowds in the stadiums and the multitude of television viewers' making up 'one fifth of our planet's population – in other words, 1,200 million people', including 200 million players, of whom 40 million were claimed to be female.

Blatter – unlike his mentor Havelange, who is stony-faced in even the most thrilling of moments of the greatest football matches – is an *aficionado* of the game. He claimed that football stands for basic education, shapes character and combative spirit and fosters respect and discipline. It can make a valuable contribution to health, he added. And it's theatre, entertainment, art. 'But, first and foremost,' he told his audience, 'it is an endless source of passion and excitement. It stirs the emotions and can move its enthusiasts to tears of joy or frustration like no other game. And it is for everybody.'

Let football keep its human touch, its spirited play and its constant challenge, pleaded Blatter, 'but above all its universality'. The key word here is 'universality', a veiled reference to the European base of Johansson's campaign. Blatter was nominated by several national associations, initially by Jamaica and the USA. Others included countries from the Gulf and South America.

Sitting in the front row in the conference hall of the Olympic headquarters was the big-time fixer, Alan Rothenberg, source of the USA nomination. North American confederation boss Chuck Blazer told us that he thought his compatriot was 'extraordinarily ambitious . . . I guess he likes to find a shorter route, maybe an attorney's route, to get there'.

The head of the French national association was also there, suggesting that the pro-Johansson European alliance was far from intact. And the presence of a man from the Elysée Palace showed that there was a French political bandwagon behind the bid of the FIFA insider. This was the dream ticket: glamorous former player, symbolic boss of France '98, hand in hand with FIFA's top civil servant Blatter. Platini's address was a masterpiece of waffle. He didn't want just to 'stand by and watch', he told us, but rather to help 'this game of ours evolve as it passes safely into the third millennium'. With schoolboy enthusiasm he announced his core ideas, 'the joy of the game and the pleasure of winning'.

He appealed to the principle of widening participation in running the game, for players, coaches and referees. Bring in more great players, Platini said, just as Blatter had done in setting up a FIFA taskforce and drawing in Pelé, Beckenbauer, Cruyff and Weah. 'Give back to footballers what is theirs,' pleaded Platini, in 'those places where there is little or no coaching at all'. And help footballers become 'mature adults', giving them a proper education and maybe a career for when their playing days are over.

Platini adapted Blatter's slogan, hailing 'FIFA for all, all for FIFA' – the second 'FIFA' replacing the 'football' in the campaign slogan. Gaffe or strategy? Handily enough, Blatter's ideas coincided, Platini noted, 'exactly with my own'.

Things were getting tough for Johansson. Blatter would hardly be standing on speculation and he had been travelling the world at confederation congresses and national association meetings for the previous 16 months, ever since Havelange announced that he would not be standing for a seventh term. In these travels he was reminding delegates who was really boss and in the know, and proposing the ideal blend of football development and personal aggrandisement that had always appealed to a certain brand of crafty football administrator.

Disquiet in the Johansson camp was tangible. David Will had much to gain as a front-runner for the European presidency should Johansson become FIFA supremo and relinquish the European position. He also had much to lose should Johansson fail. Will's position began to look less solid within FIFA's own inner circles.

Speaking to us in March 1998 the Scot put a brave face on how the campaign was shaping up. The African confederation had confirmed its support – 'The executive might not carry 100 per cent with it, but they'll carry a big percentage.' The Johansson team was not worried about rumours that the former eastern-bloc nations would desert and was fully confident that almost the whole of Europe would stay solid. Despite hopes in the Johansson camp that the campaign would make some impact in the Americas, Chuck Blazer confirmed in the run-up that his 30-odd votes could be delivered with confidence: 'In the 1996 congress in Zurich, North, South and Central America demonstrated they could vote as a perfect bloc. I believe it possible to do again.'

Asia was unpredictable. Havelange had annoyed some in the Far East over the Nigeria affair and had lost friends through his mishandling of the 2002 bidding process. But the Big Man had been good to the influential oil-rich Gulf and most Arab states would be behind whoever Havelange recommended as his successor.

Johansson had not been idle while Blatter was waiting to make public his last-minute entry. In January he was busy handshaking and hugging the top brass of the South American confederation, in Ascunción, Paraguay, celebrating the inauguration of its new head-quarters building, the New House of South American Football. Here, for five or six days, doyens of the world football élite gathered for what Havelange called 'the best of South America's football meetings in the last 40 years'.

It was a heavyweight line-up for the ribbon-cutting ceremony in front of three thousand guests. Paraguayan president Eng Wasmosy dubbed the occasion 'a milestone in the heart of South America', and preached that 'the passion awakened by football cannot be unheard by governments. That is the reason why we have given our staunch support to this wonderful work.' The president of Argentina, Dr Carlos Menem, announced that 'this splendid building fills us all South Americans with pride'. Havelange was on his right, holding his own bunch of posies.

In this crowded, demanding schedule, Johansson was making his pitch for some or any of the ten available votes on the South American sub-continent. He and confederation president Leoz are pictured – Swedish arm across Paraguayan shoulders – joking together. A gigantic barbecue was laid on at a country estate outside the city. It was fiesta time. A thousand guests attended. The oldest railroad line in South America was fixed to carry guests to the country estate. This was difficult lobbying territory for Johansson. He looked sweatily uncomfortable as he shared a carriage with Leoz and Japanese football boss Ken Naganuma. His inability to speak any language bar his native Swedish or English crippled him at events like this and played into the hands of enemies who saw him as too Eurocentric.

Until he declared himself, wherever Johansson was, FIFA general secretary Blatter could be there too, not an official candidate yet, but always there – shaking hands, suggesting developments, calling for ideas and promising appropriate forms of co-operation and support – in German, French, Spanish, Italian.

In February, the North and Central American confederation held an executive meeting during its Gold Cup tournament. Johansson's pitch, Chuck Blazer told us, did not convince. 'Interviewed by our exco [executive committee] and other members, he did not demonstrate, by his answers, any greater understanding of our issues,' Blazer said. Neither was the rotund American impressed with Johansson's overtures to Africa, saying the UEFA president was 'if not less Eurocentric, then more Euro-African-centric, a political policy which may be coming undone, at least from the African side'.

The Europeans also asked for and got a special session on the programme of Blazer's last confederation congress before the June election, in Antigua. Johansson was wasting his breath. By then Blatter was a confirmed candidate and the Americas had made their choice in his favour.

In Dublin at the end of April, Johansson's team snubbed Blatter, offering the FIFA general secretary no invitation to address the European constituency of the global football family. This looked like sour grapes and, rather than playing up the real strengths of the Johansson candidacy, the Swede's team was being drawn into a slanging match. This had its roots in the concern that Blatter, long before being nominated, was really campaigning behind the scenes. David Will told us, 'It's no secret that he has been widely promoted internationally by the president. The president has openly canvassed for Sepp.'

This enraged the Johansson camp so much that it planned to ask Blatter for clarification of his position at a special meeting called for by a majority of the executive committee – not, as Will was at pains to point out, as any 'attack on Sepp', but rather as a matter of procedure. 'I make no bones about my own personal view,' Will said. 'It would be incompetent for him to remain as general secretary. I cannot think that he can act as the employee of the executive committee, whilst at the same time standing to be the president of the executive committee.'

Not everyone in the FIFA family shared this view. We asked another lawyer, Californian Alan Rothenberg, at the Blatter launch whether the will-he-won't-he saga was a conflict of interests. Rothenberg saw no such problem, but the majority on the FIFA executive committee clearly did. The day before the special meeting of the executive committee, a resolution from this majority went to the FIFA president. The signatories to this were made up of the eight European, four African and one Oceania members of the committee. Dr Chung of South Korea, though widely associated with this grouping, hedged his bets and declined to sign. But this betrayed the divisions within FIFA's central, most powerful committee.

TO THE MEMBERS OF
THE FIFA EXECUTIVE COMMITTEE

Resolution proposed by members of the FIFA Executive Committee

Mr President
Dear Members
Prior to the extraordinary meeting of the Executive Committee of FIFA on Friday, 13 March 1998, members of the Confederation Africaine de Football (CAF), the Oceania Football Confédération (OFC) and the Union des associations européennes de football (UEFA) met for consultations concerning the option that the acting General Secretary of FIFA would present himself as a candidate for the presidency. Based on the statutes of FIFA and considering the political implications which such a candidature would have, the representatives of the respective confederations agreed on the following principles:

1 The duties of the General Secretary of FIFA are strictly non-political.
2 The General Secretary of FIFA is bound to a work contract. One of the most important duties of the General Secretary is to organise the FIFA Congress and the FIFA World Cup. Without permission of the Executive Committee a person employed by FIFA cannot, at the same time, be a candidate for presidency.
3 Three months before the World Cup and the Congress in France it is the most important duty of the General Secretary to ensure, by his function, a smooth

---

running of these events and to safeguard the unity of FIFA in this crucial period of world football.

4 According to Art. 43, paragraph (e) of the FIFA Statutes, the General Secretary is responsible for the relations between the Federation on one hand and the confederations and the national associations on the other hand. It is hence not acceptable that the highest-ranked employee in the FIFA administration would challenge a candidate who has been presented in due form by members of FIFA.

5 Keeping in mind all these observations, it is evident that the duties of the General Secretary are absolutely not compatible with the ambitions to become president of FIFA. The European members of the FIFA Executive Committee recall the fact that, four years ago, UEFA unanimously declined the offer of the General Secretary to stand as a candidate against the actual FIFA president.

6 Finally it must be stated that nobody should be hindered to be elected in a democratic procedure provided that this initiative is not in conflict with the duties as member of the FIFA administration.

Consequently and considering the developments in the recent months, the undersigned members of the Executive Committee as the supervising body of the FIFA administration take the following resolution and ask the other members of the Committee to give it their support for such decision based on Article 62, para 1 of the FIFA Statutes (Matters not provided for):

Answer	Decision
-Mr Blatter is standing as a candidate	-In which case he has to leave his office immediately
-Mr Blatter is not standing as a candidate	-In which case he has to commit himself in writing to fulfil his contractual obligations
-No decision is expressed by Mr Blatter	-In which case his contract will be suspended with immediate effect until the elections are over

- To be informed about the wording of the contractual relationship, the General Secretary is requested to submit to the Executive Committee a copy of the employment contract with FIFA.

Les membres du Comité exécutif de la FIFA:
Dr João HAVELANGE
Julio H. GRONDONA
David H. WILL *(signed)*
Lennart JOHANSSON *(signed)*
Issa HAYATOU *(signed)*
Dr Antonio MATARRESE *(signed)*
Dr Mong-Joon CHUNG
Jack A. WARNER
Viacheslav KOLOSKOV *(signed)*
Abdullah K. AL-DABAL
Slim ALOULOU *(signed)*
Michel D'HOOGHE *(signed)*
Isaac Davi SASSO SASSO
Ram RUHEE *(signed)*
Gerhard MAYER-VORFELDER *(signed)*
Carlos COELLO MARTINEZ
Ricardo Terra TEIXEIRA
Per Ravn OMDAL *(signed)*
Mohamed BIN HAMMAM
Senes ERZIK *(signed)*
Mustapha FAHMY *(signed)*
Charles J. DEMPSEY *(signed)*
Chuck BLAZER
Worawi MAKUDI

Lined up alongside the status quo, and the established FIFA hierarchy of Havelange and Blatter, were the South Americans, the Gulf Arabs, at least one further Asian confederation delegate, and all delegates from the Central and North American confederation.

Within the FIFA executive committee, the anti-Havelange faction looked stronger and more determined. But the executive didn't elect the president, the national associations did. In any wider vote involving all national associations and where more than a simple majority was required – which was the basis in the statutes of the FIFA presidential election – much would depend upon the extent to which confederations could deliver bloc votes.

When it came to it, the resolution was simplified to the basic point that Blatter must stand down from his position within FIFA if he declared himself as a candidate for the presidency. But the committee never even got to vote on the issue.

Chuck Blazer, wielding his thirty-odd votes which could have such an important influence on the outcome (remember, the vote of US Virgin Islands has the same weight as that of Argentina or Germany or England) was scathing about the style and impact of the Euro–African pact. It was widely reported that Havelange simply stormed out of the meeting, so making a vote impossible. Blazer denies this, offering an account which highlights the consummate holding powers of Havelange, as well as the ill-preparedness of the Johansson camp.

Blazer told us that the meeting lasted four and a half hours, and Havelange also read to the committee the legal advice of FIFA's lawyers working within the boundaries of Swiss law. This was a strong point, for Italian delegate Antonio Mattarese admitted that the document had been drafted without legal advice or, in Blazer's words, without any adequate consideration of 'the legal issues in Switzerland'. There was, it seems, under Swiss law, no legal obliga-tion to remove Blatter. All agreed on this. In Blazer's words, the resolution was amended, changing the word 'removal' to 'suspension'. Havelange then asked David Will 'three times, in the capacity of chairman of the legal committee', said Blazer, 'to propose the restrictions he deemed appropriate to have a fair election'.

Will refused on the basis that he was too implicated to make a truly neutral judicial-style ruling due to his being a signatory to the original resolution. If legal momentum had to give way to moral appeal then in Havelange's FIFA the pragmatism of the manipulator was always going to retain the upper hand. Havelange concluded that if no one would take the job on, that was in effect it for the day and he would recall the body – if appropriate – to make a decision on 8 April, the day after the deadline for nominations to the presidency. Then he, along with everyone else, walked out of the meeting.

Blazer portrays Havelange as the voice of reason. 'The president did a good job of trying to gain consensus,' he told us, 'but none are so deaf as those who wouldn't hear. Personally, I believe the president did the right thing and that the Europeans and Africans behaved like asses.' And Blazer is right. By failing to take control of the issue, Johansson and his backers made themselves look weak and handed back the initiative to Havelange and the protégé.

Blatter came out of his first skirmish in the election battle looking a lot more dignified than his accusers and smarter and quicker on his political feet than his opponent Johansson. By the time his formal declaration was scheduled he had disarmed his critics by getting Havelange to announce that he was to stand and that 'the general secretary asked for dispensation from certain duties so as to avoid any possible conflict of interest – a request which complies with a wish expressed by the executive committee.' Problem? What problem?

Until the vote, Blatter chose to conduct all his other duties away from the FIFA offices, which would include continuing to supervise preparations for France '98. Blatter added that this would enable him to comply with the wish of the majority of the executive committee, as expressed at the meeting of 13 March. 'This solution,' he said, 'I'm sure, would also be in the best interests of FIFA and football in this very delicate situation.' The Blatter statement was dated 27 March, as was the Havelange announcement – no danger of getting any wires crossed on this one.

By this one stroke, Havelange and Blatter answered the committee critics. Maybe Havelange would look to move against the committee later. Blazer believed that in the tempestuous meeting of 13 March Havelange wasn't trying 'to break the axis, to split them at all'. But he'd certainly outmanoeuvred his critics again and Blazer recognised that the 'Euro–Africans felt insulted'.

'But they were so into being dogmatic,' scoffed Blazer, 'that they didn't see conciliation when it was in front of them.' The Johansson camp had been chasing both strategic advantage and the moral high ground. Havelange and Blatter ensured that the Europeans crept away with neither.

As the date of FIFA's first contested presidential election for almost a quarter of a century drew closer, the Euro–African alliance was looking increasingly fragile. One of the most experienced FIFA watchers on the European mainland observed that Blatter would never have declared himself if he wasn't sure he could win: 'Johansson is not as sharp as Blatter, not as clever,' the Dutch journalist remarked. 'Blatter is a good administrator. Johansson's campaign is built around anti-corruption. But he's up against too many faceless people who have been implicated in that corruption, that's why he will lose.'

Johansson had even offered to keep Blatter on as general secretary should he win, but Blatter, Johansson reported, turned him down point blank. Here was serious evidence of the Swiss's confidence.

Also, Johansson hadn't managed to prise open the financial issue, to get his hands on FIFA's books. He'd tried at the Cairo executive meeting the previous September. 'He failed and with that went the chance of his presidency,' the Dutchman told us. 'At the bottom of it all are the billion-dollar deals with ISL and [the German company] Kirch. It's like Horst Dassler is still running FIFA.'

The European campaign had looked desperate since an aborted campaign launch in Ghent, in January 1998. This was planned alongside the draw for the forthcoming European nations championship. Some 150 reporters turned up for a non-event at which Johansson's campaign team spent as much time bad-mouthing the FIFA hierarchy as talking up its own case.

Because of family commitments, Blatter was not at the draw. He turned European arguments back on his opponents when executive committee member Antonio Mattarese wrote to him requesting that he openly declare his candidature. 'It is mystifying that an organisation that preaches about democracy, unity and fair play could launch such a personal attack, particularly as I was not present because of a family engagement,' said Blatter.

Experienced FIFA and Olympic observers detected panic in the Europeans. Blatter was the one man other than Havelange himself who frightened the Swede – not because of who he was, but because of what he knew. 'Blatter, the man that knows every bit of wheeling and dealing that's going on, because he's the one that has actually had to deliver,' the Dutch journalist told us. 'Johansson had it all tied up and the fact that Blatter was hinting that he would come forward scared the hell out of him, scared the hell out of the Europeans.'

Another veteran FIFA insider put it this way. 'Havelange and Blatter are chained together,' he said, banging his wrists together. It wasn't so much that Blatter wanted to stand, he told us, 'but that he had to stand'.

Once in the open, Blatter's campaign moved up a gear and he hit his strategic targets in Africa hardest. In May he went to Nairobi, his first trip to East Africa for 20 years, to talk to the Confederation of East and Central African Football Associations. In his 12-hour visit to Kenya he met officials from Djibouti, Eritrea, Ethiopia, Malawi, Rwanda, Somalia, Sudan, Tanzania, Uganda, Zambia, Zanzibar and Zimbabwe, as well as the hosts, Kenya, all keen to listen to his promises. 'After a lengthy meeting with the CECAFA officials, I feel tremendously positive,' said Blatter, splitting the Africa–Europe alliance to bits, warning Johansson that 'no candidate had a right to be imposed on the voters'. He also reiterated his pledge to support South Africa's bid to host the 2006 World Cup, and announced a new financial windfall for all the continent's soccer federations – including annual payouts of $250,000 to associations for improving their facilities, and for technical, administrative and marketing expertise.

The previous month he'd targetted Eastern Europe, visiting Zagreb and exposing the fragility of Johansson's European front. He met the Croatian president, Franjo Tudjman, took in a Zagreb v FC Croatia match, and sat alongside Croatian FA boss Branko Miksa, who said that he was delighted that 'the next FIFA president' had come to the city. At this point a top FIFA insider confided that at least 15 European votes were in the Blatter bag.

Blatter continued to busy himself confidently, liaising with national associations in the two months of open campaigning. In one of his initiatives, dispatched from his independent address down the road from FIFA House, he offered a reminder of his concern for the poorer members of the FIFA family. 'Dear friends,' he began, *how about a hand-out from your million-dollar allocation from World Cup television and marketing rights? If you lack money, and need facilities for administration, this can help you out* – a 'tailor-made solution,' Blatter called it. The letter was dated 22 May, just days before the Paris election. Platini's Paris address was also at the top of the letter, but Blatter was the sole signatory – an indication of the division of labour should the dream duo's campaign succeed.

JSB
for
President

To the national associations of FIFA
To the confederations

JSB – MESSAGE no.3

Tailor-made solutions

Dear President
Dear General Secretary
Dear Friends
This information is principally addressed to those national associations which are
– as is unfortunately far too often the case – less priviledged than others due to
a lack of money and the appropriate technical infrastructure and hence the means
to run their administration efficiently at national level.
The share of the revenue from the television and marketing rights that the
Havelange administration has already apportioned to each national association
(one million dollars each payable in four annual instalments of USD 250,000, of
which USD 50,000 can already be paid out this autumn) is intended to enable
those who need our support to set up a permanent office equipped with
indispensable facilities such as a telephone, fax and computers with E-Mail. After
FIFA technical experts have taken stock of the individual situation for the
national associations on the spot, I want to make sure that these associations
receive tailor-made assistance in establishing their technical, administrative and
marketing programmes. For this purpose, every national association should have
suitable possibilities for training and adequate resources for advancement at their
disposal. This will in the end also be beneficial to football and instrumental in
providing better opportunities.
Thank you for your attention
Yours sincerely

Joseph S. Blatter
Zollikon, May 22, 1998

Le Football pour tous – tous pour le football

There was nothing technically wrong with such an offer. You couldn't call it a bribe. It was 'officially given by FIFA', said David Will the day after the opening match of France '98, but 'nobody knows by whose decision. Nobody knows who took that decision. The finance committee didn't take that decision, the executive, the emergency committee didn't. This $50,000 has been paid out to a number of countries last week by FIFA, officially.' Will paused for breath. Then, choosing his words carefully, he told us, 'Mr Blatter has apparently said that these are poor countries that needed the money in a hurry. It's bound to be queried, somebody will have to ask "On whose authority was this done?".' But in the end, nobody did.

So it wasn't a bribe. But it was at the least an abuse of bureaucratic power. It seems strange that, having relinquished his FIFA role for the duration of his campaign, Blatter could still be so closely involved in decisions and initiatives concerning FIFA finances. Tailor-made indeed, with Blatter and Platini cannily at work gathering up the vote for judgement day on 8 June.

At the World Cup draw in Marseille in December 1997, Havelange had said that his protégé would make an outstanding president. The old partnership played the following fixtures nimbly on a global anti-European card. As early as the beginning of March, a top FIFA insider confirmed, Blatter was assured of at least 15 European votes, not least as 'UEFA doesn't give a shit about world football. UEFA thinks it can go all round the world giving gongs – some Africans will accept anything, any gong – but all they're pouring into Africa is another form of neo-colonialism.'

With Blatter working behind the scenes to fragment the European front and the Johansson energies all but spent in his long-running confrontation with Havelange himself, the scene was now set in the starkest of terms. The elected democrat was up against the hand-picked career administrator – a reformist package or a continuity card?

At the Equinox Conference Centre on 8 June, freelance heavies and government agents patrolled the razor-wired fences. A few hours later the FIFA family anointed Blatter as its new president. With public fanfare, England had jumped ship from Europe at the last minute. Alec McGivan, England's 2006 campaign manager, looked smug. Graham Kelly of the English FA looked as mournful as ever, as if he was yearning for a wet day back at Football League headquarters in Lytham St Annes, when life must have been so much simpler. Maybe he was just uncomfortable in his seat, or perhaps he saw his future.

As a parting gesture, Havelange the magnanimous eased the passage of several nations to full membership status before the vote. Now Eritrea, American Samoa and Palestine each carried as much electoral weight as Germany, Brazil or England. There were three more votes Johansson could kiss goodbye to.

As it turned out, an African haemorrhage ('I doubt Johansson polled more than ten African votes,' Jimmy Boyce of Northern Ireland speculated to us) and many European defections meant that the three new votes made no difference. Blatter won with a landslide majority of 31, taking 111 votes of the 191 associations polled. In his thank-you speech Blatter pledged to unite football. Why it needed uniting now, after years of his own administration, had obviously not occurred to the majority of voters.

In his last presidential address Havelange said that he took his leave with indelible memories of 'Sepp Blatter at my side for 23 years. I leave, with a clear conscience, the governing body of the world's, the planet's, most popular sport.' With his protégé in charge, Havelange would remain close to the action for the foreseeable future.

In the Equinox hall the post-mortem on the result was under way. Questions were swirling. Mihir Bose of the *Daily Telegraph* asked Blatter: 'Was your campaign corrupt? Is FIFA not clean?' Blatter's face tightened, his smile subsided. 'The accounts were cleared in congress,' he snarled, 'no questions were asked then.' Show me my accusers, demanded Blatter. 'It might become uncomfortable for anyone whose name you mention.'

The day after Blatter's victory, Kenya's *Daily Nation* reported how grateful the Kenyan football federation was to Havelange for promising to pay team travel costs to an obscure regional tournament in Rwanda. Chairman of the federation, Peter Kenneth, said in Paris, 'It has been a gruelling battle but in the final analysis we are proud to have been associated with the winning candidate.'

Inside the Paris hotels, as the football started, the FIFA family closed ranks. *Omertà* became once more the order of the day. Copies of documents which we'd been promised disappeared from history, or at least from our grasp. 'It's all gone dead,' conceded one tough veteran at the heart of FIFA's inner circle. 'It's gone absolutely flat.

It wouldn't do them any good to try to open things up.'

Everybody knew the game was lost. 'You've got the FIFA you want, you want this FIFA of corruption, that's what you've got. Get on with it,' said one executive committee member to another. The pompous and acidic response said it all. 'Sure it's all about money. Your side didn't spend enough money.'

So the protégé became the president. Blatter is nimble and cunning, but he lacks the Big Man's gravitas. Nobody stands up in FIFA House when Sepp phones. Havelange filled the public spaces he entered. Subjects sought him out and, when allowed, came cap in hand for an audience. Sepp has to work the floor, but he is good at it. What he lacks in awe-inspiring presence, he makes up for with his quick wits, charm and affability. Asked how the new boy was doing in the first weeks of his presidency, Northern Ireland's Jimmy Boyce told us, 'Sepp's PR skills are excellent. He's good at winning friends and influencing people, he seems determined to get what he wants.' The Irishman said that the majority of the FIFA executive were satisfied with his overall approach. We are not surprised.

Once in power President Blatter moved swiftly to neutralise his enemies. In his first exco meeting he dropped a controversial proposal to create a special bureau – an inner circle empowered to take decisions outside of the executive committee 'to cope with FIFA's increasing volume of work'. Johansson and his supporters would never have stood for this. Cleverly, Blatter withdrew his proposal at the last minute, proposing instead to double the number of full exco meetings. More meetings, more five-star treatment.

In his second meeting he reshuffled the FIFA committees, giving his supporters key positions, but also making sure that potential opponents were kept in the club. David Will was punished for his open commitment to Johansson by being removed from the chairs of the prestigious referees' and legal committees. But he wasn't bounced out of the club altogether. Instead he was handed the grand-sounding but practically irrelevant national associations' committee. Ernie Walker of Scotland wasn't so favoured, and was banished from the FIFA family for not smarming up to Blatter after the Equinox vote, unlike many turncoats from the defeated Johansson camp. 'I wouldn't shake the bastard's hand,' he said bitterly.

The Big Man would have been hard pressed to match his protégé's next stroke. Blatter proposed that for the first time exco members should be paid in addition to already generous expenses. He suggested $50,000 a year. Keep your mouths shut for ten years, boys, and you can bank a cool half-million. Few dissenting voices could be heard when this motion was tabled. No wonder the trail went so cold on the pre-election accusations. We recalled the words of top football marketing man Jürgen Lenz. Speaking of the FIFA club, he said, 'It has become so openly corrupt that they do not know that they are being corrupt.'

After his first year at FIFA's helm, Blatter looked to be secure in his tenure. He got more prestige, status and influence a little over a year on from his election, when the International Olympic Committee elected him as its 104th member, at its 109th meeting in Seoul. FIFA's last two presidents were now the longest-serving and the newest members on the IOC, which had announced to the world that it would be cleaning up its act. And Blatter was keeping up Havelange's style in big deals. In May he'd also been in Seoul, signing up the Hyundai Motor Corporation as the official car for the 2002 World Cup. Hyundai beat off competition from Toyota and Opel, France '98's supplier. The chairman of Hyundai is Chung Mon Koo, brother of Chung Mon Joon, FIFA vice-president and son of Hyundai's founder.

Blatter was slipping smoothly into the presidential style. He'd had some awkward moments. Although he'd got an injunction to stop the publication in Switzerland of British author David Yallop's book covering the election of June '98, a Dutch judge concluded that the story of cash inducements for votes 'was sufficiently concrete that Blatter and the FIFA can defend themselves against it'. FIFA's media machine went into overdrive, saying in April 1999 that 'all the payments were entirely above board and there was no question of such payments being "bribes" relating to Joseph Blatter's election to FIFA'.

But as Ernie Walker reminded us, the world was alerted to the serious scale of corruption at the heart of the Olympic movement by a veteran member of the IOC. 'Too many know too much,' he said, hinting that it was only a matter of time before the truth would out, exposing FIFA's malpractices.

Blatter's honeymoon didn't last long. The simmering dispute between the Asian and the South American confederations over the allocation of places for the 2002 World Cup finals boiled over on the eve of the Women's World Cup in the USA. With Korea's and Japan's co-hosting arrangement guaranteeing each country a berth, the Asians, who had occupied four places in France '98 requested five next time round. Peter Velappan, secretary general of the AFC, said that in January 1999 Blatter was 'sympathetic to our case and assured us of a solution'.

But Blatter dragged his feet, deferring the item at the March 1999 meeting, saying that he would deal with the issue 'personally'. the new president was cornered because he could only give the Asians an extra place at the expense of some other confederation. The Asians targeted South America, saying, 'They have four guaranteed places plus a play-off with the Oceania champion and the possibility of five seats for a confederation of ten members! This is not fair and we cannot accept such a greed.'

Blatter had secured precious votes from Asia and there was a deep sense of betrayal. The seriousness of the Asian concerns was demonstrated when, *en masse*, they walked out of FIFA's Extra-ordinary Congress in Los Angeles in July 1999 and declared that 'Asia is compelled to boycott the World Cup 2002'. Further, they ostracised the South Americans, barring them from attending any of their events, and the Qatari, Mohamad bin Hammam Al-Abdulla, resigned from all FIFA standing committees. The other Asian representatives on FIFA's executive committee threatened to follow suit. Suddenly, the FIFA family looked more disunited than at any time since Sir Stanley Rous's difficult relations with Third World members three decades before.

Blatter was stung by the Asian boycott and his response was far from conciliatory. 'Naturally, I am personally disillusioned by the way the Asian national associations behaved,' he fumed. 'I made a point of stressing the desire to seek an open dialogue . . . Alas, this appeal for common sense fell on deaf ears.' The Asians, he said, 'misused FIFA's most important body . . . an affront against our organisation and an insult to the FIFA member national associations'. With only a thinly veiled reference to the largesse enjoyed by the FIFA family, Blatter went on: 'If one is a guest at a sumptuous banquet, it is certainly not good form to get up and leave before the meal is over.'

Appealing to principles of trust, democracy, universality and, of course, solidarity, Blatter worked overtime to hold his 'vision of the house of football together'. 'A boycott,' he thundered, 'would shake its foundations and cause its ruin.' These words, if uttered by the Big Man, may have brought the Asians into line at once. But the Protégé remained unproven. Unlike Havelange, he had not been able to keep all of his promises and neither did he have his old boss's presidential gravitas. A resolution of sorts was thrashed out between Blatter and the AFC's president HRH Sultan Ahmad Shah of Malaysia in early September 1999. Asia had been offered 'half a slot' for the finals, from the Europeans, the play-off issue to be decided at the end of the year. It remained unclear against whom the play-off would take place – obviously, the Asians would be pushing hard for a deciding game against a country from Oceania, rather than a strong European side. FIFAspeak dominated the reconciled parties, which bore 'no ill-will' and 'underlined their commitment to work together for the good image of FIFA and for the good of the game'. The new FIFA president was not having the easiest of rides. If the Asians had followed through on their threats, under Blatter, FIFA's House of Football could have tumbled like the proverbial house of cards.

10. THE POLITICS OF THE BELLY

Let's suspend disbelief for a few pages and listen to a good story. It is Sunday, 7 July 1998. Tomorrow the elections for the most powerful and important job in world sport will take place. The campaign teams for the two runners, Sepp Blatter and Lennart Johansson, have had an exhausting day, rallying the faithful and making last-minute pleas and promises to voters who may yet be persuaded to mark X for their man.

It is getting close to midnight. Ensconced in separate wings of Paris's luxurious Hotel Le Bristol, the candidates and their close advisors are making their final calculations. Both men know that the result is going to be close, but Johansson, with the African executive's endorsement in his pocket and written assurances of support from the overwhelming majority of European delegates, feels he has the presidency in the bag 'by about ten votes'.

Let's now nip across town a few miles to the huge Hotel Meridien in Montparnasse. This is where most of the members of the national associations are staying. The hotel's extensive lobby and lounge area is packed with the lesser movers and shakers of world football administration. Tomorrow is their big day. Tomorrow they will be king-makers.

Sitting around the lacquered hardwood tables, sipping cocktails and coffee, or submerged in over-stuffed easy-chairs, the hubbub of the king-makers' excited election-eve gossip all but drowns out the melodies from the grand piano. Who is going to win tomorrow? Some say Johansson and others say Blatter, but almost everybody agrees that it is too close to call.

Tomorrow's congress promises to be a marathon and by one in the morning most of the delegates begin drifting off to bed. Similarly, back at Le Bristol, in the lobby, cocktail lounge and inside the exclusive FIFA Club, things are beginning to wind down as FIFA's glitterati make their way upstairs to their ample suites in preparation for the next day's epic.

It is now 2 a.m. and, as he prepares for bed, Issa Hayatou is a worried man. He has much to gain and even more to lose, depending upon the outcome of tomorrow's poll. He has promised to deliver the African vote for the UEFA president, knowing that, if Johansson wins, he himself will be next in line for the throne when the Swede steps down.

His trademark white suit is hanging in the wardrobe and he has changed into a flowing, ice-blue jellaba. His deep-brown eyes, set in a broad, handsome face, stare back at him from the bathroom mirror. In a secret ballot, if the incentives are big enough, he fears that the votes which Johansson is counting on will end up on Blatter's pile.

Hayatou has always known it would be difficult to hold Africa together behind Johansson. The Swede's racist gaffe hasn't helped. Issa had been in Dublin for Johansson's final campaign convention – thinly disguised as the UEFA congress. Hayatou had been introduced as the 'man who will deliver Africa' for Europe. But things are coming apart at the seams.

Issa had bumped into Emanual Maradas, the editor of *African Soccer*, in the gent's toilets at the Dublin congress. It was a strained, chance meeting. Maradas was there to dish out free copies of his magazine to Europe's delegates. His editorial castigated Hayatou and the African executive for backing Johansson. Instead, Africa must vote for Blatter, trumpeted Maradas's piece. Some Johansson supporters believed that Maradas was 'Blatter's agent in Africa'. Was this true? Had Maradas succeeded in splitting the African vote? Hayatou is trying to put such thoughts out of his mind when his phone rings.

Back at the Meridien, an African delegate who will cast the secret vote on behalf of his national association is also preparing for bed when somebody knocks softly on his door. Dressed only in a starched white jellaba, the delegate dries his hands, leaves the bathroom and opens the door. Two men dressed in expensive pale-blue suits stand on the threshold. 'Assalaam alaykom,' says the shorter visitor. 'Alaykom assalaam,' responds the delegate. 'Please, come in.'

The taller man carries two large briefcases, one of which he places on the table. He clicks it open, revealing rows of neat packages of $50 bills. 'We have come from our country,' says the other, in clipped, Middle-East English, 'and we are authorised to offer you, personally,

$50,000 if you pledge your vote for Mr Blatter.' Blatter did not authorise this, but there were powerful forces propelling his run-in.

The delegate stares at the money. In his country, $5 per week is a decent wage and most people don't make that in a month. $50,000 would go a long way. All he has to do is take the duplicate ballot paper marked for Blatter and switch it with the official one marked for Johansson on the way to the ballot box. Who is to know? Besides, England has said that it is switching from Johansson to Blatter, and the Swede did make those racist remarks. Anyway, they are both Europeans, so what is the difference? Hands are shaken, the briefcase is clicked shut and the two Gulf Arabs move on to the next customer. The trouble is, the delegate is a man of principle who is fiercely loyal to Issa Hayatou.

Issa reaches slowly for his phone. He is yet to sleep, but already his worst nightmare has arrived. His loyal supporter tells him the bad news. Hayatou slams down the phone and rushes down the corridor where he finds Johansson sharing a nightcap with his right-hand man, Gerhard Aigner, the general secretary UEFA. Both men are stunned by Issa's report.

Aigner hurriedly gathers a posse of influential Johansson supporters and dashes across town in taxis to try to stop the rot. Upright Norwegian Per Omdal is among them. But it is too late. By the time Aigner reaches the Meridien the Emirs' briefcases are empty. 'Johansson's African vote has haemorrhaged,' is how one delegate put it, 'and Blatter has the election in the bag.'

Fantasy or fact? As yet nobody who knows has broken the silence to confirm the details of this election-eve bribe scandal. But Omdal is adamant that many votes ebbed away from Johansson as a direct result of the Gulf's last-minute intervention. Reading and listening to the carefully chosen words of key insiders leaves us in little doubt that something seriously wrong happened in the Meridien on the night of 7 June.

Johansson was gracious in defeat, but clearly nonplussed by its scale: 'I do not want to appear a bad loser and I congratulate Mr Blatter on his success. But we were very sure of a certain number of votes and maybe something happened to make them change their minds.'

David Will was angrier and slightly more forthcoming when he told us, 'As far as I'm concerned this is just hearsay, but we heard that a Middle East country was actually paying out $50,000 for buying votes. I know this because money was offered to countries who remained true to Issa Hayatou really, and would not take the money. I know that many of the people here [Hotel Le Bristol] who were supporters of Lennart Johansson left very quickly from here to get to the Meridien to try to stop this.'

If anybody knows the truth it should be Hayatou. However, in the wake of the election disaster, he was fighting for his political future and choosing his words carefully. Like Johansson and Will, he too hints at shenanigans at the Meridien: 'We had the majority on the eve of the ballot. It was during the night between 7 to 8 June that things changed. Why? I don't know. There were rumours, but I am in no position to confirm the reason for the reversal of some delegates.' No position to confirm, but in a position to deny, which Hayatou flatly refuses to do. Issa's from Cameroon and he understands how the politics of the belly works in African football.

The Confederation of African Football (CAF) was formed in 1956 by Egypt, Ethiopia, Sudan and South Africa – the only independent nations on the continent at that time. The proposal to form an African confederation met stern resistance from the South Americans who, misreading their own history, viewed the African nations as potential dupes of their former colonial masters. However, with strong support form Sir Stanley Rous and Granatkin of the Soviet Union, CAF was formerly inaugurated at its first constitutional assembly in Khartoum in 1957.

In one of the first attempts to use sport as a political tool in the fight against apartheid, the leaders of the new-born confederation expelled South Africa the following year when it insisted on sending either an all-white or an all-black team to the first African Cup of Nations in Khartoum.

With only three members throughout the following years, CAF was a weak political force. By the early 1960s, however, things changed radically as the European powers shed their colonial authority. Newly independent African nations discovered in football a way to advertise their presence on the world stage.

For the post-colonial Third World, however, affiliation to FIFA and participation in international football represented a tacit acceptance of the deep structure left behind by the colonists. Football was a European game and, while some of the names might have changed, the shape of the new nation states which affiliated to FIFA were the same as those imposed by the old colonial powers a century earlier. By playing international football, Sudan, Nigeria, Sierra Leone and South Africa were confirming a social and political map imposed by the First World.

One of the Africa's oldest colonial legacies – and one which finds its clearest expression today through football – is the division between Arab-Africa and sub-Saharan or black Africa. This expression is rooted in the slave trafficking which took place from the south to the north of Africa many years before the Europeans and Americans turned African slavery into a global industry. The extent of this antipathy was made brutally manifest during the 1986 African Nations Cup finals in Morocco. The semi-finals saw Cameroon line up against the hosts and Nigeria face neighbouring Algeria. These games were very violent and in both cases the black African players were subjected to extreme forms of racial abuse from predominantly Arab crowds. These events led some senior sports writers to question what lay behind the façade of pan-African unity.

A decade later, in Bloemfontein, South Africa, a group of Egyptian officials and supporters, who had just attended their national team's defeat in the quarter-finals by Zambia, were stoned by local black Africans as their coach left the stadium. Later, in the lobby of the hotel where the Egyptian team were staying, it was suggested that FIFA might be considering South Africa as a venue for the 2006 World Cup. A disgruntled Egyptian official gave a sarcastic laugh and said, 'They would never trust niggers with the World Cup!'

As Havelange had discovered and exploited earlier, and as Rous was to learn in 1974, there is no love lost between French-speaking and English-speaking Africa. As the Europeans pulled out of the continent and CAF grew, the balance of power within the African confederation shifted away from the ex-British possessions towards the former French and Belgian colonies. With the Arabs and black Africans at each other's throats, and the Francophone and Anglo-phone Africans on uneasy terms, the prospect of Hayatou delivering an African bloc vote for Johansson in Paris always looked remote.

When football emerged from colonialism as one of the few institutions which captured the imagination of diverse populations, it became the target for political interference and economic exploitation by powerful political élites. Such is the power of the game that, the world over, where the activities of military dictators have stifled open political debate, football has been used to buy time for moribund administrations.

Football administrators are often appointed and fired at the whim of unelected political leaders who want to have control of national teams and get their hands on any money which football generates. 'In 1959 we had a junta government,' recalls Dr Halim of Sudan, one of CAF's founder members. Halim gave up his post as president of the Sudanese FA in protest against outside political meddling. 'They wanted to interfere in the work of the FA. They wanted to select the president and all of the committee members.' His old leathery face cracks a wry smile. 'I would not work in this situation. They put in a Minister for Sport who could have been my son! How could I be told what to do by a soldier?'

African heads of state have taken excessive and often manipulative interest in national football affairs. Nkrumah and Rawlins promoted great teams in Ghana. Babingida and Abacha saw the political potential of the game in Nigeria. Doe in Liberia, Numeri in Sudan and Mubarak in Egypt are others who have used football for political ends. Hayatou's Cameroon has been suspended from international football on at least three occasions by FIFA because of the intrusion of the government into football affairs.

Worse than political interference, extreme poverty is the most serious obstacle to the development of football in Africa. Frequently countries are forced to withdraw from international competitions because national federations can't afford to send their teams abroad. In the qualification series of the 1996 African Cup of Nations, a combination of civil war and lack of funds forced 16 countries out. Mali let it be known that, owing to economic problems, they would not be taking part in the World Cup qualifiers for France 1998. Pleading poverty, Gambia withdrew from the qualification stages of the 2000 African Cup of Nations to be held in Zimbabwe, and the government of neighbouring Tanzania announced that in order to finance the country's participation five dollars a week would be deducted from the wages of each policeman!

'With so much poverty, we simply cannot afford to fund football properly,' said Emanual Maradas over breakfast in his hotel in Johannesburg. 'The situation is made worse through the stance taken by the World Bank, which has very strict criteria for money lending and equally strict monitoring procedures.' The World Bank's loan conditions forbid spending on sport.

The imposed financial misery of African football is accentuated by the corruption which so often goes hand in hand with the administration of football there. Modern Africa is made up of 'artificial states', many of which are ruled by jumped-up and corrupt heirs of the colonialists. These artificial states, over which a succession of dictators have ruled, are so rent by tribal factions and ethnic rivalries that it has been all but impossible to construct meaningful and durable civic democracies. Immature democratic experiments have, more often than not, perished, replaced by a range of authoritarian, military régimes and single-party systems with little or no effective civil opposition. Feudal-like traditions of power, patronage and exploitation operate in settings of bureaucratic breakdown.

Corruption and the abuse of political power have flourished and become institutionalised. Men in key positions – police, customs officials, immigration officers, military personnel, civil servants – are able to prey upon the civilian population, extracting tribute for services which should be rendered free.

In these countries, where a life of poverty and starvation is the lot of the ordinary people, the most powerful, greediest and corrupt men – the men most on the take – become the fattest. They carry their over-indulged stomachs like status symbols. This is the politics of the belly, and it is ruining African football.

Football generates income through grants from sponsorship deals, television contracts, gate receipts and FIFA subsidies. Too often the money which should be spent on football development ends up in the pockets of corrupt administrators and government officials. Maradas refers to this as 'the cancer of African football'. AC Milan's George Weah sees these corrupt officials as the 'main problem' for African football: 'Our officials are too selfish. Everything is money. They use us, the players, to get money, to steal the money.'

Take Zaire. With its mineral deposits it was once one of the most prosperous countries in Africa, but its post-colonial history tells of a progressive decline into despotic exploitation and economic chaos. Under the rule of the dictator Sesi Seko Mobuto Zaire's economy has been ruined. In 1994 inflation was running at 6,000 per cent. For decades, commentators have claimed that Zaire's natural wealth has been creamed off by the Mobutu family and there have been no official denials that the deceased President for Life had a numbered account in Switzerland containing more than $4 billion. When they get paid, Zaire's army of civil servants receive as little as $3 per month. It is hardly surprising that corruption is rife. If possible, things have only got worse since Laurent Kabila seized power in 1997.

During the African Cup of Nations in South Africa the Zaire national team checked into the Holiday Inn hotel in Sandton City. Immediately a rumour spread among the hotel staff that $500,000, which was earmarked for the players' and manager's wages and bonuses, had disappeared *en route* between Kinshasa and Durban. Back in Zaire people whispered that the Minister had recently purchased an expensive holiday home in South Africa, paying for it in cash. The team's Turkish-born coach, Muhamed Ertugal, resigned and several of the players refused to play in the next game unless they were paid up front.

The image is conjured up of a Zaire official slipping away in the dead of the night carrying two battered suitcases full of used dollar bills. This becomes less of a fantasy when it turns out that most transactions in African football are conducted on a cash-only basis. According to Kalusha Bwalya, the captain of the Zambian national team, many players do not have bank accounts. 'In Africa nobody trusts cheques anyway,' he said. 'We expect to be paid in cash.' When teams travel they bring along with them sacks full of money. It is little wonder that, with so much poverty in Africa and so much hard cash lying around in football circles, so much of it goes missing.

Manfred Honer has managed the Nigerian national team and worked in 14 different African countries as a coach and technical adviser. Manfred explained how the rip-off works. 'Someone from the federation or the government minister – sometimes they are one and the same – has all of the money in a safe in this hotel or another hotel and at the end, if everything works quite well, then he is paying some money to the players, but the biggest amount, more than 50 per cent, is staying in his pocket.' He can say that he has paid the team's expenses, even though he's taken the lion's share of the money.

Joseph Antoine Bell was one of Cameroon's goalkeepers in both the 1990 and 1994 World Cup finals. Prior to Italia '90, the squad had gathered at a training camp in the former Yugoslavia. According to Bell, they only had eight battered footballs 'and only one of them was any good'. The team doctor and trainer had no medical gear and the players had to have a collection to buy bandages and other essentials. Yet Bell knew that the federation had already received enough money from FIFA to help the team's preparations. Bell, who in 1990 was a senior professional in France, decided to act to protect the players' interests. He got the team to agree that on the eve of the first game in Italy, the opening match against the host nation, they would refuse to play unless the federation paid them their wages in advance. He was experienced enough to know that if they were not paid in advance, the money would disappear into the pockets of officials and politicians back in Yaoundé, the capital of Cameroon. In the meantime, he persuaded the players to train and prepare like European professionals, instigating a system of fines to ensure that his team-mates turned up on time to practices, meals and team meetings. Bell's strategy worked, at least partially, when at the eleventh hour the federation came up with a proportion of the team's wages.

Player power was not enough to prevent the president of Cameroon imposing his personal friend, Roger Milla, on the squad (perhaps just as well, as he turned out to be the team's most influential player), nor could it spare Bell from being dropped as first-choice keeper because of his shop-steward's role.

Cameroon went on to make Italia '90 a truly memorable competition, beating Italy in the curtain-raiser and almost dumping out England in a thrilling quarter-final. They got far enough in the competition for the players to merit bonuses from FIFA. They never received this money, though, because, after the event, the threat to withdraw their labour became meaningless. Instead, the cash ended up in the pockets of greedy administrators and politicians.

Bell explained that Cameroon's USA '94 campaign was just as chaotic and corrupt. In the build-up to the tournament the papers were full of stories of a repetition of the 1990 stand-off over wages. Once in America itself, the situation deteriorated. 'For two days, Henri Michel, our coach, couldn't sleep because he was constantly taking calls from here in America and from Cameroon,' said Bell. 'It is people trying to interfere, trying to be big men with the team.' Demoralised and in disarray, Cameroon lost their final first-round match of the tournament 6–1 to the Soviet Union – another under-achieving team which likewise was on its way home. After the competition, the bulk of an estimated $4 million which should have accrued to the players and been used for football development in Cameroon disappeared.

The Cameroon government disbanded the federation and imposed a new régime which, according to Bell, was likely to be as corrupt as the out-going body. FIFA's response to this political *coup d'état* was to suspend Cameroon until a democratically elected federation resumed control. It was only through the intervention of

CAF that Cameroon were allowed, under a special dispensation, to participate in the 1996 African Cup of Nations.

For the 1996 African Cup of Nations, the Cameroon team received their tickets to Johannesburg late and lost a night's sleep over a flight delay. They had to play South Africa at altitude in the opening match less than 24 hours after arriving. Not surprisingly, they were hammered 3–0. A further twist to Cameroon's story was added when, much to the dismay of team manager Jules Nyongha, two days after this defeat, the former captain of Brazil, Carlos Alberto Torres, arrived at the team's hotel to be introduced as the new 'technical adviser' to Cameroon. Torres had been flown from Brazil by MBM Multimedia Inc., the company which brokered Nike's $7 million sponsorship of Cameroon football. Torres, who had previously worked as technical advisor for Nigeria for eight months without getting paid, said that this time he wasn't doing anything until he had a big fat contract in his hand.

Nyongha got a stay of execution when his team managed to scrape a 2–1 victory over Egypt, but Yves Yopa, the MBM representative and Torres's chaperon, was confident that after the tournament, Carlos Alberto would be installed as Cameroon's new manager. Nike's directors demanded to see a return on their $7 million investment and believed that a world-respected figure such as the Brazilian would be good both for Cameroon football and for the profile of Nike products in Africa. This could have been the first case of an international team manager openly being appointed by the sponsors. As it turned out, unable to get the contract that he wanted, Carlos Alberto rejected the Nike/Cameroon proposal.

People often view big corporations such as Nike as villains in the political economy of world football. However, Yopa explains that in order to receive instalments of the $7 million sponsorship, the Cameroon Federation must stick to a budget which ensures that most of the money is spent on football and related projects. Where the politics of the belly rules, financial control by the multinationals may be one of the few ways to stabilise African football.

Two years later at France '98, amid more allegations of fixing and corruption, Cameroon performed wretchedly as a team. The president of Camaroon's football federation, Vincent Onana, languished in jail awaiting trial over ticket fraud and, once more, there was evidence of high levels of political interference in the national association. Much to the embarrassment of Issa Hayatou, FIFA suspended Cameroon for the second time in three years.

The politics of the belly could also severely damage South Africa's bid to host the World Cup in 2006. Not long after South Africa's victory in the 1996 African Cup of Nations, scandal was engulfing the black people's game. As African football expert Mark Gleeson put it, 'After just four years back on the world stage, revelations of corruption and farcical on-field incidents have threatened to retard this remarkable progress after almost 30 years of apartheid-enforced isolation.'

At the centre of these scandals was Solomon 'Stix' Morewa, the president of South Africa's FA and the man who, next to Mandela, had bathed most in the afterglow of the national team's 1996 triumph. He certainly gained most financially. After serious allegations of corruption and mismanagement, Sports Minister Steve Tshwete appointed a Supreme Court judge, Benjamin Pickard, to investigate the affairs of the South African FA. Judge Pickard found that Morewa had sold all the marketing and television rights of the South African national team to an Irish-based marketing company called Awesome Sports International. In return for a modest fixed fee, the company made millions of dollars from ticket sales, advertising sponsorships and TV rights. Awesome indeed!

In return for his 'co-operation', Morewa received a $100,000 'loan' from Awesome as well as being given a new Mercedes Benz from a grateful sponsor. Morewa, a trusted member of FIFA's bid inspection team, was found to have paid himself a performance bonus of $10,000. After the African Nations Cup, the SAFA executive voted themselves $3,000 bonuses. However, Morewa's pickings look paltry compared with those of former South African league president, Abdul Bhamjee, who was sent to prison in 1992 for embezzling $1.5 million from South African football.

Ignoring Judge Pickard's warnings about selling out to the multinationals, SAFA has since voted to retain its ties with Awesome. It has also struck a deal with a US-based marketing company to promote South Africa's bid for the 2006 World Cup. Danny Jordaan, who took over from Morewa, pledged to purge South African football of corruption. If the country's World Cup bid succeeds, he may have an even harder job on his hands as the big money pours in and the big bellies rumble.

What marks Africa out is not the fact of corruption but the scale of it. As Bell says, 'In France, you might expect that for every $100 coming into football, $10 might disappear. In Africa, for every $100 coming into football, $90 disappears!' Africa may, from time to time, yield teams of world-beating potential, such as Cameroon in Italia '90 or Nigeria, Olympic champions in 1996. An African country may one day win the World Cup. But, so long as the politics of the belly dominates African football, its tremendous potential will be stunted.

In revelations about the extent of bribery which has accompanied recent attempts to secure the winter and summer Olympic Games, the finger is pointed in the direction of certain African members of the IOC. Marc Holder, a Swiss lawyer and respected member of the IOC, estimates that between 5 and 7 per cent of the committee were open to bribery and that most of these were Africans. Among them was Congolese wheeler-dealer *par excellence*, Jean-Claude Ganga, the man who mustered Africa for Havelange back in 1974. Ganga bestrode the Equinox in 1998 at the Big Man's last congress. He stood up and recalled Havelange's historic 1974 victory: 'There were no booths in Frankfurt, no cubicles. The vote belongs to the association,' insisted Ganga. 'The associations should be allowed to do as they wish in an absolutely free vote, an absolutely transparent ballot.' Then he addressed not so much the congress floor as Havelange himself: 'Mr President, you came through the front door in full glory, and I would like you to leave in the same glory through the front door. The vote must be clean, and may the best man win.'

This is the last thing it would be if Ganga had anything to do with it. Famous for years as a hard man of FIFA and IOC politics, he became infamous within months of France '98 as one of the most extensively and consistently corrupt IOC members in the Olympic movement's shakedown on bribery and corruption related to cities bidding to stage the Games. Ganga was exposed within the IOC for, amongst other things, making £30,000 from a land deal set up by those running Salt Lake City's bid for the winter Olympics. When for the first time in its history, the IOC expelled members, in March 1999, Ganga got just two votes of support out of 90. Maybe the Big Man stayed faithful to his old ally. The corrupt Congolese looked in his element at the Equinox in June 1998, toadying to Havelange and electioneering to the end. That Ganga could prosper for so long at the heart of the Olympics and FIFA is testimony to the hold of the culture of corruption in world sports politics.

11. TOUT HEAVEN

The ferry chugged beneath the gaze of Zinedine Zidane, whose brooding image filled the gable end of a building overlooking the entrance to Marseille harbour. Fat Tommy adjusted his ample frame, making himself as comfortable as he could on one of the hard wooden benches that covered the small vessel's outer deck. The ferry was bound for Archipel du Frioul, a scattering of fortified rocks that once guarded Marseille harbour. For centuries the islands were used to isolate victims of the plagues which had ravaged the city. Today it would play host to another pest: Fat Tommy and his gang of ticket touts were having a day off.

The gang had been working flat out in the build-up to the very popular Argentina *v* Holland quarter-final match which had been settled in Holland's favour the day before. There were now three days to go before the semi-finals. Marseille was to host Brazil *v* Holland. With Brazil's globetrotting yellow-and-blue fans about to arrive in town, and with the ranks of Holland's Orange Army swelling by the hour, a black-market ticket for this game was one of the hottest in the entire tournament. Most of the serious trading would not start to heat up until this evening, so Fat Tommy had decreed that the boys should have a well-earned day at the seaside.

Fat Tommy's broad Manchester accent pierces the chatter and laughter of French day-trippers as he holds court on the tiny ferry's forward deck. He is a big man, but without much sign of muscle. His flabby pink belly sticks out between his T-shirt and the top of his Bermuda shorts. In his plump hands he grasps a can of lager and a mobile phone – symbols of the ticket tout's trade. Rick, his second in command, is almost as flabby as Tommy. Bob, another member of the gang, is a Londoner with sharp blue eyes set in a tanned, unshaven face. In a former life he might have been a pirate. For the time being, in this life, Bob is working with Fat Tommy on a kind of subcontracting arrangement: he uses his contacts and works the streets to get tickets which he sells to Fat Tommy, who in turn sells them on at a higher price to 'clients' from England and elsewhere. For Bob, hustling is a way of life. Even on his day off, with a skinny French girl he picked up in a bar the night before, he can't resist sneaking on to the ferry without paying. Chris, the apprentice, is the youngest member of the gang. He is absent without leave from his job in a Manchester warehouse. His young wife's not sure where he is either. For Chris, the excitement of working with Fat Tommy during France '98 is irresistible. He's slim and quick on his feet. The gang have nicknamed him The Rat because of the stealthy way he works the streets, scavenging for tickets and setting up punters.

Fat Tommy explains that for him and the rest of his gang touting is a logical progression from hooliganism. When he was younger he used to follow Manchester United everywhere and was a key member of their élite hooligan fighting crew. 'But when I got older, had a wife and kids and that, I realised I had to settle down, start making some money. What better than this game?' Fat Tommy and the boys do most of the things they used to do *and* make a living out of it – usually without getting arrested or beaten up.

Fat Tommy's story is interrupted by the chirping of his mobile. His thick Mancunian accent suddenly becomes respectable middle England. 'Hello? Yes. How many? Six category one, Brazil Holland. Right, hang on.' He puts the caller on hold. 'Bob, can you do me six bits, cat one, let's say for . . . carpet chink? Come on, you know you'll get a drink out of that! Yes? Yes. Good!' He goes back to the caller: 'Yes, we can do that, yes . . . four hundred dollars a ticket. Okay, good. Flying in from Amsterdam tomorrow. That's no problem, you've got my number. Right. What? You could take up to 30 more. Okay, I'll see what we can do and get back to you. Bye.' He switches the phone off. 'Here, lads,' the Manchester back in his voice, 'we can get a proper drink out of this if we can pick up 30 bits by tomorrow.'

The touts have their own coded language – toutspeak – through which most of their transactions are conducted. It's a mix of cockney rhyming slang ('cockel', a trimmed-down version of 'cock and hen', is 'ten'), back slang ('ruof' is 'four' backwards and usually means '400') and 'foreign' words picked up on the road and adapted ('chink' means '500', from the Italian *cinque*, a term the touts picked up at Italia '90). A 'carpet' is '300', a 'monkey' is '500' and £25 is a 'pony'.

The more money the touts make, the more they spend on drink. 'Getting a drink' means 'making money'. 'Bits' or 'gear' are tickets. Use toutspeak, and the punter won't understand the deal taking place. Working the streets, Rat finds a punter with tickets to buy or sell and gets on the mobile to Fat Tommy. Rat speaks with the punter in English, but he deals with Fat Tommy in toutspeak to get the buying or selling prices, so the punter has no idea of the touts' profit margins.

Tickets turned out to be one of the 1988 World Cup's biggest stories. From the moment that FIFA announced that France was to be the venue, the touts knew that Christmas was coming early that year. The first ever 32-nation tournament meant the biggest ever black market.

France is surrounded by countries with football's most populous, prosperous and most easily mobile fan bases. Once Germany, Holland, Belgium, Denmark, Sweden, Spain, Italy and, of course, Scotland and England qualified, the touts knew that business would boom. The well-supported giants of South and Central America – Brazil, Argentina and Mexico – were also coming to France. *Nouveau riche* football nations such as Japan, South Korea and the USA, were through. The surprise qualification of Jamaica, with its large European diaspora, added to the clamour for tickets.

France's stadiums were tight. The average capacity of the ten venues was just 46,348. Four grounds held fewer than 40,000 fans. With the exceptions of St-Denis and the Olympic Stadium in Marseille, the French grounds were too small to host a decent English Premiership match never mind a World Cup finals game. Squeezing into the stadiums were press and VIPs and, although the French organisers would not say precisely how many seats were taken out of regular circulation and set aside for special customers, it looked to be as much as 10 per cent per game. Very high, inelastic demand (that is, infinitely gullible fans and relatively small stadiums) meant the touts were laughing.

The French organisers made things worse by rotating national teams around the ten stadiums, ensuring that some of the most high-profile games would be held at the smallest grounds. Two of England's group games, against Romania and Colombia, for example, were played at two of the smallest venues, Toulouse and

Lens, both of which were close enough to England to be easily accessible by planes, trains and automobiles. This led to a massive demand for tickets. Holding England's hugely attractive second-round game with Argentina in St-Etienne's Geoffroy Guichard stadium, capacity 42,000, was akin to squeezing a Rolling Stones rock concert into a basement jazz club.

The real bonus for the touts, however, was the way the French organisers and FIFA distributed the tickets. For the 64 matches in the France '98 programme, a record total of 2,500,000 tickets (an average just short of 40,000 per game) was issued and distributed through a complex formula that was open to abuse. Here are the facts. French residents received 60 per cent or 1,500,000 tickets; FIFA received 20 per cent or 500,000 tickets for distribution around the national associations; sponsors and the grasping 'FIFA family' took a 12 per cent or 300,000 ticket share; and the remaining 8 per cent or 200,000 tickets went to approved tour operators (ATOs) – organisations which came to be known as the licensed touts.

Tickets to French residents went on sale early in 1997, months *before* the draw allocating teams to venues was made. So the vast majority of tickets had been sold before anybody knew who was playing against whom and where. The French organisers justified this by claiming that they needed the cash flow to help them to complete their preparations for the tournament. At first glance, this may look like the French government joshing their citizens into taxing themselves to pay for rebuilding and other public projects associated with the World Cup. The opposite is true – the 60 per cent allocation for French residents turned out to be little short of a tax rebate. Until the national side were on the verge of winning the tournament, the World Cup generated little enthusiasm throughout the country. We watched game after game, in bar after bar with only ourselves and the bartender for company.

There was little or no evidence of the French in Nantes or St-Etienne flocking to see Yugoslavia take on Iran or Spain against Nigeria. But there was plenty of evidence that the vast majority of the French who pre-bought tickets sold them on to touts at a considerable profit. If the composition of the crowds at England's games is anything to go on, the black market must have been enormous. The English FA's allocation hovered around 6 per cent, yet stadiums in Marseille, Lens and St-Etienne were up to two-thirds full with English fans.

Fat Tommy and the boys had been busy in Marseille for England's first game with Tunisia. Trading had been brisk before the riots kicked off. It was standard stuff – gangs of lads spilling into the city, many already half-drunk, swelling the ranks already occupying the bars and cafes around the Old Port harbour and adjacent squares. More ale, then run up the cross of St George and sing for 'Ingerland'.

In the gathering gloom of the evening, gangs of local youths, mostly of North African complexion, massed to taunt the English. It was all premeditated stuff. Once it became dark, some of the locals sped around the area on motorscooters, carrying knapsacks full of empty wine bottles. They slowed down as they passed the English-occupied pavement cafes and hurled bottles grenade-like to shatter in the middle of the drinkers. This was the catalyst, turning a simmering showdown into a full-scale running battle in which some of the drunken English fans were only too pleased to engage. Many others wanted none of it but, hemmed in by the security forces, were too scared to run away down the menacing back streets and alleys of the Old Port.

All this was done under the noses of France's finest – the gendarmerie, the national police, the French navy, the French foreign legion, and, of course, lined up in full battle gear like Roman legionaries, the notorious CRS riot police. The French *résistance* were probably already among the English fans. Softly-softly policing this was not. When the first bottles began to fly, the combined security forces did little or nothing.

Why? Local ticket touts who were working with Fat Tommy explained that this was a deliberate strategy by the police. In the weeks building up to the finals there had been sporadic clashes in the city between the police and groups of North African youths, embittered by high unemployment and their lowly status in French society. When the rioting broke out, the police stood back and let the English and the North Africans battle it out. The police couldn't lose. The English gave the locals a bit of a hiding, something that the police had been wanting to do for weeks. Then, once the locals melted away into the darkness, the security forces moved in and gave the exhausted English a battering. Revenge for Algiers and Agincourt all in one good night's work.

Article 58 under EC law makes it illegal for any member country to operate a trading system which disadvantages national, racial or ethnic groups from other member nations. The ticket distribution system with its overwhelming bias towards the French clearly violated this principle. A group of individual Euro MPs took the matter to the French courts but lost their case on a technicality.

Under pressure from all quarters, the organisers introduced a telephone hotline, ostensibly to give non-French citizens a better chance of getting tickets. However, the French telephone network could not cope with the demand when, on the first day of the new system, an estimated 20 million calls were made and only 15,000 people got through. There was also a separate hotline number for French citizens only, and it is estimated that they were almost ten times more likely to get through and obtain even more tickets. And, if you had a friend working for France Telecom, your chances improved astronomically if you were given the 'secret' number which bypassed the queuing system and gave direct access to the switchboard. A Paris newspaper reported that one caller had been able to buy up to 400 tickets this way.

It is easy to understand why Fat Tommy calls France '98 'tout heaven'. He explained how his gang worked the streets in the days leading up to games, buying as many tickets as they could from the locals and selling them on at huge profits to clients around the world and, closer to kick-off, to the tens of thousands of fans who came to France in the hope of buying a ticket on the street. The sign 'I buy tickets' in several languages accompanied by an English mobile phone number was a common sight in the towns and cities of France during the summer of 1998. Nine times out of ten this was held aloft not by ordinary fans, desperate for a single ticket, but by a tout eager to get hold of as many tickets as possible. Hopeful fans usually arrived in Paris, St-Etienne or Bordeaux only to find that the touts had already bought up all available local tickets. And, the more tickets the touts held, the more they were able to control the market price.

The French organisers claimed that this sort of activity would be impossible because tickets were issued with individual names on them, meaning, theoretically, that black-market tickets would be worthless. Prior to the tournament, television advertising campaigns in France and across Europe bombarded the public with images of disappointed fans being turned away at the stadium gates because their IDs did not match the name on their black-market tickets. In fact little, if any, checking of tickets took place. 'It was ridiculous of the French to think they could check tickets,' said Ernie Walker, a senior UEFA and FIFA official who was in charge of stadium security in Marseille and who is also involved planning Euro 2000 in Holland and Belgium. Any advantages gained in terms of curbing the black market, he claimed, would be far outweighed by the security problems caused by having 'tens of thousands of fans queuing for hours on end as the police tried to check each ticket'.

The names-on-tickets fiasco, according to Fat Tommy, also led to another great scam. A group employed by some of the French staff in their central distribution office in Paris used names taken from the telephone directory and issued thousands of tickets to themselves which they then sold on to the black market.

The enterprising French citizenry and the incompetent and corrupt French organisers were not the only source of tickets for Fat Tommy and his gang. Through its partnership with FIFA, ISL Worldwide acquired 180,000 or 7.2 per cent of the total allocation of tickets, most of which were earmarked for the tournament's 12 top sponsors. The practice of giving large numbers of tickets to sponsors has crept into sport without seriously being questioned. FIFA/ISL try to justify this practice as part of a larger marketing strategy, but how the acquisition of tickets contributes to sponsors' commercial success is unclear. That FIFA/ISL need to keep their big sponsors sweet is less of a puzzle.

Sponsors either used their tickets as perks for senior managers and favoured employees or passed them on to the public as prizes. As the tournament approached, we were inundated with inducements to eat, drink, drive and pay by plastic for long-shot chances of winning coveted tickets for the World Cup. Inevitably some of these tickets ended up on the black market, as did some of the 120,000 tickets for FIFA's designated VIPs. The most outrageous case of this, with potentially disastrous security consequences, happened when VIP tickets for the England v Colombia match in Lens were sold onto the black market. Television cameras scanning the VIP box revealed a group of ordinary fans occupying seats a few rows behind Prince Charles and his sons.

The gangs of professional English touts who were roaming around France faced competition not just from local organised criminals but also from sophisticated teams of North American 'scalpers', many of whom operated from home via the internet. Web pages offering tickets for sale and/or exchange became increasingly common in the build-up to France '98. At the push of a few buttons, corporate executives in Miami or Toronto could offload their complimentary tickets for huge profits.

All of FIFA's 200 or so members were entitled to a share of tickets for France '98. Some, like England, attempted to distribute their relatively paltry allocation as fairly as possibly by operating loyalty-based membership schemes. Unfortunately, membership of the England Supporters Club was ten times greater than FIFA's allocation of tickets to the English FA.

Many other national associations, particularly of smaller countries who hadn't qualified, got rid of their tickets in fairly opaque ways – through a friend of a friend or on-the-nod. Sometimes corrupt officials simply stole tickets and sold them privately.

'They may be in prison, but they are also human beings,' said Pong Moni, the head warden of Yaoundé's Central Prison in Cameroon, announcing in June 1998 that eight television sets were to be made available so that inmates could watch the national side's progress during the World Cup. This was good news for the disgraced head of Cameroon's Football Association, Vincent Onana, detained at Yaoundé's international airport and prevented from travelling to France after a British TV documentary revealed that he had sold 3,000 tickets, the whole of the Cameroon's allocation, on to the black market. Instead of occupying his VIP seat in Toulouse, Onana would watch Cameroon's debut against Austria from his prison cell.

Fat Tommy boasts that he'd made a killing on France '98 even before the opening match. He set up a travel company and advertised packages comprising travel, accommodation and, crucially, tickets. 'The phones never stopped ringing,' he grinned. 'People were lining up to give their money away.' Tommy had no tickets, at least not for the people who had forked out in advance. Two weeks before the tournament kicked off, he declared his company bankrupt and disappeared with the loot.

The way FIFA and the French organisers handled the distribution of tickets made this kind of scam far too easy for Fat Tommy and his friends. Approved tour operators were allocated 200,000 tickets. These were companies which, with the blessing of the organisers, put together exclusive packages which included travel, tickets and, sometimes, accommodation and hospitality. Travel companies were invited to submit tenders for ATO status. Seventeen were successful, including five European firms, three of which were British. Massive profits were assured. The standard package for round-one matches consisted of flights, taxis to and from the stadium and a $50 face-value ticket. The actual cost of such a package was $350, but operators were selling them for more than $1,000. They were nothing short of licensed touts.

Companies attempted to justify this high mark-up by claiming that they had to pay the French organisers more than $500,000 for the privilege of ATO status. The French raked in an additional $12 million from this. Only relatively wealthy people or those ordinary fans who were prepared to go into debt went to the World Cup via FIFA's licensed touts.

If there is anything worse than paying ten times the face value for a ticket, it's paying for a ticket which does not exist. Because ATO status was conferred by the French before they distributed any tickets – before operators or anybody else knew the quantity of tickets that they would get – fans had to buy packages on the promise that tickets would eventually materialise. Many of the 17 operators sub-contracted the sales of their World Cup tickets and packages to other, usually smaller, travel agencies. Fans couldn't tell whether they were dealing with officially sanctioned companies (with FIFA-guaranteed tickets) or with one of a plethora of non-accredited companies, like Fat Tommy's, which sprang up in the months preceding the tournament. Many, if not most, of such companies had no guaranteed access to tickets and yet nobody prevented them from advertising in newspapers and on the internet. Tens of thousands of phantom tickets were bought. Countless fans fell victim to these bogus companies, paying hundreds of pounds, pesetas, dollars and yen upfront, only to discover, often on the day of the match itself, that there were no tickets. When they went to get their money back, they found that many of these travel companies had been liquidated. In the UK alone, at least eight such companies declared themselves bankrupt. There was Great Portland Entertainments, established in 1996 by David Spanton, an undischarged bankrupt with a history of failed ticketing businesses. The Official Receiver estimated that between December 1997 and May 1998 Great Portland 'sold' 40,000 tickets which it did not possess in the first place. After a damning Department of Trade and Industry investigation, the company was wound up with debts of up to £2.5 million, leaving thousands of fans brokenhearted and in debt.

Despite recession at home, the Japanese turned up in France in force – 35,000 made the trip – and many came hoping to buy tickets on the black market. When it comes to bartering, most ordinary fans are no match for an experienced tout, and the Japanese proved to be particularly vulnerable. Bob boasted of how he had cleaned up in Toulouse for the Japan *v* Argentina clash, 'Yeah, the Japs were great, you could charge 'em more or less what you liked and they would pay it.'

Along with the British, Brazilians, Germans and Dutch, the Japanese were amongst the biggest losers in operator-related ticket scandals. For their game with Argentina, nearly 15,000 Japanese fans had reserved package tours only to discover that fewer than 3,000 of these delivered on tickets. Consequently, either individual Japanese fans, or representatives of 'dishonoured' travel companies, wandered round the streets looking for tickets. This played right into the hands of the touts, who had already bought up most of the local supply.

One particularly greedy North American company, Prime Sports International, not satisfied with the obscene profits that it made through the 'legitimate' sale of tickets and related packages, tried to get more of the green stuff through an insurance fraud. The company filed a report of the theft of thousands of tickets and hundreds of thousands of dollars in cash from its Paris office. This was followed by an insurance claim for the value of the tickets and the missing cash. This company, one of the 17 awarded ATO status by FIFA, was already under investigation for not delivering 1,000 tickets which a Madrid travel agency had paid for. French officials and the police became suspicious when they checked the seats corresponding with the missing tickets at the France *v* South Africa match at St-Denis. They discovered them occupied by people who had actually bought their tickets from Prime Sports. When US agents visited the company's Florida headquarters they found the place deserted.

As the World Cup wore on and the ticketing scandals got worse, FIFA officials tried to pass the buck to the French organisers, who in turn claimed the operators were to blame. The aloof, holier-than-thou stances of FIFA and the French organisers became difficult to maintain when the chief executive of ISL France, Marc Loison, and Philippe Magraff, a senior consultant working for the French-based subsidiary of FIFA's main global marketing partner, ISL Worldwide, were charged with fraud in connection with ticket sales. According to Glen Kirton, senior vice-president of the parent company, ISL Worldwide had only a minority, non-executive shareholding in ISL France and, anyway, 'ISL France came nowhere near the sponsors' tickets.' From whom, then, did Loison and Magraff get the 2,000-plus tickets which they were peddling using ISL headed paper? Is it possible that the two men used their positions to steal tickets designated for some of the company's biggest customers? Kirton went on the defensive, saying that ISL France had no ties with FIFA and that ISL Worldwide would 'take whatever necessary legal action to protect its good name'. In the end, ISL Worldwide solved the problem of its delinquent relative by buying a majority, executive shareholding in ISL France.

Fat Tommy's gang are not the only ones working Marseille. On the return trip, as the ferry approached the dock, it sailed under the shadow of the Sofatel, one of the city's grandest and most expensive hotels. Naturally, that's where FIFA's top brass and other VIPs are staying. A gang of touts from London sets up shop right in the middle of the lobby. As they checked in, or sat at their tables in the restaurant, well-heeled guests were approached with offers of tickets – all right under the noses of senior FIFA officials.

When criticised for their mishandling of ticketing, the initial response of both the French organisers and FIFA was to point out that no matter how big the stadiums were, demand was always going to exceed supply. 'The only way to do this is the way it has been done,' said Keith Cooper, FIFA's director of communications.

Fat Tommy believes that FIFA and the French organisers tolerated the touts because they valued the black market as an efficient distribution system, especially at the knock-out stages of the competition. People with money waited at home from match to match, watching the progress of their teams before committing themselves to travelling for, say, quarter- or semi-final matches. 'Only the touts,' claimed Tommy, 'with their extensive networks, could shift the tickets in the time available.'

With FIFA failing to operate a system that was for the good of the game and its supporters, it was only through the intervention of the touts that large quantities of tickets did get into the hands of ordinary fans, albeit at highly inflated prices. Not that the supporters respected the touts for this. On the contrary, the touts were generally despised. 'Treated like scum, worse than drug-dealers,' is how Fat Tommy puts it. Some of them faced physical violence in France. Bob tells of inexperienced touts finding themselves isolated in back streets or alleys, beaten up by angry fans who then stole their tickets. The police tended to ignore the touts working the streets and they took the same attitude when the touts got into trouble.

Most touts are sensible enough not to be caught with large amounts of tickets and cash, and usually losses are small. But it is not always so. Fat Tommy recalls an incident in Paris when an English mob bought a large quantity of tickets from a French team for $12,000. The following day one of the Frenchmen came to the touts' hotel and explained that when he counted the money he had discovered that the English had paid $2,000 more than they should have. He wanted to return it. Scarcely believing their luck, the English accepted the cash. Several days later, the ringleader of the French outfit phoned back, offering a second, considerably larger, consignment of tickets for which he needed $25,000 upfront. Remembering the returned $2,000, the English touts believed that the French gang must be trustworthy and went for the deal. On the day of the transaction one of the French team came to the hotel room and told the English that they must come outside, bringing the money, where another gang member was waiting with the tickets in a parked car. Two of the English touts went down with the cash and jumped in the back seat of the car only to find themselves facing a mean-looking Frenchman brandishing an automatic pistol. He promptly relieved them of their cash, dumped them out of the car and sped off into the Paris traffic.

Getting an extra 30 tickets for tomorrow's big game is a tall order, but Fat Tommy's confident that with Rat on the job, the gang will be able to deliver. After a day's rest and relaxation, the lads are ready for the challenge. 'Let's go to work,' barks Fat Tommy, sending his men scurrying into the thronging warren of streets and squares surrounding the Old Port. He and his gang are a pretty ugly bunch, yet the real villains of this story are the people who created the conditions that were so favourable for the touts' trade: FIFA, ISL and the French organisers – the real spivs of the 1998 World Cup.

12. THE BEST CLUB IN THE WORLD

Perched on the edge of the avenue Montaigne, Paris's prime designer-store highway, the Hotel Plaza Athénée smacks of conspicuous wealth. The mahogany revolving door is embossed with gold panels depicting prancing ladies, while a traditionally glossy oak reception desk stands opposite vast antique mirrors, whose extravagant gilt frames shine against the deep brothel-red of the decor.

In the marble-tiled hallway, a pianist in a tuxedo feeds the *nouveau-riche* clientèle of the bar opposite with clichéd classics. But the Bar Anglais is hardly a bar at all, more a long lounge serving the obligatory Kir Royales at expensive prices. Football folk and their companions are at home here, oblivious to the prices as FIFA handles the tab. The leather armchairs and flamboyant historical portraits are all bathed in a yellowy light that flatters the over-made-up customers.

Here, a few months before France '98 kicked off, top FIFA people arrived for the annual meeting of the International Football Association Board. This is the little group that is in charge of the Laws of the Game. It was set up by the British, and has been going since 1886, long before the formation of FIFA in 1904. The British first let FIFA representatives on to the board in 1913. Now it is an equal partner, with four votes alongside those of the English, Welsh, Scots and Northern Irish. Britain had bankrolled FIFA back in 1947, gifting it the proceeds of the Great Britain *v* Rest of the World game played at Glasgow's Hampden Park. Now FIFA bankrolls the board. It only meets for an hour or two a year. These meetings used to be in Llandudno, Portpatrick or Torquay. Now board members have to pack their bags for Paris, or further afield.

There's not a lot of arduous work to do at these meetings. As one veteran board member put it, it's a 'rubber stamp'. The 1996 meeting was scheduled for Belfast, but at Havelange's whim the venue was changed. He wanted to welcome old colleagues to his home town. The board met in Rio. No one objected, exchanging the frosty climes of Ulster for the beaches of Ipanema – a nice little late-winter break for the Brits and the Zurich-based FIFA members and their entourage.

The board meeting in 1997 was switched back to Belfast and the FIFA family turned up for a long weekend at the Culloden Hotel on the shores of Belfast Lough. Once the Saturday-morning meeting was over and the press conference was out of the way, folk could get down to the normal business – catch up with the global gossip, relax at the banquet, look forward to next year's meeting in Paris. There was a lot of talking to be done. Alhough Scotland had just one member on the board, six members of the Scottish Football Association turned up in Belfast, all accompanied by their wives. The SFA assured us 'that FIFA did not pay the Scottish expenses for the IFAB meeting at the Culloden Hotel in Belfast in 1997'. It can be an expensive business, then, keeping up with the club.

But the Athénée and the fashion houses of the avenue Montaigne wouldn't be the FIFA select's base for the World Cup – Havelange ruled out the Athénée because the lobby isn't big enough. And even the Big Man can't block book the Ritz for six weeks in midsummer. For France '98 the family's inner-circle – the FIFA Executive, their partners and respected family elders – decamped *en masse* to Hotel Le Bristol. That's also in the eighth *arrondissement*, one of Paris's most exclusive neighbourhoods. It's on rue du Faubourg-Saint-Honoré, parallel with the Champs-Elysées. Le Bristol is not quite the French capital's most exclusive hotel, but it's better than the local B&B. Established in 1924, it claims to pride itself on discreet class rather than the swanky luxury of its 'palace hotel' rivals. It strives to recapture an historical, regency-style elegance that, nowadays, is distinctly unfashionable. The good-sized lobby, a wash of cream and gold, is an exercise in quiet, if uninspiring elegance – a theme which continues into the spacious, pillared bar, where piped muzak alternates with the tinkling of a grand piano and where the powerful scent of stylish lilies is unmissable.

The style here is refined mismatch: well-crafted sofas and ruby-red armchairs; Chinese-style lamps sit on spotless glass tables and Persian rugs are decorated with bold but old-fashioned primary-coloured prints. Cream-coloured walls are finished off with delicate mouldings, though everything, given the hotel's proud boasts of its history, is suspiciously, inauthentically glistening. The raised bar is reminiscent of something you would find in a Merchant-Ivory movie; immaculate waiters flit discreetly among the clusters of tables. At the far end of the lounge, broad windows look on to the stunning walled courtyard, where guests – such as Claudia Schiffer, Naomi Campbell and Stephanie Seymour (who held a private party here) – can catch some Parisian sun while keeping out of the way.

This was the heart of the Havelange empire during France '98. Always in a collar and tie, immaculately attired, the Brazilian held court here, shook hands in the lobby, dispensed patronage, usually looked mean and occasionally smiled. He may have been a regular at Le Bristol when he's in Paris, but the hotel management wasn't ecstatic at the prospect of more than a month of footie types hogging its halls. In the end, only 40 rooms were kept for non-FIFA clients. But Havelange had brought in the heavyweights to clinch this. It was rumoured that he'd asked the Minister of Culture to pressurise the management. 'We were like this,' the hotel manager said, locking his arms together to mime a straitjacket. 'It was difficult,' he added, grimacing at the memory of dealing with the Big Man.

Le Bristol is not cheap. A night in the cheapest room costs £250. The presidential suite, occupied by Havelange himself for the duration of the competition, set our weary traveller back £3,500 per night. The remaining suites and apartments range from £760 to £2,800. Typically, the FIFA family took the best rooms. Le Bristol won't reveal exactly how much the Paris sojourn for FIFA's grandees cost, but it's safe to assume that for the same money a mountain of footballs could have been bought, acres of pitches built and thousands of needy children coached and kitted out.

But Le Bristol is Havelange's favourite Paris hotel. The Big Man can be faulted on many things, but an appreciation of style and the finer things in life cannot be included. From the outside, with its beige-marble façade, sparkling picture windows and understated revolving doorway, Le Bristol oozes class. This is the Big Man's Paris bunker and it's all action when he's in town. On the street an opaque, gilded-glass canopy shelters the busy commissioners in their blue-and-gold livery. Armed gendarmes patrolling the nearby pavements watch the prim and sprightly bellboys as they fetch and carry the expensive leather suitcases, gifts and shopping bags of FIFA's glitterati from the fleets of limousines in front of the hotel. Silver and gold chandeliers cast a mellow light throughout the foyer, dancing off gold necklaces, inlaid bracelets, diamond crusted rings from Mauboussin, one of Paris's top jewellers, which are displayed in the lobby in gilt-glass cases – no prices of course.

One wall of the lobby's inner lounge is dominated by a heavy burgundy-and-gold tapestry depicting a rustic sporting event from the nineteenth century. A game of *boules* perhaps, or even an historic evocation of French folk playing football? Wrong. The scene is an early English cricket match, appropriately enough, for the style and atmosphere of Le Bristol is more class-consciously English than classically French – more Pall Mall than Champs-Elysées.

Day and night, FIFA's executive members, its elder statesmen, wannabes and, of course, the wives and courtesans (without which no FIFA event would be complete) deport themselves in the lobby of Le Bristol. Most days the imperious Havelange sweeps through, entourage in tow, pausing here and there to kiss the cheeks of a FIFA relative, friend or sycophant.

The busy Blatter, fresh from his election victory, darts in and out of the revolving doors on his way to or from some urgent strategy meeting or PR appearance. On the evening of his election victory we saw him enter the lobby of Le Bristol as we were on our way across town to the Meridien Montparnasse hotel. We jumped in a taxi and, ten minutes later, marched into the Meridien. There he was, in the centre of the lobby with his daughter, glad-handing more well-wishers. Had we at last found the secret to his ever-present impact on the election trail? Are there two Sepp Blatters?

The Meridien's where a lot of the business is done and the more public receptions are held. Right in the middle of once-bohemian Montparnasse, its pseudo-1920s style is unintentionally kitsch. The hotel's numerous floors and labyrinthine corridors cater for the mass-market, flashy needs of an international (but in no way top-notch) business clientèle.

On entering the vast lobby, everything from the burgundy abstract-print armchairs to the quasi-abstract art on the walls smacks of bulk-purchase excess. It's just the spot for the lesser lights of FIFA and for the congress delegates from the national associations. Some big names gather here, too – George Weah, the saint of Liberian football, was mingling here within hours of Blatter's presidential triumph.

Back at Le Bristol, Americans Rothenberg and Blazer, key players and winners in Blatter's election gamble, are frequently found in the lobby. Rothenberg is often accompanied by his smartly dressed wife. Chuck Blazer – the man who made his first million inventing and marketing the smily face badge – grins as he barrels his way through the foyer, arm in arm with his attractive companion.

The vanquished have to stay in Le Bristol too, and confront their conquerors on a daily basis. A downcast Lennart Johansson is a familiar sight as he lumbers by, going through the motions of his role as chairman of France '98's organising committee. The diminutive Scot, David Will, still a FIFA vice-president but vulnerable and nervous after heavily backing the wrong horse, darts in and out. Head down, pacing the marble floor, a step ahead of his minder, another Johansson backer and now deeply worried man, Mong Joon Chung, of South Korea, slips by.

The president of Oceania passes through the lobby with his spry wife, Annie, and stops for a chat. Charlie Dempsey is in his sixties. He is a short, slight man with a weathered face, wispy white hair and big, horn-rimmed glasses. He too had backed Johansson all the way, but in defeat Charlie remains unbowed. We had interviewed him first in Cairo on the way to our audience with Havelange. Charlie's a no-nonsense expatriate Scot in the sytle of Jock Stein or Bill Shankly. He emigrated to New Zealand when he left the navy shortly after the Second World War. Like many migrant Scots, Charlie took his football everywhere. He played, coached and administered football in New Zealand before climbing the ladder to become confederation president. Oceania is the newest confederation (formed in 1966) and one of the smallest. American Samoa and New Caledonia were granted full membership of FIFA at the 1998 congress, bringing the total membership of Oceania up to 12. As a vice-president who sits on a number of influential FIFA committees Charlie's in the know. He tells us how Blatter's people plotted to get rid of him as president of the confederation.

In what promised to be a tightly fought election, Oceania's 12 votes were highly valued. The problem for Blatter's people was that Charlie was very loyal to Johansson. Dempsey believed that 11 of the 12 football associations were equally faithful to him – they would vote for the Swede if Charlie advised them to do so. Australia, the strongest football power in the region, was the odd one out.

Usually Australia easily dominates FIFA's World Cup qualification tournaments. Because of the small size and relative weakness of the teams in Oceania, there is no automatic qualification place for the finals of the tournament. Instead, the winner of Oceania has to play off, home and away, against the fourth-placed team in either Asia or South America. The Australians are afraid of the banana-skin potential of such a system. Their worst fears were realised in the qualification stages for France '98. After being 2–0 up at home in the final leg of a play-off game with Iran, Terry Venables' Kangaroos conceded two late goals and were eliminated on the away-goals rule.

Believing that his country would stand a better chance of qualifying in a more straightforward league, David Hill, president of the Australian FA, for several years threatened to quit Oceania and join the Asian Confederation. Dempsey, from his Oceania base, led the resistance to Australia's ambitions to play in Asia. Hill wanted to get rid of Dempsey. He mounted a challenge to Charlie's position as president at the 1998 Oceania Congress. Conveniently for Hill, his ambitions coincided with those of Blatter, who wanted Dempsey's authority removed from the region before the elections for the FIFA presidency. According to Dempsey, Hill, backed by FIFA's marketing partner, ISL, flew to the Cook Islands, Fiji and Vanuatu offering officials help if they would back him against Dempsey. None would accept. 'They came to me and explained what had happened and told me that they would vote against Hill,' said Charlie. Staring defeat in the face, Hill withdrew his challenge. Not long after France '98, he resigned his position with the Australian FA to pursue a career in Australian parliamentary politics.

Today we stood with Charlie in the lobby chatting about this evening's match between England and Argentina. We had wanted to see this game live, but St-Etienne's hotels were fully booked. Charlie said he could have gone too, but didn't fancy the long journey or the overnight stay in St-Etienne's FIFA hotel, which wasn't up to his standards. Charlie had been FIFA's rep for all of the games in Lens. Again, he didn't like the FIFA hotel so for the few weeks that he was engaged in Lens he chose to make the four-hour round trip from his base at Le Bristol. Charlie may be one of the good guys, but he still knows how to get the most out of FIFA's five-star, globetrotting lifestyle.

'Would you like to come and watch the game with me in the FIFA Club?' asked Charlie. When they are not in business meetings, VIP seats or on junkets, the grandees take their ease in the FIFA Club. Unlike the lobby, this club is open only to members of the Executive and their special guests. It's the place where the family goes to relax and socialise, away from the prying eyes and ears of journalists and related investigators who dog their every move in more public spaces. It is the last place that we would be welcome, but Charlie insists that we join him.

The FIFA Club is housed in a downstairs wing of Le Bristol. Its French windows open out on to a tranquil garden, set in an elaborate quadrangle rimmed with off-white, mock-Grecian pillars. Neat emerald lawns surround an ornately sculptured fountain. Running water and the tinkling of the fountain's spray blends with the buzz of honey bees as they hover and hop around the garden's fragrant pink and yellow flowers. The drone of the Paris traffic is barely audible. This is a centre of tranquillity in the middle of the storm of France '98. In the cool of the evening the family and their guests gather here. They sit under broad, white canvas parasols, in the comfortable basket-weave garden furniture which adorns the patio, relaxing, smoking, sipping cocktails and gossiping.

The game is scheduled for nine o'clock and we return to meet Charlie in Le Bristol at eight. He is waiting for us in the lobby with a four-pack of bottled Guinness tucked under his arm. Guinness is Charlie's favourite tipple and, even though the FIFA Club has a well-stocked and, of course, free bar, it doesn't serve Guinness. Charlie brought in his own.

The hairs on the back of our necks bristle as we march down the long corridor past the security checkpoint and into the main lounge of the FIFA Club. It is a large room, set as if for a night of cabaret, with a scattering of tables, a piano and a small dance floor. In a side room is the bar. On the club's opening night the weekend before the World Cup, mezzo-soprano Julia Weill warbled a Parisian welcome to the weary members. As a warm-up to the football final iself, you could look forward to Melbra Rai's 'strong, dark, rich tones and her soft appeal which leave the audience overwhelmed'. Peace missionary Melbra was celebrated by her FIFA hosts as a world figure. She'd marched with Dr Martin Luther King, 'and in 1996 met another Nobel Peace Prize winner, Nelson Mandela'.

But tonight's cabaret is to be provided by England and Argentina, televised on the three large-screen TVs spread around the room. We are presented with the FIFA Club's designer cocktail menu, 'Drinks by Ernst Lechthaler'. It's a lush's wish list. Shall we try a special France '98 creation? What about the 'FIFA Cocktail' (cointreau, lemon, blue cherry, Spumante Rotari Metodo Classico Brut) or the

'Fair Play' (orange juice, maracuja juice, Cognac Remy Martin, Jaya Mango Liqueur, Galliano)? How about a couple of magnums of Piper Heidsiek champagne? In a gesture of solidarity with the fans back home, we settle for beer. That it has to be Budweiser or nothing else comes as no surprise. We are the only Northern Europeans in the place, but a cluster of executives from Coca-Cola, Adidas and ISL are hanging out at the bar. Most of them are American. With them is the tall, bespectacled, white-haired boss of ISL, Jean-Marie Weber.

A few feet to our left there is a glass cabinet displaying the World Cup itself, surrounded by sponsors' logos. Nobody else seems to notice it. We are mesmerised, thinking of the passion of millions of people around the world focused on this 18-inch object. In its shadow, the Family dispassionately ponders the choice of free cuisine from the FIFA Club's special menu.

What's on offer tonight? Yummy! The 'hen stock' soup with Royans' raviolis looks good. Then we'd be nicely set for the Italian-style veal scallop 'pané' of herbs, mushrooms, cream and carrots, or codfish garnished with red pepper and zucchini olive oil, followed by bitter- and white-chocolate mousse and the cheese board. We settle for peanuts.

Charlie finds us a table near to one of the screens. As kick-off approaches, the lounge fills up, mainly with Latinos, Arabs and Africans. Just before the game gets under way we are asked by an elderly gentleman to move our position a little so he can get a better view. 'Who's that?' we ask Charlie. 'Ach, him?' replies the Scot. 'That's old Lacoste, the guy who organised the World Cup in Argentina in 1978.'

Argentina had been awarded the 1978 World Cup by FIFA in 1973, the year before Havelange took over. It was, after all, South America's turn. But with a failing economy, political upheaval and rampant terrorism, Argentina was still an unusual choice. Few were surprised in 1976 when for the fourth time in two decades, the military seized power there. Not long after, the 'dirty war' began. Thousands of civilians, particularly students, intellectuals, journalists and any critics of the junta, were picked up by paramilitary gangs before being tortured and killed. To this day, many bodies have never been recovered. This was hardly the right place or right time to stage the World Cup, but when he became president, Havelange insisted that FIFA stand by Argentina as hosts for the 1978 tournament.

The organising committee was run as a sub-committee of the junta, with the army's General Actis in charge and the navy's Vice-Admiral Lacoste as deputy. Within the junta itself, the greatest rivalry was between President Videlo and Admiral Massera, the latter a close friend and supporter of Lacoste. As 1978 drew closer Videlo and Massera struggled for control over the World Cup organising committee. When General Actis was assassinated, despite terrorists being 'officially' blamed, 'Everybody in Argentina, including the generals, knew that he had been killed by the navy,' said Pablo Alabarces, a professor of philosophy at the University of Buenos Aires, 'Lacoste took over the World Cup.'

Like the other members of the military, Lacoste realised that a successful World Cup could boost the junta's popularity. It also meant he could become rich. Against all sound economic advice, he spent hundreds of millions of dollars on new infrastructure – stadiums, international airports, communications complexes, television systems – none of which the country could afford and much of which would be useless once the World Cup was over. In Argentina it's an open secret that as the cash was released to fund his programmes, Lacoste made a personal fortune. After the dictatorship years ended, an investigation was held, but nothing could be proven. Pablo Alabarces speaks for many Argentinians when he says that 'the level of corruption during the preparation for the World Cup in 1978 was the biggest fraud in Argentinian history'.

Argentina had to beat by Peru by at least four clear goals if they, rather than their greatest rivals Brazil, were to progress to the knock-out phase. The Peruvians collapsed to a 6–0 defeat and Argentina went on to win the competition. It was Havelange's first World Cup and he basked in the inglorious victory of the host nation.

In 1986, though, on the day of the Argentina *v* England match that was to become infamous for Maradona's 'Hand of God' goal, the *Sunday Times* ran its lead front-page story on the 1978 match. The Peruvians were reported to have received their bribe in two ways: 35,000 tons of grain shipped to a Peruvian port over the following two months and the unfreezing by the Argentine central bank of a $50 million credit account. Citing two football officials and one senior civil servant who worked for the Argentinian junta, the journalist Maria-Laura Avignolo alleged that the match was fixed through direct negotiations between the two governments.

'An extraordinary game,' recalls Sir Walter Winterbottom, the former England coach. For the first quarter of an hour he remembers that the Peruvian side 'overran the Argentinians. They played marvellously. They wouldn't have done that if there was a fix-up.' But then something happened which changed Sir Walter's view. A Peruvian missed what he called 'the best chance of goal-scoring I had ever seen in my life. The bloke miskicked it and he was only about four yards out and he had an open goal . . . it looked as though it had been specially cooked, this thing, this match.'

An Argentinian journalist, Carlos Ares, expressed his suspicions to Lacoste. He said that the FIFA vice-president 'threatened me. I had to take exile in Spain.'

Of course, the people of Argentina took to the streets after their team's victory. It was the first chance that they had had to gather in large numbers in public since the 1973 military takeover. The glow of winning the World Cup would not last long, though, and the generals knew that even if Argentina went on to retain the trophy in Spain in 1982, the junta, faced with continuing political chaos and economic collapse, was running out of time. If success in football could generate, albeit fleetingly, popular support for the government, they thought, what more could be achieved through fighting a war?

When Argentina surrendered to the British after the Falklands conflict, junta leader General Galtieri resigned in disgrace (he is now a janitor in a Buenos Aires apartment complex), and Lacoste, who had been promoted to admiral, took over as head of the junta for a week while Galtieri's successor was decided. Once democracy returned to Argentina, Lacoste found himself out of a job but, while he undoubtedly had blood on his hands, unlike many of the other military leaders he escaped prison, instead exiling himself across the River Plate in Uruguay. He continues to live there in some luxury and occasionally travels as a privileged emissary of the FIFA Family. Havelange is ruthless with enemies, but he takes care of old friends.

We looked around the room, wondering how many more crooks, torturers and murderers surrounded us. Then the emotional roller-coaster which the game became kicked off. Argentina's early penalty, Owen's wonder goal, Beckham's sending-off, England's heroic ten-man resistance and, ultimately, Batty's dreadful spot-kick miss. We were up and down in our seats as the FIFA Club, for the briefest of moments, became like a real football bar. When it was all over, we accepted Lacoste's condolences. Charlie finished his last Guinness and shuffled off miserably to his room as we made for the bar and FIFA's free beer.

The family saves the best cuts for its own, but other branches of the wider football family are well fed, too – such as the 12,500 accredited journalists who had converged on Paris for the opening stages of the competition before dispersing around the country, following the fortunes of their respective teams and their supporters. Many went home once their national team had been eliminated, but many others stayed on, returning to Paris for the closing stages of the competition. With no matches to cover, this was party time, as most of the sponsors threw celebrations for the media and other VIPs. The press had been pretty kind to France '98. The French organisers repaid the friendly reporting by throwing the biggest party of all for accredited media in the Equinox Centre, the same venue that had staged Blatter's under-reported spurious election to the FIFA presidency. It was some bash, held in three linked halls, each the size of an aircraft hangar. It started at eight and finished at six the following morning. Everything was free, with endless supplies of every drink imaginable, including hundreds of gallons of Bolly to wash down a dazzling array of food. All night long, in one hall, a succession of live entertainers kept the dance floor heaving with sweaty bodies. Top of the bill were France's equivalent of the Spice Girls and a leggy Brazilian Tropicana dance troupe. Another hall had been turned into a casino. Journalists and photographers crowded the tables, playing blackjack, poker and roulette with free chips. In the third hall a booming disco attracted most of the younger crowd.

Status meant little here as the press-agency men, the paparazzi, writers for the heavies and the glamour boys and girls from television and radio let their hair down and partied till dawn. It must have cost the French organisers a fortune, but for them and FIFA, if it kept the media happy, it was money well spent.

There are some journalists and lazy academics who toady to organisations like FIFA and the International Olympic Committee because they get too fond of the junketing good life which so often accompanies the administration of international sport. 'We may be mere nibblers at the droppings of the cornucopia,' concedes veteran sports writer Peter Corrigan, 'but largesse does come our way.' He claims that the 'media, however, are not very sophisticated in their anticipation and are so overcome by gifts, little pens, T-shirts, baseball hats and the like, that we would have sold Manhattan for even fewer beads than did the Red Indians'.

It was easy to see what he meant when you saw the thousands of journalists marching around France with their World Cup blue rucksacks, stuffed with gifts that would thrill the kids back home and provide fond reminders of the big event. The England 2006 bidding team understood the message, too, issuing invitations to the party on the British Embassy lawns and coming up with a few spare tickets for the Three Tenors concert for chaps from the international news agency, Reuters.

Some become part of the organisations which they started out by reporting on. Some even collaborate in producing edifying 'official' histories and heroic hagiographies of past and present leaders – all done, of course, on five-star expenses.

During the World Cup, what Ronaldo ate for breakfast was more important to most Brazilian journalists than discovering the connections between Havelange and Nike – just as finding out Glenn Hoddle's team selection was given a higher priority by the English media than the shadowy tactics of England's 2006 campaign. This, of course, is what the public wants. It fuels the gossip of the fans. But maybe fans want more than just the ebb and flow of World Cup trivia which is carefully controlled by FIFA in its press conferences and releases.

The FIFA Club has both a real and a metaphorical existence. We'd been inside the real one, but were more familiar with the other one – the one that includes the media, the sponsors, the secretariat, the retired officials and the rest of those keeping their noses in FIFA's trough. The FIFA family is not cheap to run. It has almost charity status in Switzerland, so doesn't make profits. It spends all its money on football and itself. For the period between 1998 and 2001 the FIFA accounts project income of a little over 691 million Swiss francs, around £288 million. Virtually all of this gets spent, or redistributed, with total expenditure pitched at around 658 million Swiss francs. A lot goes back – unmonitored – to member associations. But plenty is kept in hand to get on with the business.

Expenses for 'presidential activities/executive committee' were budgeted at a cool 20 million or so Swiss francs, including the executive committee's expenses of £1.25 million per year. From 1998 'presidential offices' got by on around £638,000 per year. 'International relations/presents' weren't forgotten, claiming about

£19,000 for 1999. But the real gift was membership. And FIFA accountants know how to keep members comfortable.

Outside of the FIFA Club and the close family, ordinary fans are kept in the cold with their noses pressed up against the windows, watching the feasting while Fat Tommy and the boys pick their pockets.

'This [FIFA] is the best club in the world' is how one truly canny veteran UK survivor of global football politics described it. 'Come on, lads, do you know a better one? World travel, cars at the airport, five-star hotels, lavish lunches and a daily allowance to boot?' He couldn't give it up. Could we? Could you?

There is a price, though, said the same insider. 'They give you this and they give you that and then they come back and call in your debt. You, over there, go and kill.' Family rivals were united on this front at least. Democracy and transparency in the FIFA accounts wasn't worth dying for. What price opacity if it meant losing your membership card to the best club in the world?

13. LANCASTER GATE

'We will provide full backing to the bid to host the 2006 football World Cup in England,' proclaimed the Labour Party's manifesto of 1997, on the eve of its historic landslide victory. A few months later cameras flashed as Prime Minister Tony Blair clasped hands on the doorstep of 10 Downing Street with Dr João Havelange, president of world football's governing body, FIFA. Alongside the prime minister and the president were members of the FA top brass, Keith Wiseman and Graham Kelly.

Kelly started in football politics as a pen pusher in the salty breezes of the old Football League's headquarters up on England's Irish Sea coast, at Lytham St Annes. He moved to the FA's headquarters at Lancaster Gate as secretary. When football became sexy in the 1990s, Kelly's fly-away hair, crumpled suits and face to match hardly fitted the game's slick media image. Off-the-peg trousers were replaced with designer Italian suits. Out went the barber's shop and in came the hair salon. With a new diet and regular exercise, Kelly shed a few pounds and the chief executive's new look was complete.

The FIFA president emerged from a half-hour meeting with Blair fluent in the rhetoric of the English bid – you are the cradle of the game; you have a great pedigree, hosting (and winning) the 1966 World Cup and staging an exemplary Euro '96; and, by 2006, you will have the ultimate stage for the game, a rebuilt Wembley Stadium. 'It's the personal wish of President Havelange,' FIFA's interpreter, communications boss Keith Cooper, recited, 'that the FIFA executive committee will decide, in two years' time, that the World Cup of 2006 will indeed take place here.'

For Havelange, the handshakes at Downing Street offered a chance to show that, despite his imminent retirement from the job that he'd monopolised for the last quarter of the twentieth century, he was still the Big Man. He may have been stepping down, but he still had an agenda – not the least of which was to secure the presidency of FIFA for Sepp Blatter. England still had some influence in the world. If by dangling the prospect of hosting the World Cup Havelange could persuade the English to ditch Johansson and declare instead for Blatter, it would be a good day's business.

For Blair, it was an opportunity show off his French. What a change for Havelange to deal with an English official who actually spoke more than one language! A few months earlier, the sports minister, Tony Banks, had spoken in favour of South Africa's bid for the 2006 World Cup. Alluding to the sports minister's lack of foreign-language skills, Graham Kelly joked that Havelange's visit was the first occasion he'd known Banks to be lost for words.

Maybe Havelange had been persuaded by Banks's earlier arguments. Four months before his visit to Blair, at the draw for the France '98 World Cup in December 1997 in Marseille, Havelange had also backed the South African bid. Earlier still, back in 1993, a German delegation visiting FIFA House in Zurich had received the Big Man's endorsement for *their* campaign. Talk up all the bids and rule out nobody – until the votes were counted at the Paris Congress.

Havelange's encouragement was enough for Blair. Together, the National Lottery, the FA and the Premier League had assembled a bid development fund of £9 million, and the Prime Minister reiterated his wholehearted support for a process which involved showering information and favours on FIFA's executive committee at the tax-payers' expense. At one time the race to host the World Cup was settled by voting in the FIFA congress, but in the Havelange era the decision came to rest with the executive committee. Nobble them and you got the big prize. In May 1999 football's 24 most pampered men and their womenfolk were to be flown to and from London and put up in the best hotels for their hectic, publicly funded holiday. Shopping at Harrods, circle seats at *Phantom of the Opera*, and a royal party with Prince Charles at Highgrove. For dessert there would be VIP tickets at the FA Cup final.

When England hosted and won the World Cup in 1966, things were different. The world came to England then. Sir Stanley Rous was the key figure. He was FA secretary when the 1966 tournament was awarded to England, and FIFA president soon thereafter. African nations withdrew from the qualifying rounds and England played all of their games at home, at the national stadium. It was a cosy, domestic scene when Sir Stanley handed the World Cup trophy to compatriot Bobby Moore in London.

Even Jacques Chirac, on France's World Cup victory in July 1998, could not claim this degree of stitch-up. As Sir Walter Winterbottom, the England team manager from the post-war period until the early 1960s, told us, 'Stanley could use his influence. Personality goes a long way.'

Huddersfield Town fan Sir Harold Wilson, the Prime Minister of the time, milked the glory of the summer of '66 for all it was worth, squeezing into the post-victory photos with Moore, Stiles and the Charlton brothers. Rous, ever the defender of the boundary between sport and politics, sardonically commented that it was the players, not the Prime Minister, who had won the trophy.

A few months after Havelange's visit, Alec McGivan, leader of the England 2006 bid, sat nervously among the media players and interested parties at the back of FIFA's congress hall as the vote for FIFA's new president took place. The solemn-faced Graham Kelly was there, and did not seem happy in the exalted company in the Paris Equinox Centre. Glum at the most relaxed of times, he looked fidgety, shunned by European colleagues who were offended by the bellicose arrogance of the England 2006 bid and the clumsy attempts of England to gatecrash the corridors of European football power.

The stakes were indeed high. Kelly's man, FA chairman Keith Wiseman, had polled a measly 12 votes out of 51, trying to get on to the European federation's executive in Dublin back in April. Since Bert Millichip had retired from the FA, England did not have a single representative in any of the big committees of UEFA or FIFA. Wiseman had hoped to use UEFA as a springboard to FIFA where he could push the 2006 issue. Without a presence in the corridors of power, England's 2006 bid looked lost. Kelly was only too aware of this: 'We're seeking to strengthen our international position,' he told us. 'We see ourselves as one of the major nations and not to have a seat on the UEFA executive committee is unfortunate to say the least, but we are doing everything possible to rectify that. We are hoping to secure representation in the near future.' Speaking to us before the UEFA vote, he boasted, 'We have a very broad strategy to get people out and about, within UEFA and FIFA.'

Jürgen Lenz of TEAM told us that the aggressive England 2006 campaign had 'alienated England and was the cause of such a low vote for Wiseman at the UEFA Dublin congress'. Jimmy Boyce, the ebullient, curly-haired president of Northern Ireland's FA agrees: 'Let me tell you,' he said, 'I think that in terms of grounds and facilities England are the ideal hosts. Personally I want them to get it, but I don't think they will.' The clumsy and arrogant way England handled its 2006 bid ensured that few voted for Wiseman, explained Boyce. He raised his voice, 'The trouble with the English is they think they are superior to everyone – and they are not!'

According to Boyce, there are three reasons why England will not win enough support for their 2006 bid. First, there is the FA's betrayal of Bert Millichip's unwritten agreement with the Germans. When we caught up with him in his Birmingham law offices, the former FA chairman said he had made no formal deal, but he did hint that some kind of accommodation had been made. Millichip was close friends with German and French colleagues. In the late 1980s, when hooligans had English football's reputation in tatters, Millichip had managed to persuade them to back England's unfashionable bid for Euro '96. Without that support, Sir Bert told us that England would never have landed the tournament. He didn't bid for the 1998 World Cup because he knew that France had the edge. At that time, 'Germany said that it would like to announce its interest to run at 2006,' he told us. 'All I have to say is that I may well have indicated we will support you, at that time, but there was no agreement.' No agreement, no contract, but maybe a promise and a handshake.

The leadership of the European federation supported the German bid for 2006. It claims 'to have taken a decision in favour of Germany' in 1993, though there was no formal record or communication of the decision. When the UEFA secretary faxed the English FA, confirming support for a German bid, David Davies of the FA reported he had Blair's full support for England's counter bid.

The Conservative government's sports minister, Ian Sproat, said that the 'undemocratic hole-in-the-corner way UEFA has acted' had caused him extreme concern. Tony Blair called it 'a cosy stitch-up', and Davies claimed that the politicians and the sports administrators were 'deeply shocked by actions which run counter to all democratic instincts that we believe world football should stand for. Informal, unannounced pacts behind closed doors are no substitute for democracy and fairness.'

How inconvenient for Blair and his chums that somebody had stayed awake at a meeting of the FA's International Committee in August 1991. It was minuted that : 'It had been decided, further to a conversation between Sir Bert Millichip and Lennart Johansson, and discussion with the French Football Association, to withdraw the English application to stage the World Cup. In return, the French had agreed to support the English application to stage the European Championship in 1996.' This may explain why no English bid for 2006 surfaced until after Millichip's retirement as FA chairman and the euphoria of Euro '96.

Within mainland Europe it was widely understood that the 1991 agreement carried through after Euro '96. 'Kaiser' Franz Becken-bauer, figurehead of Germany's 2006 bid, says England would never have been given the chance to host Euro '96 without German backing. 'But Germany supported England and, in return for that, Millichip assured Egidius Braun [president of the German federation] that England would back Germany's bid for the World Cup.' The FA's denials rankle with Beckenbauer: 'We were very disappointed by the behaviour of the English FA. We still are.'

Lennart Johansson was equally adamant on this issue. 'We had a gentleman's agreement,' he told us. 'All the big nations were present and they know we said "Let's go to England for Euro '96 and to Germany for World Cup 2006".' The honourable Swede felt that he had no choice but to back the German bid, a stance which would cost him votes in Paris.

It was obvious to the FA's men that the England bid wouldn't stand any realistic chance if Lennart Johansson became FIFA president. Twenty-four hours before the presidential election, Kelly and Wiseman pledged the English FA's vote to Blatter. This, according to Boyce, was their second big mistake. The English FA had already joined with more than 40 other European national associations and signed a letter promising that they would vote for Johansson. When, at the last minute, they switched to Blatter's side, they earned the enduring contempt of most of Europe's biggest football nations, many of which were represented on the FIFA executive and would still be there when the 2006 decision was made.

The third and most damning error of judgement by Wiseman and Kelly was their bungled attempt to get rid of David Will as the four UK associations' representative on the FIFA executive. Thwarted at Dublin's UEFA Congress, Kelly and Wiseman thought they could muscle their way into the FIFA Club by ousting the Scot and replacing him with Wiseman. To do this they would have to gain the support of at least one, and probably two, other home associations.

It was unlikely that the Scots would turn against their own man, so Kelly and Wiseman shifted their attention to the Welsh and the Irish. Kelly claims that turning on Will was suggested by Havelange and Blatter in March 1998; and also advised by 'our own government'.

When we met up with Jimmy Boyce at Paris's festival of football in the Place de la Concorde on the eve of Brazil's opening game with Scotland, he was furious with the treachery of the English FA. 'It happened just a few days after the Dublin Congress,' he told us. 'I was walking around the boundary at Clontarf cricket ground, watching Glamorgan play Northern Ireland, when I got a call on my mobile.' Boyce raised his hand to his ear mimicking the call. It was the secretary of the Welsh FA. 'Hello, this is David, David Collins,' said Jimmy, rehearsing the other end of the line. 'Has Keith [Wiseman] or Graham [Kelly] called you yet?' Boyce told Collins they had not. 'Listen, they will. They want to get Will out of the FIFA exec. They need our support and are offering big development money to persuade us. I think, if the money's big enough, my board will vote for it.'

For a moment Boyce, who was due to succeed Will when the Scot's tenure was up in two years' time, thought the English were trying to bounce him back in the queue. 'No,' Collins told him, 'they want rid of Will now, and for Wiseman to take over immediately. All we have to do is sign a letter telling FIFA that we no longer support Will as our rep.'

Boyce told Collins that he thought Will was doing 'a superb job', and that he would see him removed 'over my dead body' and hung up.

Not long afterwards, Kelly contacted Boyce and invited him and the secretary of the Irish Football Association, David Bowen, to London for the FA Cup final. The night before the game the two Irishmen were wined and dined by Kelly and Wiseman at the Royal Garden Hotel. After the meal Boyce and Bowen listened to the proposition. An unspecified amount of money, at least as much as had been promised to the Welsh FA, would be granted to Northern Ireland for football development. For a small and relatively poor football country, the offer must have been tempting. Kelly claims that Boyce 'promised to think about our request'. To their credit, though, Boyce and Bowen stayed loyal to Will and rejected the English offer totally. Back at Lancaster Gate, Alec McGiven complained to his staff that 'we can't budge the Irish'.

The Welsh FA weren't so high-minded and soon £3.2 million was on its way from Lancaster Gate to Cardiff at a rate of £400,000 a year over the next eight years. Not long after, Michel Zen-Ruffinen, then the acting general secretary of FIFA, received a letter from the English and Welsh FAs suggesting that because David Will no longer had majority support from the UK associations he should be removed from the FIFA executive. Right on the eve of the World Cup, Graham Kelly was still trying to oust Will. He pledged the English vote to Blatter, and immediately spoke with the Swiss, asking him to 'remind Havelange to speak to Jim Boyce about the FIFA British vice-presidency'.

But no FA committee had been consulted on the deal with the Welsh. Millichip and the old guard had bided their time, watching as the men in suits, led by Kelly and Wiseman, turned their beloved FA into a laughing stock. They saw their chance and struck, accusing the two men of operating independently of the FA's constitution. With realism and dignity, Kelly resigned on the spot, 'because at the end of a lot of discussions we were unable to convince the executive committee of the appropriateness of what we did'. Principles at last, but too little and too late to save Kelly or his former chairman who, with less pride, was forced to resign a few weeks later.

So in the political context of the world game, the England bid for the 2006 World Cup looked cocky and the FA leadership appeared sadly out of its depth as it dived into the murky waters of European and FIFA politics. Graham Kelly's efforts 'to strengthen our international position', as he put it, by 'being on the inside track, knowing what's going on', will look like one of the most embarrassing own-goals in the history of football politics.

England's bungled coup achieved the opposite of what its protagonists had hoped for. Long before the story broke, David Will knew of the FA's underhand attempts to unseat him. In the early days of France '98 he told us that FA vice-chairman Geoff Thompson was opposed to a strategy that had not been placed before the FA's own committee. Will told us that the plotters 'have not thought the consequences through, they've isolated themselves in Europe'.

When the story came out it looked like the English would be reprimanded. But in true FIFA style – no agenda, no paperwork – Blatter called the English in to a meeting at Zurich in early 1999. By now the English FA had publicly backed David Will as FIFA executive member through his full tenure, way beyond decision time for 2006.

The old guard at Lancaster Gate had gone. All could be swept under the thick carpets in the meeting rooms and halls of FIFA House. FIFA never mounted any serious investigation into the affair. Boyce confirms this: 'No, nothing. Not even a phone call. I was really surprised when Northern Ireland wasn't contacted. Of course they [FIFA] were up to their necks in it anyway. Once it came out and England went cap in hand, they could hardly discipline them. FIFA wanted David Will out. I don't think they knew the details of the deal with the Welsh, but I don't think they cared so long as they got rid of Will.'

Boyce agrees that the incident damaged the case for the UK association's special vice-presidential position in FIFA. Some committee members – Chuck Blazer and Jack Warner of the North and Central American confederation prominent among them – went on to oppose the position, but in Los Angeles at FIFA's 1999 Congress the decision over the position was taken away from the executive committee. 'David is a popular guy,' sighed Boyce, 'but England's actions have severely weakened our position.'

The FA could now wash its hands in public. Geoff Thompson announced that the FA had 'had a lot of problems to deal with', and now it must get the 'ship back on the proper path, bring integrity back to the FA, build bridges with the UK associations, and FIFA and UEFA'.

As the bid was self-destructing at home, the 2006 team made their presence known abroad. Sir Bobby Charlton found himself on the manicured lawns of the British Embassy in Paris a couple of days before the World Cup final, in a gathering of diplomats and politicians, FIFA Club members and hangers-on, football wheeler-dealers and media folk. He spoke fluently and wistfully of memorable World Cup moments and was ushered back on stage after omitting to mention the 2006 campaign. And a few months later, one of the newest elected members of the FIFA executive, Dr Joseph Mifsud, was welcoming Sir Bobby and other campaign team members to Malta. Charlton, Sir Geoff Hurst and Tony Banks were the high-profile members of the delegation.

Sir Bobby was a practised globetrotter. His company, Bobby Charlton Enterprises Ltd, had changed its name in September 1993 to Bobby Charlton International Ltd, and was looking to expand its worldwide markets. It was famous for its football schools but the company's annual report also pointed to 'promotional and consulting services based mainly in the field of football' as its principal activity. In 1992 the company reported pre-tax turnover as £902,008 on the sports school and related activities, and £132,130 on corporate hospitality. This report identified the UK as the biggest market – £782,143 against just £34,979 from the Far East. The 1993 turnover saw the Far East figure almost halved, and the UK figure reduced dramatically to £217,564. The company's fortunes and the balance of the finances were to change dramatically during the following years, as Sir Bobby lent his support to Japan's World Cup 2002 bid. The 1994 report showed a revival of turnover in the UK, up to £664,957, and a dramatic rise in Far East business, £221,569. Corporate hospitality now accounted for £242,990, almost 30 per cent of total turnover. The company's two major markets in the 1995 report were again the UK (£571,023) and the Far East (£515,549), the chairman's salary now hitting £133,501, plus a few emoluments including one of between £50,001 and £55,000. By the mid-1990s the soccer schools were seen as less important: 'The company's principal activity' was now 'the running of an international soccer consultancy service based around soccer coaching schools and a hospitality business'. The 1996 figures were still high, the UK generating £434,533, the Far East £375,583. But the directors described the year's trading performance as 'disappointing'. The 1997 report, after the decision on the hosting of the 2002 World Cup, showed a loss of over £200,000. Soon Sir Bobby had resigned, on 2 October 1997, and the company moved on to a 'principal activity' of 'the receipt of royalties for the use of its name and the management of sports images'.

Maltese member Mifsud is new to the FIFA committee and, despite welcoming the England delegation, believes that bidders should not impose themselves upon individual committee members. 'A presentation should be made,' he said. 'There should be a code of ethics for exco members. Giving the World Cup should be a decision which is for the real good of football – it should be outside our scope to gain personally from our position.' Said with sincerity, but Dr Mifsud was one of those invited to speak with Tony Banks in London later in the year. Of course he came.

The England 2006 beanos will roll on. You have to do this to get the World Cup, as the exco members (and Sepp Blatter) have independent secret votes. And the serious players in the race to win the 2006 finals will all be equally praised by members of FIFA's technical committees when they visit the bidding countries.

One veteran member of such visiting delegations confirms that you have to accept the promises of the bidding teams. Faced with pretty pictures of designs of future facilities, you can't call them con-men or liars. The facilities looked thin in Korea when its bid was rated of equal merit to Japan's, but you couldn't tell the top *chaebol* in South Korea and their chums in the government that you thought that their bid had about as much substance as Brazil's warm-up for the France '98 final.

On top of the £9 million kitty, the England bid has had lots of help in kind. Whitehall has seconded personnel on to the bidding team. Partners have come on board as the race heats up – British Airways, Marks & Spencer, Nationwide and Umbro initially, with the *Daily Telegraph* and Deloitte & Touche joining these 'official supporters' of England's bid.

In Japan and Korea, where they know a lot about alliances between the institutions of state, finance and civil society, experienced football bureaucrats comment on the political credibility of the England bid. They are impressed when a starry-eyed Blair beams bonhomie from the glossy campaigning literature. And Sir Bobby is immensely liked and respected throughout world football. His column in *Target 2006*, the bid's official newsletter, is restrained, a touch lighter than some of the earlier more bellicose outpourings from the bidding team: 'Our bid combines professionalism with passion and our visits have provided an opportunity for us to present our case to stage sport's greatest occasion. We have set out England's strengths clearly and succinctly rather than drawing comparisons with other bids.'

Do the English people want the World Cup finals? Who knows? Nobody's asked us. The success of Euro '96 excited the FA so much that they broke promises left, right and centre to grasp for the World Cup. This coincided very nicely with the Labour Party's development of its manifesto and its aim to stage mega-sports events.

Imagine what might happen. Three years into its first administration, the Labour initiative lands the finals and boosts its chances for a second term. During the election campaign for not-so-New Labour's third administration, England hosts and wins the World Cup. Well, who knows what a devolution-reshaped United Kingdom would make of that. But it would be a dream ticket for the central floating vote of middle England. Even if none of that comes to pass, the 2006 bid looks like the closest alliance of interests, around English sport, of the state, finance and civil institutions. It may not be enough. Labour's people are finding it tough going dealing with the politics of world football. It seemed to be tiring former sports minister Tony Banks. But when in November 1998 the *Financial Times* reported that Banks was withdrawing active support for England's bid, he countered this with a reassertion of the Prime Minister's 110 per cent support for the bid.

'The bid is a national one based on an alliance between the whole of English football, the government and business', proclaimed the Football Association in a minute to the Culture, Media and Sport Committee of the House of Commons. Tony Banks was only the most visible element in a huge government operation to secure World Cup 2006 for England. Behind him are amassed the faceless legions of Whitehall. The Foreign and Commonwealth Office and related government 'intelligence' brokers have been central to England's 2006 bid. The FCO makes no secret of its role in the bidding wars. It listed as its major functions: gaining access to key decision-makers; providing assessments of the attitudes of international sporting bodies and key decision-makers; offering ministerial and other high-level official hospitality on the UK to key decision-makers and opinion-formers; offering sponsored visits to the UK and the bidding authority to specially targeted decision-makers, opinion-formers and others likely to be able to influence the bidding process; facilitating the visa applications of visiting personnel connected with the bid; helping with the production and dissemination of publicity/propaganda; identifying and briefing UK-friendly journalists to be used in the promotion of positive image; organising special events and other functions at overseas missions and residences for the promotion of the bid; and arranging formal and informal approaches to influential decision-makers by the head of mission and senior diplomatic staff.

This is nothing short of a spook's charter. The 2006 team is not just backed by one of the world's oldest and most extensive intelligence-gathering networks, it is part of it. A former ambassador serves as international adviser to the bid. Together with two other staff, also on the FA payroll, a junior FCO officer and a member of the support staff, they all have offices in the FCO 'enabling them to liaise between the FA, the Department of Culture, Media and Sport and other government departments and diplomatic posts.' It is this unit of specialist fixers which, behind the scenes, runs England's 2006 bid.

As the summer 1999 deadline for the submission of bids approached, the FA's 2006 campaign went into overdrive. All members of the FIFA executive, with wives and partners in tow of course, were invited to London for the Cup final in May. Wining, dining, theatre-going and an audience and dinner at No. 10 with Prime Minister Blair were added attractions. The main lobbying event was lunch, hosted by Prince Charles. Wembley, Downing Street, Harrods, Covent Garden and now the Royal residence at Highgrove. This was the hardest of hard sells.

Only days before the deadline, the FA played its trump card and launched England's Welcome to the World. 'An invitation to the whole FIFA family,' read the glossy promotional magazine, 'to all 203 footballing nations.' They were invited to send a group of 12 children with up to four adults to spend two weeks in England during the World Cup finals – should England be awarded those finals. This is the catch: you only get this if your country votes to have the party in England.

Anyone who has been involved in sport will know that there is a gift culture. Teams exchange pennants, players swap shirts, town councils host civic dinners and visiting athletes and administrators give each other mementos to remind them of their stay in 'our town'. We should not be surprised to see this gift culture in operation at the upper reaches of world football. Reflecting on his inspection trips to the Far East, Scotland's Ernie Walker recognised this as part of international sports rituals. 'What do you do when the mayor of Nagasaki offers you a present?' he asked us. 'Stick it up his arse?'

But the gift culture should not be boundless and it must be distinguishable from the graft culture which has grown up around the bidding for sports events like the Olympic Games and the World Cup. England's 'Welcome to the World' is couched in the language of sport's gift culture. 'We want our World Cup to be for young people everywhere,' beams Sir Bobby. 'England 2006 will offer everyone a World Cup that young people will remember for the rest of their lives.' Had this offer been made *after* England's bid had been successful we could have applauded it as a wonderful gesture. That it was made *in advance* of any decision shows it to be nothing short of a very expensive inducement. Consider the costs for the 812 accompanying adults (who are these 'youth leaders' anyway?). Even using restrained costings, it is unlikely that it would be anything less than £2,000 per head, which adds up to £1,624,000. Now let's add in the 2,436 children. Even if they are hosted free by English families (and this is by no means certain), it is unlikely to cost less than £1,200 per head, which adds up to £2,923,200. This puts the total estimated costs of the junket at over £4.5 million, surely the biggest financial inducement ever in the history of football or any sport, including the Olympics.

The financial detail of the England 2006 bid will make interesting reading. At least some of the money, from the National Lottery, must at some point be accountable to the English Sports Council. Regardless of costs, though, the bosses certainly moved quickly, getting Sir Bobby Charlton on board, as well as Sir Geoff Hurst (opportunistically knighted by New Labour). And these top names weren't in it just for fun. Sir Bobby was accounting for his time, invoicing the bid as he went. But concern inside the bidding team was expressed at those having more of a figurehead role. Gary Lineker was rewarded with a hefty annual retainer for his name and profile. Some members of the team were apprehensive that Sir Bobby might get to know just how much Lineker was getting. Also, some of the committee felt that it was a pity that Lineker didn't see his role as a more active one, and as a way of putting something back into the game. Most in McGivan's creative team – one of whom moved on to become a spin doctor for Prince Charles – are not paid. But the consultancy gained by Matrix Communications was paid, though never tendered for: (Lord) Dick Newby's conversations with McGivan didn't always find their way into wider strategic discussions about the bid.

Meanwhile, in the wake of confirmation of Olympic scandals around bribes for votes in bidding processes, FIFA issued its guidelines for the World Cup: no excessive hospitality, no personal gifts worth more than £70. Ho hum. What's the cost of a suite for a heavyweight FIFA exco member and his lover, garlanded with flowers, at Claridges?

The English FA and other bidders would continue to pay lip-service to FIFA's guidelines and provide room service to the men with the votes. Come to England. Look, in our video promo, at Stonehenge, at mock-ups of the new Wembley, backed by The Lighthouse Family crooning the campaign hope, 'We can be lifted, lifted from the shadow'. Then we'll take you wherever you want to go.

In seeking to light this particular New Labour beacon, however, some tricky questions arise. Not least, who is wooing whom? Asked

179

whether it was Blair or Havelange who suggested the Downing Street visit, press spokesman Alistair Campbell, uncharacteristically vague, replies, 'To be honest, I can't exactly remember. We certainly anticipated that he [Havelange] would get involved in the bid.' Cancel your appointments, Prime Minister, the Big Man's in town.

FIFA guidelines notwithstanding, the bidding war won't stop at theatre tickets, maybe not even at £9 million. It makes you wonder if Downing Street has quite figured out the nature of the global game it has so cheerfully joined. World Cup 2006 may yet prove a poisoned chalice. But a bit of spin about the dangerous streets of Johannesburg and the untrustworthiness of the typical African football administrator and, hey presto, the exco member, urged on by his wife or partner perhaps, may well vote for five weeks in Knightsbridge and comfortable seats at the new Wembley next to the Blairs.

With the exception of the high-profile interventions of Banks, the government has been at pains to conceal from the general public its heavy involvement in the bid. Manchester United's decision to withdraw from the 1999–2000 English FA Cup forced the government to reveal its hand. Against the wishes of most of the strong football nations in Europe and contrary to the views of Lennart Johansson and other senior officials at UEFA, one of the first things Sepp Blatter did when he graduated to the FIFA presidency was to launch the first world club championship. Scheduled to be held in Brazil in January 2000 and organised along the lines of the World Cup, the new competition proposed to bring together the world's regional club champions to compete for global supremacy.

Like Havelange before him, after his successful election Blatter had promises to keep. The inauguration of this 'World League' would give the minnows of football an opportunity to display themselves on the global stage. Teams from the Gulf, North and Central America, Australasia, Asia and Africa – regions where Blatter garnered many votes in his election – would be given the chance to measure themselves against the might of South America and Europe. The new league would also facilitate further money-making opportunities for FIFA's precious commercial and media partners and provide yet another regular, five-star party for FIFA's extended family.

Western Europe is where the world's best players perform in the game's strongest and best-supported domestic leagues and cups. They do this in the context of an already congested pan-European competitive calendar and international schedule. There is not the need, the room or the appetite for another global football competition. Manchester United, one of the biggest names in the game, won the European Champions League in 1999. In the same year they won the English FA Premier Division and, in front of specially invited FIFA guests, they also won the world's oldest football competition, the FA Challenge Cup. The introduction of the World League notwithstanding, with domestic titles to defend and involvement in the expanded format of the European Champions League, the 1999–2000 season already promised to be the busiest in the club's illustrious history. The World League was a competition too far, particularly as it was scheduled to be played at the height of the English domestic season. Something had to give. It should have been the World League. Instead, prompted by the English FA, newly knighted manager Sir Alex Ferguson announced that Manchester United would not be participating in the FA Cup. Ferguson made it clear that the decision was taken under considerable pressure from the FA, the 2006 team, and the British government.

As veteran journalist Peter Corrigan points out, Manchester United becoming European champions at this juncture provided an opportunity for pandering to Blatter and his cronies that the FA could not miss. By delivering the European Champions to the boys in Brazil in January 2000, McGivan and his team believed England's bid in the minds of Blatter and his executives would be hugely enhanced when they made their selection for 2006 a couple of months later. McGivan was a veteran of the political scene in Britain, and had worked for the Gang of Four breakaway Labour politicians, as the first ever full-time member of staff of the Social Democratic Party, before boosting his profile as events manager for Euro '96. But he was outfoxed when FIFA executive committee member Chuck Blazer had the decision date put back to its original date of July 2000. New sports minister Kate Hoey passed the buck to her predecessor, Tony Banks, stating: 'I think it is absolutely imperative that Manchester United play in the FA Cup. I would not have felt it was the role of the Minister of Sport to be asking Manchester United to go to Brazil. A number of errors were made.' This upset United's chief executive, Martin Edwards, who claimed that it wasn't the club's decision to withdraw, that it was a decision made 'with the full backing of the government and the FA . . . a joint decision. Now, for a new sports minister suddenly to enter the arena . . . I suggest she does her homework properly and I suggest the government gets its act together because we did this in support of the last sports minister.'

Keith Cooper, FIFA's media spokesman, denied that Manchester United's participation in the World League would have any bearing upon the 2006 decision. However, FIFA executive members Jack Warner and Chuck Blazer praised the sagacity of England's position and hinted that it would stand them in good stead. Cooper's view was confirmed by Blatter himself, who in October urged Manchester United to play in the FA Cup, and suggested that the FA make this happen.

Government-driven, the England 2006 bid was presented in Zurich on 9 August 1999. The English flew in, bidding team and press pack together, and irritated FIFA by arriving late. Tony Banks, by now moved aside as Minister of Sport, had been handed the role of special envoy for the bid. This was a canny piece of positioning by Blair – *all credit for me if the bid comes off, not my fault if the envoy loses it*. To FIFA, this sub-ministerial presence was downgrading the bid, an insult to them. The English stagemanaged the bid submission for the press, then left. They saw no other bid, spoke to nobody else, saw nothing of the informal lobbying.

Meanwhile, after all the bids were presented, a Bavarian oompa-pah-pah band played on the terrace of FIFA House with its spell-binding view over Lake Zurich, and wild mountain flowers framed the flow of wine and beer as President Blatter entertained FIFA insiders, hangers-on and self-selecting press. In dark shades and casual shirt, and cracking jokes revolving around double beds in Africa, Blatter rubbed shoulders with, among others, the Brazilian Ricardo Teixeira, former son-in-law of João Havelange. The Brazilians and Germans – let alone the emotional favourites, the South Africans – showed real savvy in the bidding process. For Teixeira, the stakes were high. Under pressure and under investigation for his activities in Brazil, his slate would be wiped clean if he were to land the 2006 finals – just as Havelange had been cleared of charges and spared investigation by the junta when he'd slipped into the FIFA presidential seat. Within weeks, Havelange would be announcing that the Brazilians might consider withdrawing – 'I'd prefer to lose a finger than lose a hand; in order to win you also have to know how to lose,' he said. 'If Brazil are not to be hosts of the 2006 World Cup, I can guarantee they will be in 2010.' If Havelange himself was unlikely to be sitting in the stands of the rebuilt Maracaná in his mid-90s, the mid-term strategy would certainly suit his surviving nearest and dearest. By now, the Brazilian television and marketing agency Traffic – broker of Nike's deal with the Brazil national side and Ronaldo – had clinched the TV contract for the FIFA World Club Championship. And, of course, Havelange would want to lull the oppostion into a false sense of strength. Blatter had promised continuity in the FIFA family.

At last the cat was out of the bag. Forget the separation of sport from politics, forget tradition, forget the fans: anything, including the FA Cup, was expendable in the pursuit of 2006. A House of Commons Culture, Media and Sport Committee has commended the bid, saying, in prominent bold type in its summary volume: 'So far, the Football Association's bid to stage the 2006 World Cup appears to be well conceived, well managed and well executed. The support offered by the government, most notably the Minister for Sport and the staff of the British Embassies and High Commissions, appears to have been exemplary.' This might just be the most integrated and fully developed political exploitation of sport in the history of the country. Towards the end of her first administration Thatcher grasped at the Falklands conflict to help secure a second term in office. Securing the World Cup for England might achieve the same for Blair in 2002. Never mind broken promises, underhand deals or England's reputation for honesty in the gutter, just listen to the people sing.

14. FIFALAND

In France '98 we were part of post-modern football – the massive media circus, the orderly audiences, the wars of the sponsors and the almost-choreographed games themselves – performances which bore little or no resemblance to the matches we used to watch a lifetime ago at Goodison Park and Turf Moor.

The media guide claimed that 2,000 spaces were reserved for the press for the final. From our vantage-point it looked like half the Stade de France was filled by the media. The remaining seats were occupied not by a traditional football crowd, but by a restrained and well-behaved audience. Is this the future of football, we thought, with stadiums redeveloped as studios for over-privileged live audiences providing colour and atmosphere for the masses to consume from their couches?

The people of France poured on to the streets for a two-day party which merged with their traditional Bastille Day celebrations. We went back to our temporary home to sleep, like the dead in Montmartre cemetery opposite our apartment. While we slept we dreamt.

We look skywards and gasp as a laser-guided fireball lights up the Nevada night. 'Ladies and gentlemen,' a disembodied voice booms around the packed auditorium, 'welcome to Fifaland Las Vegas where Players Win and Winners Play!' More fanfare. 'Welcome to the Championship Game of the 2024 World Soccer Series!' We had made our pilgrimage to Montevideo to visit the site of global football's beginning. Now, in our dotage, we were in the pleasure capital of the world to witness its end. FIFA Incorporated had grown out of the rubble of its crumbling, amateur parent. This tainted body had finally collapsed after shenanigans and controversies which surrounded the awarding of the World Cup to South Africa in 2006 and Saudi Arabia in 2010 were made public. Then, when two German journalists finally proved that presidential elections had been rigged, its very latest president was forced to step down. An American lawyer was installed as caretaker president. He at once abandoned FIFA's charitable façade and floated the organisation as a limited company on the world's stockmarkets. He raised billions of dollars, mostly from the media and marketing industries which already had a huge stake in making sure international football, in one form or another, survived. One by one the confederations, who were by now totally dominated by business interests, followed suit and were themselves gobbled up by FIFA Incorporated.

No longer concerned with massaging their over-inflated egos or buying their votes, one of the first acts of FIFA's new board was to get rid of the hangers-on, the sycophantic relics of the *ancien régime* who themselves had grown fat as modern football perished. FIFA also gave up the unpredictable and damaging practice of auctioning the World Cup to the highest bidder and instead searched for a permanent site.

Las Vegas was the obvious choice. FIFA bought the Tropicana Hotel on a prime site on the Strip and razed it to the ground. In its place they built Fifaland, a 20,000-room hotel complex, with ten acres of casinos, bookies and slot machines, 200 bars and restaurants, an underground shopping mall, 20 swimming-pools and a state-of-the-art media centre equipped for 10,000 journalists.

Fifaland dwarfed the MGM Grand and New York New York across the street and towered above Mandalay, Luxor, Excalibur, Bellagio, Paris and the other theme palaces which had turned Vegas into the dream capital of the world. Its centrepiece was a 100,000 all-seater auditorium with retractable roof. With the roof closed a range of artificial weather conditions could be created, to make the game seem more like the real thing. The spectators, of course, were protected from these fake elements. The arena also had a playing surface which, like pulling open a drawer, could be manoeuvred out of the complex and into the open air. Once outside it was watered and manicured by an army of groundsmen. Inside, the auditorium floor could now be used for concerts, business conventions, political rallies and a host of other money-making ventures.

As Fifaland took shape, FIFA's enforcers set about restructuring world football so that it would feed into the yearly World Soccer

Series. Domestic and continental franchises still played their annual competitions but there were no longer senior national teams. Those larger clubs that had survived the financial madness of the 1990s and the first decade of the twenty-first century were mostly owned by the same interests which now ran FIFA. They were allowed to keep their players until they peaked, which FIFA set at 26 years of age. Up until that age they could also represent their countries and play in the biennial Olympic-FIFA Junior World Cup in Disney's Olympus complex in Florida.

Each year, as the best players reached their prime, they became FIFA's property and were placed in an American-style draft system. The 24 commercial franchises who participated in the World Soccer Series (Team Nike, Team Adidas, Team McDonald's, Team Ford, Team Microsoft and the rest) had players allocated to them according to how they and the players were rated from the previous season. The most highly rated players went to the teams that achieved least and vice versa. This way FIFA kept their competition competitively balanced. Some thought that this system resembled a rigged slave auction. But Fifaland was the only show in town and few turned down the opportunity to play there.

In return for putting their names on the backs of the greatest players in the world, FIFA demanded and received generous payments from the blue-chip companies who owned the precious franchise teams. An unintended welcome by-product of replacing national teams with company ones was the end of football hooliganism. Years ago, fuelled by misplaced national pride, thuggish fans might have fought one another on the beaches of Marseille, but no one rampaged in Vegas for the sake of a company logo.

Seamlessly, the announcer's voice faded and the honky-tonk piano introduction to Jerry Lee Lewis's 'Great Balls of Fire' assaulted the eardrums. Team Nike, captained by the bald 40-odd-year-old Ronaldo, and Team Adidas, led out by his slightly younger rival, Michael Owen, jogged into the arena. Tackling of any sort had been outlawed by FIFA after the 2006 World Cup and certain forms of steroids were now legal. This enabled many of the best players to continue their careers well into their forties.

The game itself was entertaining enough. The goals were bigger: ten metres long by four metres high. A new scoring system had been invented by FIFA, one that awarded one point for a penalty, two points for a goal scored from inside the area and three points for one from outside the box. Off-side disappeared ten years ago. There was plenty of action at either end. The arbitrator in his instant-replay, virtual-reality helmet, ensured that there was absolutely no room for physical contact. With weary grace and circus trickery, the ball was lobbed, dribbled and pinged around the field.

It was a bit like watching one of those old Play Station video games. In the last minute of the final quarter, Ronaldo's 30-metre pile-driver almost broke the net. Team Nike won 27–25 and succeeded Team Budweiser as World Champions. Like the rest of the audience, we applauded politely as the octogenarian president handed over the World Series trophy, the Golden Goose Egg, to the captain.

We filed out of Fifaland heading for the Strip with time and money to spend. Having been bombarded with special effects for three hours, it was hard to tell whether it was night or day, whether we were inside or out. The casinos would be open all night and we could take in the professional bull riders competition over at the MGM. We might even catch the together-again Spice Girls' late show at Caesars Palace. All of a sudden we felt nostalgic for a flat pint of bitter, a pie, brown sauce and a copy of the *Football Pink*.

Dream? Nightmare? Or vision of the future? Do we see as inevitable this depressing future?

While Fifaland may itself never happen, the wholesale transformation of football is more likely to come to pass. It is inevitable if the people – that is, all of us – passively accept that there is no choice but to allow the game to be driven with the bullish and ultimately self-destructive logic of big business. We cannot turn back the clock but we can still have a say in the shape of things to come.

Either through incompetence, greed or vainglorious notions of destiny, the league of gentlemen, the blazer-and-slacks brigade, forfeited their right to rule world football a long time ago. There is a danger that their places will be filled by slick-suited chief executives or high-flying commissioners who have scant regard for football's traditional culture. What the game needs at every level is representative and responsible government. For this to happen the administration of football has to be rooted in accountable institutions and be subject to the rule of law.

We would not want national governments to run football. But at a domestic level democratically elected governments should, through a legally constituted and independent agency, exercise a guiding and, if necessary, a restraining influence over the game. If other important and formerly nationalised utilities such as gas, water, electricity and the railways have to be accountable to government watchdogs, the same should apply to something as important to the national psyche as football.

At a European level, a similar arrangement could be worked out between UEFA and the European Commission/Parliament, itself (in part at least) a democratically elected and representative body. At the least, such an arrangement would force these two bodies to come together and work out a sensible legal framework for the development and continued vitality of football in Europe, one through which the EC could protect football from business predators rather than inviting them in.

FIFA itself must be brought within the embrace of an accountable international organisation such as the United Nations, perhaps under the wing of this organisation's cultural framework, UNESCO. Under such an arrangement, FIFA's offshore financial status would have to end. All of its important decisions would be scrutinised by officials, themselves accountable to a broader electorate and within a wider legal framework.

We would revive Johansson's Visions proposals, and cut the number of continental confederations from six to four. Europe and Africa could remain the same. South America could be combined with North and Central America and Asia and Oceania could join forces. We'd rotate the World Cup every four years around the confederations, and they would select the host countries. To qualify as host, a country must have staged its confederation's championship no more than two years before the World Cup in question. This would guarantee good facilities and reduce costs. Bidding processes would be strictly regulated. The FIFA presidency would also be rotated around the confederations. A term of office would last four years and nobody would be allowed to serve more than two terms. Similar regulations could be worked out for the presidency of the confederations.

Obviously, these are ideal solutions with huge practical problems. When it comes to corruption, the UN and the EC have their own problems. Outside Europe, many countries passionate about football lack stable democratic governments or transnational bodies equivalent to the EC. A restructured and more accountable FIFA would continue to exercise authority over all member associations, and teams from non-democratic countries, with questionable football administrations, could compete in FIFA competitions but would have no voting rights at FIFA's congresses.

There are some indications that supporters are no longer prepared to stand idly by as a game which used to be theirs is ruined. In England, the enhanced voice of the football supporter and the success of the Manchester United Independent Supporters Club in having BSkyB's attempted takeover blocked is encouraging. The emergence and popularity of seriously critical football publications, such as *When Saturday Comes,* and the vitality of the fanzine movement indicates that organised resistance at the grass-roots level is taking shape.

In the wake of the Lancaster Gate fiasco, the British government is taking an increasingly proprietorial interest in the future administration of the national sport. This can be a good or bad thing. The establishment of the 'Football Task Force' – a government-sponsored, cross-party study group which has brought together all those with an interest in and love for the game – looks to be a step in the right direction. Its first report, *Investing in the Community,* points to the game 'being awash with money at the highest level while facilities in schools and at the grassroots are in a poor state of repair and clubs in lower divisions struggle to survive'. A key recommendation is that out of monies made through deals with BSkyB, the English Premiership should set aside a minimum of 5 per cent for 'investment in grassroots facilities and projects'. This could only benefit the people's game – clawing back cash from the profit-seekers of the new football business.

The Premiership barons are not fools. They are happy to go along with this recommendation only so long as they are guaranteed exclusive, collective negotiating rights for TV contracts. This is a position deeply resented by the 20 member clubs, who anticipate a lot more money might come their way if they could negotiate separate deals. Once more the Office of Fair Trading was called in, ruling in favour of the clubs. The Premiership responded with a writ, leading to a long and bitter court case which found in the cartel's favour. With the fans sidelined as usual, it will increasingly be left to men in wigs to pronounce on the future of football. Even when the government does become involved, it is either unable or unwilling to stop the big-business bandwagon.

Football will always have an important commercial dimension, and rightly so. But we need to return to the guiding principle which allowed the game to flourish so magnificently in its golden years: football first, business second. To achieve this, 'for the good of the game', supporters, current and former players, politicians and honest sports administrators need to collaborate in the fight for the soul of the people's game. The current beneficiaries of FIFA's flawed system of governing and regulating the game won't give up their privileges without a struggle. See you in the trenches – or in Vegas.